THE
SURVEY METHODS
WORKBOOK

THE SURVEY METHODS WORKBOOK

From Design to Analysis

ALAN BUCKINGHAM

AND

PETER SAUNDERS

polity

First published in 2004 by Polity Press Ltd.

Reprinted2007

Polity Press
65 Bridge Street
Cambridge CB2 1UR, UK

Polity Press
350 Main Street
Malden, MA 02148, USA

Library of Congress Cataloging-in-Publication Data

Buckingham, Alan.
   The survey methods workbook: from design to analysis / Alan
   Buckingham and Peter Saunders.
      p. cm.
   Includes index.
   ISBN 978–0-7456-2244-6 (alk. paper) – ISBN 978–0-7456-2245-3 (pbk. : alk. paper)
   1. Social surveys–Methodology. 2. Social
   sciences–Research–Methodology. I. Saunders, Peter, 1948-II. Title.
HM538 .B83 2004
300'.7'23–dc21   2003013538

Typeset in 10 on 12 pt Sabon
by Kolam Information Services Pvt. Ltd, Pondicherry, India
Printed and bound in Great Britain by MPG Books Ltd, Bodmin, Cornwall

For further information on Polity, visit our website: www.polity.co.uk

CONTENTS

DETAILED CONTENTS

On the Website

(www.surveymethods.co.uk)

Section 1: Summary of findings from the Smoking Survey

Section 2: Smoking Survey files and documentation

Section 3: Issues in research design

    Appendix A: Longitudinal survey designs
    Appendix B: Coding occupational data to social class schema

Section 4: Further statistics and choosing statistical tests

    Appendix C: Standardizing variables as z scores
    Appendix D: The binomial distribution
    Appendix E: Choosing statistical tests

Section 5: Further techniques in data analysis

    Appendix F: Principal Components (Factor) analysis
    Appendix G: Path models
    Appendix H: Logistic regression
    Appendix I: Loglinear modelling

Section 6: Appendix J: Guide to further reading

Section 7: SPSS updates, using SPSS syntax, links and reader inputs

Section 8: Guide for teachers

ACKNOWLEDGEMENTS

We wish to thank Rod Bond and David Hitchin for their help and advice on data analysis; two anonymous referees for invaluable comments and guidance on earlier drafts; and the production staff at Polity for their professionalism, patience and efficiency. We also owe special thanks to the 1997 cohort of sociology research methods students at the University of Sussex who carried out the survey on which this workbook is based.

The authors and publishers are grateful to the following for permission to use copyright material:

Associated Newspapers for the cartoon by Mac on p. 286;

British Sociological Association for the extracts from their ethical guidelines on p. 86;

Guardian Newspapers for the reproduction of the report in the *Guardian*, 9 Dec. 1997, on the ICM poll on p. 78;

Herald & Weekly Times Ltd, Melbourne, for the reproduction from the *Herald Sun*, 3 August 2000, on p. 102;

McGraw-Hill Education, New York, for tables 4.2, 9.2 and 9.4 reproduced from Hubert Blalock, *Social Statistics* (London and Singapore: McGraw-Hill, 1972 and 1979);

Open University Press and the University of Queensland Press for figure 1.1 from A. F. Chalmers, *What is This Thing Called Science?*, 3rd edn (Buckingham: Open University Press; Queensland: University of Queensland Press, 1999), p. 6;

Pan Macmillan for the extract from Douglas Adams, *The Hitch-Hiker's Guide to the Galaxy* (London: Pan Macmillan, 1979);

Telegraph Group for the cartoon by Matt on p. 41 and the headline on p. 50, both from the *Daily Telegraph* of 17 June 1998, and for the cartoon on p. 248, from *The Spectator*, 24 January 1998;

Universal Press Syndicate for the cartoon by Doonesbury on p. 79.

Every effort has been made to trace copyright holders, but if any have been inadvertently overlooked, the publishers will be pleased to make the necessary arrangements at the first opportunity.

How to Use this Book

If you want to learn about survey techniques, the best way to do it is to get involved in a real survey. This book enables you to do precisely this. It invites you to participate in every stage of an actual social survey – from planning the research and developing the hypotheses to collecting the data and analysing the findings.

Getting involved

The survey in which we are inviting you to participate is a small-scale study of people's behaviour and attitudes with regard to smoking.

Our society has become increasingly intolerant of smoking. As information has built up about its harmful effects, both on smokers themselves, and on the people around them, so the pressure on smokers to quit has become enormous. Yet despite this, smoking is still widespread, and many young people continue to take up the habit.

Who smokes?

The anti-smoking pressure group ASH (Action on Smoking and Health) reports that:

- There are 12 million cigarette smokers in the UK.
- 28% of adult men and 26% of adult women smoke cigarettes.
- Rates of smoking are highest in younger age groups – 37% of men and women aged 20–34 are smokers.
- Rates of smoking are higher in the lower social classes – 35% of men and 31% of women who are manual workers smoke, as compared with just 21% of men and 18% of women in professional or managerial occupations.

Information from www.ash.org.uk/html/factsheets/html/basic01.html

---

Given the mounting social pressures that they now face, as well as their knowledge that they may be causing themselves and their loved ones serious damage, there is something sociologically very interesting about people who still today take up or persist with smoking. Why do they start? And how do they resist the intense social pressures to stop?

The social pressures against smoking

'The last cigarette smokers in America were located in a box canyon south of the Donner Pass in the High Sierra by two federal tobacco agents in a helicopter who spotted the little smoke puffs just before noon. One of them, Ames, the district chief, called in the ground team by air-to-ground radio. Six men in camouflage outfits, members of a crack anti-smoking joggers unit, moved quickly across the rugged terrain, surrounded the bunch in their hideout, subdued them with tear gas, and made them lie face down on the gravel in the hot August sun. There were three females and two males, all in their mid-forties. They had been on the run since the adoption of the Twenty-Eighth Amendment . . .'

Garrison Keillor, 'End of the trail', in his *We Are Still Married* (London: Faber, 1989), p. 3

In 1997, when we were both teaching an undergraduate Social Research Methods course at the University of Sussex, we decided to investigate some of the influences on people's smoking behaviour by working with our students to carry out a survey on the population of Brighton, a city on the south coast of England. It was only a small-scale piece of research – the students spent just ten weeks planning it, carrying it out and analysing the results, and we ended up with a sample of just 334 respondents. It was also a very rough-and-ready piece of research – many mistakes were made, for this was primarily a learning exercise for our students, and in survey methods as in everything else, we learn by making mistakes. But as a learning exercise, it was invaluable, for we went through all the steps that any survey needs to negotiate and we encountered many of the problems and difficulties that many bigger surveys also have to deal with. We also ended up with some quite unexpected and intriguing results.

It is this survey in which we now invite you to participate. The Smoking Survey runs as a continuous theme throughout this book. In each chapter we address the problems that our students had to address, we reproduce and evaluate what they did, and – crucially – we enable you to join in by carrying out these procedures for yourself. At every step from survey design through data collection to the final analysis, we have written the book in such a way that you can actively use and contribute to the survey materials. You can do this in one of two ways:

◆ *Replication* If you are studying survey methods as part of a course, the best way to use this book may be to work with your tutor to set up and carry out your own group survey in parallel to the one that we carried out with our students. Provided your group is big enough to handle the interviewing that needs to be done, you can set up your own survey, with everybody participating in devising a questionnaire, drawing a sample from your local population, doing the interviews, and analysing the data. If you choose to do this, you can use this book as a detailed guide as you proceed through each stage of your project.

♦ *Participation*   Alternatively, you can work through the book on your own, but still gain practical experience of each step in doing a survey by working on our original Smoking Survey project materials. This is possible because we have included, either within the book or on our accompanying website, all the research materials developed in our project – draft and final versions of the questionnaire, sampling guidelines, the code book, original and clean versions of the data set, and so on. At each stage, you can use these research materials as if you were yourself participating in the survey, working on them, improving them, and analysing the results for yourself.

There is also a third way this book can be used, and that is as a conventional methods text. You can if you wish read each chapter without using the primary research materials we have provided. There is nothing 'wrong' with this, but we would encourage you to get more actively engaged if you have the time, for you will get more out of the book this way.

DON'T DO AS WE SAY, DO AS WE DO...

There are many textbooks on survey methods, but most of them are written prescriptively. They tell the reader what to do, which procedures to use, and so on. The problem with this is that real life practice cannot simply be read off from a set of rules. If you want to learn about survey methods and quantitative data analysis, then you will need to see how surveys *actually* get done, rather than simply reading about how they are *supposed* to be done.

The Smoking Survey which develops through the chapters that follow was originally carried out by students who (probably like you) had no previous experience of doing social research. Inevitably, therefore, they made lots of mistakes (even accomplished social researchers make mistakes, and our researchers were all raw amateurs).

Because we all learn by making mistakes (and by correcting them) we have made no attempt in the chapters that follow to cover up the cock-ups, although we do reflect on how they might have been avoided, and on what might be done to compensate for them. The book therefore presents you with a 'warts and all' guide to an actual research project, and it deliberately avoids the 'glossing' which invariably occurs when researchers normally present their material to a critical audience.

The real face of research

'Typically, the scientific paper or monograph presents an immaculate appearance which reproduces little or nothing of the intuitive leaps, false starts, mistakes, loose ends and happy accidents that actually cluttered up the enquiry. The public record of science therefore fails to provide many of the source materials to reconstruct the actual course of scientific developments.'

R. K. Merton, *On Theoretical Sociology* (New York: Free Press, 1967), p. 4

Whether all the errors, mistakes and miscalculations mean that, in the end, the results of the Smoking Survey have much value or validity is an issue which we shall consider as we proceed. But as you read through this book, and hopefully get actively involved in each stage of the research process yourself, remember the project is intended primarily as a learning device. In the end, it will not matter too much if we decide that the survey was fundamentally flawed, provided we learn why it is flawed, and how the problems might be avoided in other surveys.

Remember too that this is not a book *about* smoking. Real research has to be about *something*, and we hope that our choice of smoking behaviour as our topic of research will turn out to be an interesting one for you to investigate. In the end, however, this topic is not central to what the book is about. The research techniques and statistical procedures we shall encounter can be applied to many different areas of social inquiry – smoking is just the example we have selected as a vehicle for exploring these techniques.

Choosing a research topic

The German sociologist Max Weber pointed out that social research is always stimulated and guided by a subjective judgement about what is important and what is valuable. Everybody has their own ideas about whether and why any given research topic should be pursued, and Weber insisted that research is always grounded in some moral agenda which some people will endorse and others will reject.

So what was our agenda? Why did we choose smoking as a topic of research? There were three main reasons:

- *Personal interest*   This was a topic which we and many of our students found interesting.
- *Policy relevance*   We live in a period of increasing government regulation of people's smoking behaviour, so smoking is a topical political issue for us to investigate.
- *Pedagogy*   Smoking is *familiar* behaviour – it is something that everybody has encountered and that many of us have engaged in. It is also something that we can ask questions about without encountering too many problems, and this makes it a suitable topic for an undergraduate group project involving limited time and resources and no great fund of expertise.

Max Weber, 'Objectivity in social science and social policy', in Weber, *The Methodology of the Social Sciences* (Chicago: Free Press, 1949)

INTRODUCING OUR RESEARCH PROBLEM

In 1957 the London-based Medical Research Council issued a report which for the first time demonstrated a link between smoking and the risk of contracting lung cancer. Since then the evidence linking smoking to poor health and a heightened risk of early death has become compelling, yet millions of people in Britain still choose to smoke, and thousands of young people take up cigarette smoking every year.

On the face of it, the decision to start smoking, or to continue smoking, seems an irrational one. Assuming we all want to live long and healthy lives, why does anybody smoke? There are several different kinds of answers:

◆ Biochemists tell us that tobacco contains an addictive substance, nicotine, which reacts with neuroreceptors in the brain to produce craving.
◆ Psychologists tell us that smoking is routinized behaviour which is difficult to break (a typical smoker might puff on a cigarette about 500 times a day, and if you do anything this frequently, you are likely to become habituated).
◆ Sociologists tell us that smoking is *social behaviour*, which means it has specifically social causes and consequences as well as biological and psychological ones.

It might seem perverse to say that smoking is an example of 'social behaviour' when it is increasingly seen as asocial, or even anti-social. People often smoke when they are alone, and in today's world, smokers are quite likely to find themselves ejected from their social group and sent out into the back garden to light up a lonely cigarette. So in what sense is their behaviour 'social'?

According to Max Weber, what makes behaviour a *social action* is two things.

◆ Social action must make sense to those engaged in it – it is *subjectively meaningful and motivated*.
◆ Social action *takes account of other people*. It is learned from others and it is governed by rules and norms of behaviour shared by other members of our group.

Smoking qualifies as social behaviour on both of these criteria:

◆ Smoking is something that people do consciously. It is a subjectively meaningful activity. Think of the amount of time smokers spend contemplating and talking about how easy or difficult it is to give up, whether smoking helps keep their weight down, whether to book a smoking or non-smoking table at the restaurant, and so on.
◆ Smoking is also behaviour which is oriented towards others. It is socially learned and socially sanctioned. It is in interaction with others that we learn in the first place how to inhale, how to blow smoke rings, and how to look cool with a Zippo lighter. Smoking is also regulated socially – there are rules about who may smoke and where they may smoke – and positive and negative images of smoking are constantly presented to us through television programmes, cinema and magazines.

The meaning of smoking

'Tobacco...has meant very much to legions of human beings, brought untold comfort to sufferers, performed innumerable small acts of kindness. It has allayed fears, consoled misfortune, lulled anger...It is time for us to take leave of tobacco, but it should not be an ungrateful farewell.'

V. G. Kiernan, *Tobacco: A History* (1991), quoted in James Walton (ed.), *The Faber Book of Smoking* (London: Faber, 2000), p. 5

Smoking, then, is social action, for it is inextricably embedded in a social context. As such, sociologists should be able to say something useful and interesting about it. In fact, smoking throws up many sociological questions.

◆ How and why has the proportion of smokers in the population changed over time? (ASH reports that in 1972 nearly half the adult UK population smoked, but today it is little more than one-quarter.)
◆ What are the social factors that influence people to take up smoking in the first place, and why do they continue with it? Do smokers want to give up, and how effective are campaigns aimed at stopping them from smoking?
◆ Are young people more likely to smoke if their parents smoked? Are young people influenced to start smoking by their friends, or by advertising, or by influential 'role models' in popular music and the media?
◆ Do smokers fully understand the dangers to their health? How do they come to terms with this knowledge? Have the mounting social and legal pressures against smoking made them more or less determined to quit?

To answer questions like these, we need some *facts*, and to gather the relevant factual information, we need to do some *research*. Here, then, is the starting point for our smoking survey.

How to get started

This book is organized into three parts.

◆ Part I, 'Research Design', considers whether and when you should consider using a survey. Survey methods have often been criticized by sociologists who distrust the 'positivist' assumptions which are thought to lie behind them, and in the first chapter we ask what positivism is, whether surveys are inherently positivist, and whether it matters if they are. An appendix to chapter 1 then outlines the hypotheses that our Smoking Survey set out to test, and this is followed in chapter 2 by an exploration of the circumstances in which it is and is not appropriate to choose a survey.
◆ Part II, 'Data Collection', takes you through every stage in the development and execution of a social survey, using our Smoking Survey as a worked example. Chapter 3 looks at how to create a questionnaire working from a basic set of research questions; chapter 4 takes you through the different ways in which you can try to make a sample representative of the population you are studying; chapter 5 gives you the chance to do some interviewing while also introducing you to issues in the classification and measurement of data; and chapter 6 explains how to turn your results into an SPSS data file that can be processed using a computer.
◆ Part III, 'Data Analysis', begins with how to explore and describe your basic research findings (chapter 7) and follows this (in chapter 8) by looking at proced-ures that allow us to measure the strength of association between variables, and therefore to begin testing hypotheses. Chapter 9 introduces some statistical tests which enable us to assess how far the results we have generated from a small sample can be extrapolated to the whole population from which our sample was drawn, and chapter 10 explains how to develop and test simple causal models.

In addition, on p. 287, you will find a glossary of technical terms.

We have also included on our website a number of 'electronic appendices' which back up various parts of the book. One section of the website contains appendices which go into more detail on some specific issues about data collection. A second section develops more detailed explanations of some of the statistical issues discussed in part III of the book. If, having completed the book, you want to delve deeper into data analysis, you can go to a third section of appendices which take you through more advanced statistical techniques such as factor analysis, path analysis, logistic regression and loglinear modelling, and these can be downloaded as required. And you will also be able to download from the website all the materials that you will need in order to replicate or work on the Smoking Survey. As you go through the book, so we shall refer you to relevant sections of the website as and when you need to access them.

The book makes few assumptions about what you might know and we assume no prior knowledge or experience of survey methods or social statistics. We expect that you will have some familiarity with a social science discipline where survey methods are commonly used, but this may not be sociology, and you do not need to have a background in sociology to make sense of the book.

When we get to data analysis in part III, we assume very little knowledge of *mathematics* – indeed, we anticipate that you may be one of those people who has a fear of numbers, so we fully explain everything that might be unfamiliar at the time when we encounter it. As for *computing* skills, you will need to be familiar with the Windows operating environment (for SPSS is Windows-based), and you will also need to know how to get access to the internet if you are going to download Smoking Survey materials from our website. (Details of what is available on the website and how to access are on p. 298).

We begin, though, not with mathematics, computers or the internet, but with some philosophy. Unlike the chapters that follow it, chapter 1 is not interactive. You do not need to do anything other than read it. Many social scientists are sceptical about the value and validity of survey research, and you may share their reservations and mistrust. Given that we are inviting you to commit quite a lot of time and energy to participating in a survey, it seems sensible at the outset to explain why we believe this is a worthwhile thing for you to do. This is what we do in chapter 1.

Using this book if you only want to learn about data analysis

If you are interested in learning about techniques of data analysis but you do not want to conduct a survey from start to finish, we suggest that you start by reading chapter 4, where you will learn about sampling theory, measures of central tendency and measures of dispersal. You should follow this by reading chapter 5 for an introduction to coding and levels of measurement. You can then proceed to part III (chapters 7–10) on data analysis, and to the 'Further techniques' explained in section 5 of the website.

PART I
RESEARCH
DESIGN

DISCOVERING FACTS, TESTING THEORIES

AIM

In this chapter, we look at what positivism is, whether survey methods and quantitative data analysis are positivist, and whether it matters if they are. By the end of the chapter, you should:

- Be clear what a social survey is
- Understand the role of surveys in discovering facts (descriptive research) and testing theories (explanatory research)
- Know what is meant by 'positivism' and be aware of the implicit association between positivist social science and quantitative survey methods
- Appreciate the relation between theory and observation and how this affects attempts to test theories against factual evidence
- Understand the phenomenological critique of quantitative methods
- Be aware of Marxist and feminist critiques of surveys and quantitative methods as 'oppressive'

The chapter also includes an appendix outlining the development of ten hypotheses which will be tested in our survey of smoking.

INTRODUCTION

This book introduces you to one of the major research techniques of the social sciences – the social survey. This is an approach to research which has often been criticized in British sociology. It is not unusual to come across sociologists who refuse to have anything to do with surveys and quantitative data, and relatively few have ever carried out a survey or got involved in the statistical analysis of data.

British sociology's antipathy to quantitative methods

In the early 1980s, Frank Bechhofer published a report which claimed that many sociologists felt a 'profound distaste and contempt' for quantitative methods of research. He later demonstrated this with an analysis of articles published in four of Britain's leading sociology journals, in which he showed that two-thirds contained no quantitative data at all, and that only 16 per cent used any serious statistics. He concluded that 'the majority of the profession' in Britain was 'unable to read huge portions of the research literature'.

Frank Bechhofer, 'Quantitative research in British sociology', *Sociology*, vol. 30 (1996), pp. 583–91

This antipathy to survey methods can get passed on from one generation of sociologists to the next. Teachers tell their students that quantitative research involves mindless 'number-crunching', or that questionnaire surveys are superficial and 'empiricist', and students accept these claims, for many have a fear of numbers and need little encouragement to stay away from all the tables, graphs and percentages found in this sort of research.

Early in our study of sociology, therefore, many of us are put off this approach to social research even before we have learned what it involves. This is a pity, for it means we miss out on a potentially powerful and exciting research tool. Like all research techniques, survey methods have their problems, but we hope to demonstrate to you that these are not so severe as to rule out their use.

Empiricism and positivism

Empiricism is the philosophical tradition which believes that (a) the world consists of objects (b) these objects have their own characteristics and properties which exist irrespective of what we think they are like, and (c) our knowledge of these objects is developed through direct experience of them.

Positivism is a variant of empiricism. Positivists endorse empiricists' belief that there is a real world of objects that we can know only through experience, but they add to this some additional rules about how such knowledge is to be achieved. We shall outline the basic principles of positivist sociology a little later in this chapter.

WHAT IS A SOCIAL SURVEY?

A social survey is a method of gathering information about a specified group of people (a 'population') by asking them questions.

- Sometimes every member of the target group will be included in a survey, but more often, a *sample* of people is selected from the group, and their answers are taken to be representative of everybody in the group. For example, in our Smoking Survey, just 334 adults were interviewed out of a total target population of around quarter of a million in Brighton.

- Survey questions are usually standardized, so that everybody is asked about the same things in the same way. This does not mean that everybody is asked exactly the same questions (in our survey, for example, there would be little point in asking non-smokers how many cigarettes they smoke per day), but questions are worded in the same way for all respondents, and are asked in the same order. These questions are put together in the form of a *questionnaire* which may be administered by an interviewer or which may be completed by participants themselves.

- Information is collected on any or all of the 'three A's' – people's *attributes*, their *attitudes* and their *actions*. Surveys typically gather information on personal attributes (such as people's sex, age or occupation), on their attitudes and values (such as whether they favour restrictions on smoking), and on their activities and behaviour (such as whether they smoke).

- Surveys are not usually interested in what any one individual has to say, but are rather aimed at *generalizing* about groups or whole populations. Results are usually produced in number form, as *statistics* – so many per cent do this, so many per cent think that, and so on.

A social survey, therefore, can be defined as *a technique for gathering statistical information about the attributes, attitudes or actions of a population by administering standardized questions to some or all of its members.*

WHAT ARE SURVEYS USED FOR?

Social surveys usually aim to do one or both of two things:

- They try to *discover facts about a population* (e.g. we might want to know how many people smoke, how many smokers would like to give up smoking, and so on). We can call this *descriptive research*, for the aim is to describe a social phenomenon, and to measure its incidence in a population.

- Surveys may also try to *find evidence about some of the likely causes of people's behaviour or attitudes* (e.g. Why have so many adolescent girls taken up smoking in recent years? Does cigarette advertising encourage people to smoke?). This can be referred to as *analytical* or *explanatory research*, for it aims to explain why people think or act as they do by identifying likely causal influences on their attitudes and behaviour.

Descriptive surveys may be almost completely atheoretical. This is often the case in market research where the aim is to find out whether people like a product, or which product they prefer to buy, but there is no attempt to analyse *why* certain groups chose one product over another.

Analytical surveys, on the other hand, are driven by theoretical questions. Here the aim is to collect evidence which supports or contradicts some *hypothesis* about the causes of people's behaviour or attitudes. This normally means collecting information which will enable us to *compare* one group's answers against another.

Hypotheses

Hypotheses are statements about what our theoretical propositions lead us to expect to find. They enable theories to be tested by predicting patterns of observations that should occur. Hypotheses therefore predict patterns of association in observed data as a means for testing causal theories.

We should not exaggerate the distinction between descriptive and analytical surveys, for the difference between them may not be very sharp in practice:

◆   Many surveys set out *both* to discover facts, *and* to test some causal propositions. The same survey might be interested in discovering how many people smoke (a descriptive question) and why smokers took up cigarettes in the first place (an analytical one).
◆   Descriptive surveys can be used to help us *develop* theories and hypotheses that we can then go out to test in later analytical research.

PROBLEMS OF METHOD AND PROBLEMS OF METHODOLOGY

Sociologists who are sceptical about the use of survey methods doubt whether they should be used to describe facts or to test theories, for they reject the idea that survey researchers can simply go out and 'gather facts' in the way that we have been suggesting.

To understand what is at issue here, it will help to distinguish problems of *method* from problems of *methodology.*

◆   Problems of method are *technical* problems to do with whether research tools are used properly.
◆   Problems of methodology are more *philosophical* and relate to whether it is possible or advisable to use such tools in the first place.

Most critics of social surveys and quantitative data analysis see the problem as one of methodology rather than method. They are not really interested in whether a survey has been carried out 'well' or 'badly' – they are more concerned to demonstrate that the research should not have been carried out in this way at all.

Methods and methodology

'The term "methods" is normally reserved for the technology of research, the actual tools by which data are gathered and analysed, while "methodology" refers to the logic or philosophy underlying particular methods.'

John Hughes, *Sociological Analysis: Methods of Discovery* (London: Nelson, 1976) p. 6

Technical problems of *method*

Technical problems of survey method concern the quality of the information that we gather in surveys. For example:

◆ Do our sampling techniques really give us a group of respondents whose answers represent the whole population from whom they are drawn?
◆ Do our questions get at the kind of information we want?
◆ Do our interviewing techniques unwittingly introduce a bias into the information that we gather?

When critics raise these sorts of concerns, they are worrying about the possibility that the facts that we gather in our surveys might be distorted, and that the empirical tests that we apply to our theories might in some way be inadequate. While such concerns must be taken seriously, there are procedures we can learn and rules we can follow to minimize these technical problems. We shall see in later chapters how to ensure that samples are likely to be representative, that interviews are not unduly biased, that measures are appropriate, and so on.

Philosophical problems of *methodology*

Such reassurances are unlikely to impress those critics for whom the problem is more philosophical than technical. Their concern is not that surveys might gather 'inaccurate information'; it is rather that survey researchers make a fundamental *epistemological* error when they assume that they can use these research techniques to go out and 'collect facts' in the first place.

Epistemology

Epistemology is that branch of philosophy which concerns itself with claims to knowledge. In other words, epistemology asks: 'How can we claim to know that something is true or false?'

The philosophical case against survey methods attacks on two fronts:

- It queries the way surveys claim to *collect information*, for it rejects the notion that 'facts' can simply be observed and recorded by survey researchers.
- It questions the way information is *analysed* once it has been collected, for it rejects all attempts to express social reality in the form of numbers and percentages.

Both lines of attack derive from the same philosophical source – namely, the *rejection of positivism* which swept through Western sociology in the 1960s and which has left its mark ever since. This philosophical attack on positivism resulted in the widespread rejection of the basic principles and assumptions on which quantitative techniques are based. We can always refine our tools, but there is not much we can do if the tools are rejected as being inappropriate for the job.

Is the problem really philosophical?

'It is my contention that, behind the war cry of positivism, attacks that have been parading as fundamental criticisms of the epistemological basis of survey research have very often been either criticisms of a practical technical nature – i.e. criticisms of bad survey research, which all of us would want to agree with I'm sure – or have raised problems [common to] *any* kind of data collection in social sciences.'

Catherine Marsh, 'Problems with surveys: method or epistemology?', in M. Bulmer (ed.), *Sociological Research Methods*, 2nd edn (London: Macmillan, 1984), p. 83

WHAT IS POSITIVIST SOCIOLOGY?

Comte's positive social philosophy

In the nineteenth century, the French social philosopher Auguste Comte suggested that a new 'positive' era had opened which had abandoned the fruitless search for magical 'hidden essences' or religious 'ultimate meanings', and had come to concentrate instead on *observing things as they are*.

In this positive stage of human development, people would accept as knowledge only those claims about the world which could be authenticated through direct experience – by observing them, touching them, or whatever. Faith in intangibles would be left to religion; science dealt only in facts.

Comte believed that because of the inherent complexity of its subject matter, the study of social life was the last area of human enquiry to make this transition from metaphysics to positive science. Comte suggested a name for it: *sociology*. He believed that this new science would evolve to study social issues *objectively*, by applying tried and tested scientific procedures of observation and measurement. It would concern itself only with facts, not opinions or beliefs or wishful thinking, and it would in this way come up with explanations for why things go wrong in society, as well as prescriptions for how to put them right.

Durkheim's sociological rules

Half a century later, Durkheim set out to bring Comte's promise of an objective science of society to fruition. It was Durkheim's contention that what social science studies is not individual behaviour, but collective phenomena (what he famously called 'social facts'). For example:

- Sociologists are not interested in why any particular individual breaks the law, but in why crime *rates* are so much higher today than they were 50 years ago.
- Social science has little to say about why you may or may not choose to move in with your boyfriend or girlfriend, but it is intensely interested in why *rates* of marriage have fallen so dramatically since the 1970s.

For Durkheim, then, social science is about discovering and explaining patterns and generalizations in whole populations, not about studying the unique features of particular individuals' lives. But how can we discover these patterns and find what is causing them?

Like Comte, Durkheim argued that all sociological knowledge must ultimately be based on the evidence of our *senses*. The facts are out there – the crime rate really *has* risen, just as the rate of marriage really *has* fallen. The task for social science is to find some suitable way of observing, classifying and measuring such facts objectively, without allowing our prior theories or prejudices to get in the way of what we find. Durkheim laid down a number of 'rules' about how we might achieve this:

- He told us we should study social phenomena in much the same way as we would study objects in the physical world – we should *eradicate our preconceptions* and look at the facts as they appear to us.
- If something cannot be directly measured, then we should find an observable indicator through which to measure it indirectly – just as a natural scientist measures heat by observing the movement of mercury in a thermometer, for example, so we may measure, say, social disintegration by linking it to *observable indicators* such as crime rates or rates of mental illness in a population.

Durkheim's comparative method

'We have only one way to demonstrate that a given phenomenon is the cause of another, viz., to compare the cases in which they are simultaneously present or absent, to see if the variations they present in these different combinations of circumstances indicate that one depends on the other... [T]he method employed is that of indirect experiment, or the comparative method.'

Émile Durkheim, *The Rules of Sociological Method* (New York: Free Press, 1938), p. 125

To establish causal links between phenomena, Durkheim advocated the use of *systematic comparison* (what he called 'the method of concomitant variation'). As in the natural sciences, so in the social sciences, causation is established by comparing outcomes when a particular factor is present with outcomes when the same factor is absent:

♦ In the natural sciences, this comparative approach normally involves the use of *experiments* – we compare results in an 'experimental group' with those in a 'control group'.
♦ In social science, where experiments are rarely possible, we look for differences in social behaviour between groups by analysing *statistical patterns*.

Durkheim famously applied his comparative method to an analysis of official statistics on suicide rates in different countries at different times and across different social groups. This led him to identify clear patterns of difference – between married people and single people, men and women, the old and the young, Protestants and Catholics, the well educated and the poorly educated, in countries at peace and at war, in times of stability and times of economic tumult, and so on. Analysis of these differences then enabled him to come up with explanations for differing suicide rates, based on factors such as how strongly individuals are integrated into their social groups (married people are more integrated than singles, for example) and how successfully societies weather periods of change and upheaval.

Studying social facts by using surveys

Durkheim's *Suicide*, published in 1897, was the first important example of how a positivist social science can gather facts, classify them to reveal hitherto unknown patterns, and then develop explanations for them. Today, more than a hundred years later, we still do this. Sometimes, like Durkheim, we use official records, such as police crime records or family court divorce records. At other times, we generate new statistics using a social survey.

Social surveys are routinely used today to collect data on patterns of social behaviour, comparing one time period with another, or one type of society with another, or different social groups with one another, just as Durkheim did in his study of suicide rates. By collecting and collating survey evidence, we try to do two things:

♦ We seek to *measure objectively* 'things' like voting patterns, rates of social mobility or (as in our case) rates of smoking behaviour in different groups or populations. This is what we have called 'descriptive' research – documenting facts.
♦ We also try to analyse the results from surveys *to find evidence of causal links* between social phenomena, in much the same way as Durkheim did in his study of suicide statistics over a century ago. Like him, we employ a comparative method to see whether certain kinds of behaviour appear to be associated with particular social groups or characteristics. We have called this 'analytical' research – discovering causal associations by testing theories against facts.

Do you have to be a positivist if you want to do a survey?

There is no necessary correspondence between the use of quantitative survey techniques and a commitment to positivist philosophy:

◆ It is possible to be a positivist but to use other methods of research and analysis than social surveys – experimental and observational methods, for example, can be perfectly consistent with the basic rules of positivism;
◆ It is also possible to use survey techniques without endorsing all aspects of positivist philosophy. Indeed, most sociologists who carry out surveys or use statistical data would probably deny that they are 'positivists'.

Nevertheless, there is a connection between positivism, social surveys, and the use of statistics to analyse social phenomena. Most quantitative sociologists today are much more cautious than Comte and Durkheim were about the possibilities of measuring facts and testing theories – but that does not mean they think it cannot be done. We are just more aware today of the philosophical problems that we have to grapple with.

Reluctant positivists

'Much of sociology remains gently positivist at heart...a model of sociology which believes in a world external to the sociologist, which needs to be experienced in a systematic way. When a sociologist presents an account of his [sic] work, he is usually implicitly saying "the external world is like this: if you in the audience study it in the same way as I have done you will come to the same conclusions."'

Geoff Payne, Robert Dingwall, Judy Payne and Mick Carter, *Sociology and Social Research* (London: Routledge & Kegan Paul, 1981), p. 56

The (mildly) positivist assumptions on which survey research is based

Leszek Kolakowski (in *Positivist Philosophy,* Penguin, 1972) helpfully isolates the four key principles that define positivist philosophy:

◆ *Phenomenalism* The insistence that scientific knowledge has to be grounded in sensory experience of *phenomena*, or 'things'. If we cannot see, touch, smell, taste or hear something, either directly or indirectly, then we cannot study it scientifically.
◆ *Nominalism* The assertion that concepts are only labels for things and can never tell us more than can be gathered from experience. Labelling a group of people as

'working class', for example, does not itself tell us anything more than we already know about them – it just helps us classify them.

♦ *Unity of scientific method*   The claim that all science should follow the same method of accumulating knowledge through direct observation and rigorous testing of theories against factual evidence.

♦ *Value freedom*   The recognition that science cannot make ethical judgements about good and bad, right and wrong, because such evaluations cannot be justified with reference to knowledge based in experience.

Each of these principles is reflected to some degree in the assumptions on which quantitative survey methods operate.

1   The phenomenalist assumption in survey methods: Facts exist prior to, and independently of, research, and can be discovered by asking questions and recording answers systematically.

Survey researchers typically talk of 'gathering evidence' or 'collecting data'. This implies that the data – the factual evidence – exist 'out there' in the population, and that the task is to identify, classify and measure them accurately.

Strictly speaking, of course, the data do not 'exist' until we get people to answer our questions, and survey researchers understand this. But this approach to social research does assume that there are facts to be known about people's behaviour, attitudes and characteristics, and that these facts – 'phenomena' – have an existence before we ask our questions. It is in this sense that social survey research is 'phenomenalist', for it is premised on the belief that facts exist outside of the research process and can be discovered by it – even though this may not be as straightforward as classical empiricists seemed to imagine.

2   The nominalist assumption in survey methods: Theories guide the questions we ask, and theories can be tested against the evidence we find, but the facts themselves stand independently of the theories we may hold.

Survey researchers know that the way they collect facts about people will be guided by their theoretical interests and concerns. The way they frame their questions, classify people's answers and analyse their results will inevitably reflect their theoretical starting point. They nevertheless insist that none of this *determines* what they find – their concepts and theories give shape to their research, but they do not blind them to evidence that they did not expect to find, nor do they reveal facts that are not there.

The crucial role that theory plays in research derives from the deductive logic on which quantitative data analysis is based – we start out from theory, but we use factual evidence to test our theoretical generalizations. The assumption we make when we do a survey is that our theory guides what we are looking for, but that facts about people's lives determine what we find.

Karl Popper on the testing of theories

Positivists insist that scientific knowledge must come from experience (that is, observation). This implies that generalizations have to be built up by repeated observations (what philosophers call *inductive reasoning*). But this poses a problem, for no matter how many repeated observations you make, you can never be sure that the next one will not be different from the ones that preceded it. This 'problem of induction' has caused major headaches for positivist philosophers. How, they ask, can science develop watertight generalizations (causal laws) if scientific knowledge can only come from experience, and experience is never conclusive?

Karl Popper suggested a way out of this paradox. Instead of developing general theories on the basis of repeated observations, he said, we should *begin* with a theoretical generalization and then test it against observation (what philosophers call *deductive reasoning*). Rather than searching for evidence to confirm our theories (as inductive logic requires), Popper said science should make repeated attempts to prove theories wrong. An original hypothesis (or 'conjecture') can never conclusively be proved correct, but we can place reasonable levels of trust in theories which have successfully withstood repeated attempts at 'refutation'.

Karl Popper, *The Logic of Scientific Discovery* (London: Hutchinson, 1959)

---

3 The 'unity of science' assumption in survey methods: Survey data consist of responses to questions which can be analysed, in much the same way as observations in any other science are analysed, by means of statistical comparison.

When positivists insist that social science and natural science share the same method, they do not mean that they share the same techniques of investigation. Sociologists do not sit in laboratories heating up families in test tubes or dissecting social classes under a microscope. What they mean is that the *logic* of investigation (the 'methodology') is the same – that in social science as in natural science, we gather facts and we use them to test our theories.

All social scientists are aware that, unlike natural science (which studies *objects*), they are dealing with human *subjects*. While objects simply react to stimuli, human subjects initiate action – human behaviour is *motivated*. This means that if you want to know what 'causes' us to act in certain ways, you need to know something about the way we are thinking, and no natural science technique of observation is ever going to tell you that.

This difference between the unthinking objects of the natural world and the thinking subjects who inhabit the social world opens up research strategies to social scientists which cannot be used in the natural sciences. In particular, we can use *empathy* to understand how people may be thinking and feeling, and hence to develop plausible insights into why they are behaving as they are. There is obviously no equivalent to this in the natural sciences where we can only ever analyse data from the outside looking in.

Most survey researchers acknowledge all this, and they therefore reject a strong version of the positivist postulate of the 'unity of science'. However, the fact that we can use empathic methods in the social sciences does not rule out the use of other, more observational methods such as surveys, provided they are appropriate to the kind of information we are trying to gather. Indeed, we might decide to use empathy to develop hypotheses which can then be tested using survey methods. The stand-off between so-called 'quantitative' and 'qualitative' approaches in sociology is a false dilemma – we can use both.

4   *The assumption of value freedom in survey methods: The collection of facts is distinct from their evaluation, and the survey itself should be unbiased.*

The principle of 'value freedom' is that the results of research cannot be used to demonstrate the superiority of any particular ethical or political argument. The reason is that you cannot logically derive an 'ought' statement from an 'is' statement – knowing what the world is like (facts) cannot tell you what it 'should' be like (values).

Suppose, for example, that our research shows that young people are encouraged by advertising to start smoking. Such a finding cannot justify us concluding that cigarette advertising should 'therefore' be banned. This is because the fact that advertising influences people to start smoking cannot tell us whether protecting the health of young people is more or less important than, say, protecting the rights of free speech (which are curtailed by any ban on advertising). The research finding helps *inform* the ethical debate, but it can in no way help to resolve it.

Many social researchers do use their results to try to bring about changes in public policy, and surveys are sometimes commissioned in the hope that they will produce evidence that will help one cause rather than another. But good survey researchers will always insist that if their results do not come out as hoped, the findings should still be published and should not be altered or censored. The facts, in the end, must prevail over one's personal values.

The research process itself is also assumed to be objective and impartial. In particular, it is assumed that there is nothing about the way that data are collected in a survey, or about the way they are subsequently analysed, that favours or discriminates against any group or interest in society. The survey is simply a tool, and as such it carries no bias.

CAN FACTS BE OBSERVED AND RECORDED INDEPENDENTLY OF OUR THEORIES?

For the remainder of this chapter we shall consider how realistic and plausible each of these four propositions really is. We begin with the phenomenalist and nominalist assumptions in survey methodology. They raise the question of how far surveys can be used to collect facts about people's behaviour, beliefs and attributes without our theoretical ideas getting in the way of our observations.

The fundamental problem here is that the way we observe 'facts' about the world must to some extent reflect the ideas that we already hold about the reality we are observing. This means that theory does a lot more than simply guiding where we look – it actually helps shape what we see. This in turn means that scientific knowledge cannot after all be based in direct experience of the world around us, yet this is a fundamental axiom of the classical positivist tradition.

Is observation theory-dependent?

Have a look at figure 1.1. You probably see a staircase viewed diagonally from above. But keep looking at it, and suddenly you find that the image switches. You are still looking at a staircase, but now you are seeing it diagonally from below. As you continue to stare at this image, so your impression of what you are looking at keeps changing.

What this demonstrates is that our recognition of 'things' is not simply a function of their direct impact on our senses. What we see depends not only on the images which reach our eyes, but also on how our brains interpret these images. Observation, that is, depends crucially on *interpretation*.

This would seem to strike two mighty blows against the basic assumptions of empiricism:

- It suggests that knowledge of the world is not a function of raw experience. Our brain classifies the information which is fed to it through the various sense organs, which means that we have to learn how to 'see' things before we know what we are looking at.
- It casts doubt on the most basic assumption of empiricism, which is that 'facts' exist independently of how we look at the world. If observation depends on interpretation, then the objects that we experience in the world only appear the way they do because of what we *believe* we are seeing.

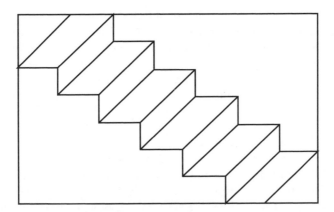

Figure 1.1   Perception depends on mental frameworks

Source: A. F. Chalmers, *What is This Thing Called Science?* 3rd edn (Buckingham: Open University Press, 1999), p. 6

We seem to be in deep trouble! Notice how we have started placing inverted commas around words like 'fact' and 'see'. Our faith that a world exists beyond our senses, and that it can be known through experience, is beginning to look very shaky – we are even beginning to doubt whether there are such things as facts.

Theory dependency is not theory determinacy

We learn to see things in certain ways by putting them into categories. That is, observation depends on prior *conceptualization*. In the process of observing things, we simultaneously *make sense of them* by fitting our experiences into a pre-existing conceptual framework. This means that if different people have different sets of concepts in their heads (for instance, as a result of being brought up in very different cultures), then they may well 'observe' the same thing in different ways.

However (and it is a big 'however'), this does not mean that we are free to interpret the world in any way we choose. There are appropriate and inappropriate conceptual frameworks for interpreting any given experience. Looking again at figure 1.1, for example, different observers might draw on different conceptual frameworks to claim that they are looking at:

◆ a set of straight lines
◆ a staircase
◆ a picture of a staircase
◆ a pattern which forms a holistic image (known as a 'gestalt' diagram)

We might accept any of these claims as factually correct – but there are millions of other claims that we would dismiss as incorrect. The object (in this case, the picture) sets limits on the range of interpretations that are appropriate.

Some enemies of empiricism suggest that there can be no objective knowledge of the world because we always have to interpret what we see, and interpretation is subjective. But this seems too strong a claim, for although there are always different ways of interpreting what we see, the range of possible interpretations is limited by the nature of the object we are looking at. *We cannot define reality in any way that we want, for while observation is mediated by the concepts which we have inside our heads, it is not determined by them.* What we see depends on the nature of what we are looking at as well as the way we conceptualize it.

This is important, for it means we can hold on to the basic assumption that there is a real world of objects, and that our knowledge of it depends on what these objects are like. Different observers may still disagree on what they see, but:

◆ *Observers will usually share some concepts in common*   Science is a community which shares an agreed set of rules and procedures for observing and recording facts. Practitioners learn these rules and procedures as part of their training, so different scientists can generally agree on how to recognize evidence.
◆ *We cannot see what is not there*   Scientists cannot simply make things up, for all scientific claims to knowledge have to be publicly tested against empirical evidence using these agreed procedures.

Can we use facts to test our theories?

We are not out of the woods yet, however! Critics have identified at least four additional problems with the position we have now arrived at:

◆ *Circular reasoning*   How can we test theories against factual evidence if our recognition of the facts depends on our existing theories and concepts? Is there not a circularity here?
◆ *The 'myth' of falsification*   Even if scientists agree that a theory has been contradicted by the facts, they often find ways of saving the theory from disconfirmation – tests are not as decisive as philosophers like Karl Popper suggest.
◆ *Paradigmatic orthodoxy*   Even if scientists all agree on the rules for observing facts, this could simply mean that the whole community of scientists will be blind to any evidence that their collective training has not equipped them to recognize.
◆ *Epistemological pluralism*   What happens if (as seems to be the case in sociology) the scientific community cannot agree on a set of rules governing the recognition of evidence?

Circular reasoning

Theories are always tested against evidence which is itself theory-dependent. We test the theory that water boils at 100 degrees Celsius, for example, by putting a mercury thermometer into boiling water and reading off the temperature on the tube – but this test itself assumes the validity of a second theory that claims that mercury expands at a uniform rate when heated! This is not, however, as big a problem as it might seem.

◆ The theory that we are testing may not be the same as the theories on which our factual observations depend (the theory about the boiling point of water, for example, is different from the theory about the expansion of metals which underpins our use of thermometers).
◆ A test will not work unless the real world makes it work (if the water is not boiling, the thermometer will not register 100 degrees). Just because our interpretation of events depends on our theories does not mean that our theories can produce successful test results out of the blue.

The 'myth' of falsification

Popper suggested that science should involve the repeated and rigorous attempt to falsify theories by looking for factual evidence that would disconfirm them. Critics have pointed out, however, that in the actual practice of science, we often try to save our theories from apparent disconfirmation. When we get a result we did not expect, we assume that something is wrong with the test rather than with the theory, and we set the results aside, dismissing our findings as a 'fluke' result.

Furthermore, scientists are often loathe to dispense with a theory, even if it has been falsified, unless there is something better to put in its place. Disproved theories can hang around for a long time until something better comes along to displace them.

Lakatos on 'sophisticated falsificationism'

'Contrary to naïve falsificationism, no experiment, experimental report, observation statement or well-corroborated low-level falsifying hypothesis alone can lead to falsification. There is no falsification before the emergence of a better theory ... Thus the crucial element in falsification is whether the new theory offers any novel, excess information compared with its predecessor and whether some of this excess information is corroborated.'

Imre Lakatos, 'Methodology of scientific research programmes', in I. Lakatos and A. Musgrave (eds), *Criticism and the Growth of Knowledge* (Cambridge: Cambridge University Press, 1970), pp. 119–20

None of this means that we cannot test our theories, but it does mean that deciding when and whether a theory has finally been knocked over by the weight of evidence is a rather more convoluted and drawn-out process than Popper originally recognized. As the history of science readily confirms, false theories *do* get refuted by facts – it's just that it can take rather a long time and can involve a lot of argument.

Paradigmatic orthodoxy

Some critics of empiricism argue that scientists are so well socialized into the procedures and assumptions of 'normal science' that their basic theories only come under sustained criticism during extraordinary periods of scientific 'revolution'. Such revolutions occur when unresolved puzzles within a paradigm build up to such a point that eventually some brave soul suggests that everybody has been looking at things in the wrong way and proposes a completely different paradigm. Other than during these periods of revolutionary upheaval, however, facts are rarely allowed to disturb our theoretical orthodoxies.

Thomas Kuhn on the incommensurability of paradigms

'[T]he proponents of competing paradigms practice their trades in different worlds... Practicing in different worlds, the two groups of scientists see different things when they look from the same point in the same direction. Again, that is not to say that they can see anything they please. Both are looking at the world, and what they look at has not changed. But in some areas they see different things, and they see them in different relations one to the other... before they can hope to communicate fully, one group or the other must experience the conversion that we have been calling a paradigm shift. Just because it is a transition between incommensurables, the transition between competing paradigms cannot be made a step at a time, forced by logic and neutral experience. Like the gestalt switch, it must occur all at once (though not necessarily in an instant) or not at all.'

Thomas Kuhn, *The Structure of Scientific Revolutions*, 2nd edn (Chicago: University of Chicago Press, 1970), p. 150

For sociologists, however, paradigmatic orthodoxy has rarely been a problem, for sociology has no single paradigm (and, arguably, we never have had one). Our problem is not that facts go unrecognized due to a uniformity of perspective. It is rather that nobody can agree on a single set of rules by which facts might be identified in the first place.

Epistemological pluralism

The key problem for disciplines like sociology is that there are *too many* differences among practitioners regarding the way research should be carried out. Rival claims to knowledge jostle each other but rarely engage with each other, and readers go with whatever appeals to their prejudices and disregard the rest.

Basil Bernstein on the rivalry between sociological perspectives

'In a subject where theories and methods are weak, intellectual shifts are likely to arise out of the conflict between *approaches* rather than conflicts between *explanations*, for by definition most explanations will be weak and often non-comparable, because they are approach-specific. The weakness of the explanation is likely to be attributed to the approach, which is analysed in terms of its ideological stance. Once the ideological stance is exposed then all the work may be written off.'

Basil Bernstein, 'Sociology and the sociology of education', in J. Rex (ed.), *Approaches to Sociology* (London: Routledge, 1973), p. 154

CAN SOCIAL PHENOMENA BE OBJECTIVELY RECORDED, MEASURED AND ANALYSED?

Just as natural scientists use various instruments to discover facts about the physical world, so social scientists try to gather facts about people's behaviour and attitudes by using survey instruments like interviews and questionnaires. From the 1960s onwards, however, 'phenomenologists' and 'ethnomethodologists' began to challenge the belief that 'social facts' can be collected in this way.

The nature of sociological accounts

Their starting point was to argue that the meaning of people's actions depends on the social context in which they occur. The 'same' action may be defined differently in different contexts, for the meaning of what we say and do is heavily dependent on where, when and with whom we do it.

Jack Douglas famously explored the implications of this for the analysis of suicide rates (in *The Social Meanings of Suicide*, Princeton University Press, 1967). He showed that an action resulting in one's own death may be interpreted by officials, relatives and others connected with the death as 'suicide' in one social context, but as 'accidental death' or 'misadventure' in another. The suicide statistics that Durkheim gathered cannot therefore be taken as 'objective indicators' of the 'actual' suicide rate, for deaths will have been defined in different ways in different situations, which means there is no 'real rate' of suicide for sociologists to explain. All that sociologists can do is develop an understanding of how coroners and others come to interpret what has happened.

The 'data' which social scientists observe and explain have already been interpreted once before, by actors themselves. There is no equivalent to this in the natural sciences, because objects in the physical world do not have any meaning attached to them until we give them meaning in the course of observing them. In the social world, by contrast, researchers are trying to study phenomena *which are already meaningful*.

What is ethnomethodology?

The prefix, *ethno*, refers to a group of people, a cultural group. Ethno*methodology* thus indicates an approach to sociology which is concerned to identify the methods used by people themselves for making sense of the world in which they live.

According to ethnomethodologists, what social scientists should be doing is producing 'second-order accounts' of how ordinary people create their own 'first-order accounts' of what happens in their world. In the case of suicide, for example, we should be looking at how deaths come to be recorded (by coroners, relatives and others) as 'suicides' in the first place.

In this way, ethnomethodologists have tried to turn sociologists away from a traditional concern with describing and explaining social phenomena, and towards a concern with how social phenomena are 'socially constructed' by actors themselves.

The social construction of survey data

From a phenomenological perspective, surveys do not *collect* facts about a population – they *create* them! This does not mean that survey researchers make up their findings. What it does mean is that they are inevitably engaged with their respondents in a *negotiation of reality*. The survey situation becomes a place where actors meet and negotiate meaning, and the researcher is just one of the actors:

- Respondents 'make sense of' the questions that are put to them and give what they consider to be an appropriate answer.
- The researcher in turn then 'makes sense of' the respondent's answer and classifies it to what he or she believes to be an appropriate category of reply.

The result of all this is not 'objective evidence' of some aspect of social reality. It is, rather, a new, negotiated account of social reality which is in principle no different from any of the other accounts which actors create in the course of their everyday lives. Sociologists' accounts of social reality are in this sense no better than anybody else's.

Intersubjective meaning as a technical problem

The phenomenological critique of survey methods is dismissed by some survey researchers as a technical rather than an epistemological problem:

- Survey researchers recognize the importance of framing questions so that they 'make sense' to respondents. Phenomenological sociology can help by alerting us to the ways in which interviewers and respondents may misunderstand what the other really means to say.
- Researchers are also aware of the importance of classifying answers to questionnaires in such a way that respondents' intentions are respected. Again, phenomenologists can inform this process by showing how language is open to diverse forms of interpretation.

Seen like this, phenomenological sociology simply makes us more aware of the problems involved in ensuring clarity of meaning when doing a survey. Phenomenologists themselves, however, see their critique of survey methods as pointing to much more than mere technical difficulties which are in principle resolvable. For them, there is a fundamental problem in attempting to discover 'social facts' as if they exist over and above actors' own accounts of their social worlds. At the heart of this problem lies the survey researcher's search for quantifiable data.

The problem with numbers

Surveys aim to *measure* some specified set of behaviour or attitudes. A descriptive survey, for example, may be concerned to establish *how many* people smoke, just as an analytical survey may be concerned to estimate the *degree to which* advertising influences people to smoke.

Phenomenologists are quite happy for sociological accounts to use numerical measures where actors themselves make sense of reality in numerical terms. For example:

- A researcher may legitimately record how many cigarettes a smoker gets through in a day, for smokers themselves think in this way, and the question therefore 'makes sense' to them when they are asked it.
- There are also circumstances where it makes sense for researchers to record information using binary measures. For example, we might ask people whether or not they have smoked a cigarette in the last 24 hours, and their answers can be measured on a simple yes/no binary scale.

Suppose, however, we try to construct a scale measuring *how strongly* smokers desire to kick the habit. We might ask them to select an answer ranging from, say, 'very much', through 'quite a lot' and 'somewhat', to 'not much' and 'not at all'.

Alternatively, we might ask them to rank their desire to quit on a scale where '0' means they do not want to quit at all, and '10' means they are desperate to stop.

Systems of measurement like these are very common in survey research – but they drive phenomenologists to despair, for here numbers are being *imposed* by the researcher to produce an account which bears little resemblance to the way the actors themselves normally think and behave. People do not go around in their everyday lives telling their friends that their desire to stop smoking has just increased from 6 to 7.

When natural scientists measure the natural world by applying their own, constructed scales of temperature, weight, mass, or whatever, they do no violence to the reality they are studying, for the data have no inherent meaning to begin with. When social scientists apply their constructs to measure the social world, however, they are imposing a second-order account which smothers the first-order accounts of their respondents themselves – yet these first-order accounts should be what we are studying.

Numbers are not always meaningful

'Er...Good morning, O Deep Thought,' said Loonquawl nervously, 'do you have...er, that is...'

'An answer for you?' interrupted Deep Thought majestically, 'Yes, I have.'

...

'Though I don't think,' added Deep Thought, 'that you're going to like it.'
'Doesn't matter!' said Phouchg. 'We must know it! Now!'

...

'Alright,' said Deep Thought. 'The Answer to the Great Question...'
'Yes...!'
'Of Life, the Universe and Everything...' said Deep Thought.
'Yes...!'
'Is...' said Deep Thought, and paused.
'Yes...!'
'Is...'
'Yes...!!!...?'
'Forty-two,' said Deep Thought, with infinite majesty and calm.

...

'Forty-two!' yelled Loonquawl. 'Is that all you've got to show for seven and a half million years' work?'

'I checked it very thoroughly,' said the computer, 'and that quite definitely is the answer. I think the problem, to be quite honest with you, is that you've never actually known what the question is.'

Douglas Adams, *The Hitch-Hiker's Guide to the Galaxy* (London: Pan Macmillan, 1979), pp. 134–6

Is quantification necessarily invalid?

A pragmatic response to this critique might be to ask whether our measures help us describe or explain aspects of people's lives. The question then is not whether our numerical categories make sense to our respondents, but whether our measures successfully translate how they are thinking and acting into a simpler, numerical language.

We shall see in chapter 5 that there are various *tests of validity* we can apply to measurement scales to gauge whether they are tapping into how people actually think and behave. We can see, for example, whether people's answers to different questions are consistent with each other ('internal validity'), or whether the scores by which we measure their attitudes actually predict the way they behave ('external validity'). Good surveys do not use numbers mindlessly – they check whether the numbers represent a reasonable translation from actors' own beliefs and actions.

Provided they are properly validated, numerical indicators and scales can help us measure aspects of people's lives, even if actors themselves do not use or even understand them themselves.

Is THE QUANTITATIVE SOCIAL SURVEY A NEUTRAL RESEARCH INSTRUMENT?

The use of survey methods (for collecting facts), and of quantification (for analysing them), has been attacked by some critics on the grounds that surveys are oppressive instruments for collecting information, and statistics are oppressive forms of presenting and analysing it.

In the 1960s, American radicals suggested that mainstream sociology was biased in favour of the powerful. Positivist sociology's protestations of 'value freedom' – that it was only interested in gathering facts, and that it was neutral as between different interests and beliefs in society – were dismissed as an ideological smokescreen, and survey researchers in particular were berated for accepting research funds from government and big corporate institutions to carry out intelligence on behalf of the dominant interests in society.

Social research as an aid to repression

'The professional eyes of the sociologist are on the down people, and the professional palm of the sociologist is stretched toward the up people ... he is an Uncle Tom not only for this government and ruling class but for any.'

Martin Nicolaus, speaking at the American Sociological Association conference in 1968 – quoted in Alvin Gouldner, *The Coming Crisis of Western Sociology* (London: Heinemann, 1971), p. 10

This line of criticism was subsequently taken up by Marxists and 'critical theorists' in the 1970s, and in the feminist social research methods literature of the 1980s.

Marxist critiques

There is no obvious reason why Marxists should shun survey methods, and not all of them have. Indeed, we shall see in chapter 3 that Marx himself used a questionnaire survey to gather information on the French working class. Nevertheless, there is a strong tradition within Marxism of criticizing social survey research as 'bourgeois' and 'ideological'.

◆   One argument is that surveys *classify* their information using categories derived from a bourgeois view of the world. Surveys reproduce existing ideological representations of reality, rather than challenging them, and in this way they help perpetuate the existing system of class domination.

The Marxist critique of official statistics

Big national surveys are expensive, and the state is one of the few players with the resources to carry them out. This means that surveys are conducted on those issues where the state needs information, and because the state's primary role is to support the interests of the capitalist class while ensuring the continued exploitation of the working class, this means that surveys get used as instruments of class rule.

Moreover, statistics produced by surveys use bourgeois categories to measure social phenomena. For example, the British census divides the population into 'social classes', but these bear no resemblance to what Marxists think are the 'real' classes of bourgeoisie and proletariat. The census categories confuse and distort the 'real' lines of class cleavage, and this helps disguise the relations of power and exploitation in society.

See Ian Miles and John Irvine, 'The critique of official statistics', in J. Irvine, I. Miles and J. Evans (eds), *Demystifying Social Statistics* (London: Pluto Press, 1979); Barry Hindess, *The Use of Official Statistics in Sociology* (London: Macmillan, 1973)

◆   A rather different argument is that surveys help the 'capitalist state' and its 'ruling class' gather information that can be used to maintain the 'oppression' of workers, ethnic minorities and other victims of the capitalist system. Just as workers in a factory or an office become 'objectified' in the labour process, so too do respondents in a survey when they are treated instrumentally as mere units of information. Surveys thus reflect and perpetuate the degradation of the human spirit under capitalism.

Critical theorists on positivist research techniques

'Insofar as contemporary life has been standardized to a great extent by the concentration of economic power pressed to the extreme and the individual is far more powerless than he admits to himself, methods which are standardized and in a certain sense deindividualized, are not only the expression of the situation but also the suitable means for describing and gaining insight into this situation.'

Max Horkheimer et al., *Aspects of Sociology* (London: Heinemann, 1973), pp. 122–3

Feminist critiques

While Marxists have attacked surveys as 'bourgeois', feminists have dismissed them as 'patriarchal'. The basic complaint is that quantitative sociology betrays an inherently 'masculine' way of seeing which prevents women's experiences from being expressed:

◆ Feminists have attacked the use of numbers (quantity) to express human experience (quality), arguing that women must be allowed to 'speak for themselves'. This requires methods which emphasize intuition, empathy and intersubjective understanding, rather than reducing subjective experience to percentages and charts.

◆ Survey methods are also criticized for treating women as objects. Surveys lock women into inferior roles in the inherently hierarchical researcher–respondent relationship, and some feminists have likened the research process to an act of 'rape' in which researchers take what they want for their own purposes, and then run away.

The critique of 'malestream' research

'The case that has been mounted against mainstream/"malestream" social research has been an important part of the project of women's studies; and within this, the dualism of "quantitative" and "qualitative" methods has played a central role. The use of "qualitative" research methods has been aligned with a feminist perspective, while "quantitative" methods have been seen as implicitly or explicitly defensive of the (masculinist) status quo.'

Ann Oakley 'Gender, methodology and people's ways of knowing', *Sociology*, vol. 32 (1998), p. 707

Are surveys inherently biased?

Some of these criticisms can be fairly easily answered. For example:

◆ If it is true, as Marxists have claimed, that the categories used to analyse survey data are commonly grounded in a 'bourgeois' view of the world, then it is open to Marxist researchers to go out and generate their own data using categories derived from their own theories. There is nothing inherent in the method of survey research itself that requires that respondents be classified in one way rather than another. Equally, there is no reason why organizations sympathetic to working-class interests – trade unions, for example – should not commission surveys to aid their objectives (indeed, they have often done just this).

◆ The feminist concern that surveys fail to capture people's subjective experiences could in principle be met by designing questions more carefully, or by training interviewers more rigorously. If surveys can successfully be used to study men, then there is no reason why they cannot also be used to study women (indeed, surveys have successfully been carried out on women's health, women's employment, and so on). By embracing 'qualitative' approaches and rejecting 'quantitative' ones, feminists reproduce the very gender stereotypes (males as 'rational', females as 'intuitive') that feminism has been so intent on challenging. Recognizing this, a number of feminist sociologists have recently argued that it is a mistake to equate feminism with qualitative approaches, and that survey methods should not be excluded from feminist research.

Problems of finance

Where there is a problem in survey research is in the sheer *expense* involved in carrying out a serious survey. Fieldwork can be cripplingly expensive, and the time taken to put the results into the computer, check them for accuracy and do the analysis adds to a hefty salaries bill. Unless you plan to do a small-scale local survey using in-the-street interviews (the strategy we shall adopt in our Smoking Survey), or a mail-out or telephone or internet questionnaire, it is unlikely that you will be able to carry out a serious survey without substantial financial backing.

This does raise a potential problem of bias, for it means that surveys tend to get carried out by those who can get access to large sums of money. This does not, however, prove the Marxist case that surveys are a tool of big business, for the principal source of funds for academic research in Britain is not private enterprise, nor the voluntary sector, but is the Economic and Social Research Council (ESRC).

The ESRC uses government money (£91.5 million for 2003–4) to fund research proposals from the academic community which have the support of expert academic referees. It is true that government does from time to time bring pressure to bear on the ESRC (this happened in the early years of the Thatcher premiership, and it happened again under Blair), but it is difficult to argue that social research in Britain has been subordinated to the interests of a dominant class when so much of the funding is dispensed by academics, many of whom are antipathetic to big business and the capitalist market system.

The ESRC responds to government concerns about the shortage of quantitative research skills

'We have become increasingly aware of a deficiency in the research skills of many of the UK's social science disciplines. This concern is reflected to us not only in the applications submitted to ESRC for funding, but also in the difficulties institutions have experienced in recruiting suitably qualified staff, and by government departments that have also experienced serious recruitment problems.'

ESRC *Postgraduate Funding Guidelines* (2001), available from the ESRC website, www.esrc.ac.uk

---

CONCLUSION: MUDDLING THROUGH?

In this chapter, we have identified four philosophical principles of positivism, and from each we have derived four somewhat watered-down assumptions on which quantitative survey research is usually grounded. These assumptions can be summarized thus:

- It is possible to discover facts about people's actions, attitudes and attributes by asking them questions and recording their answers systematically.
- The facts that we gather can be used to test our theories.
- Survey responses represent 'observations' which can validly be measured and analysed using statistical procedures.
- Questionnaires – the instruments for collecting facts in social surveys – are not inherently biased.

We have seen in each case that these assumptions can be challenged, but in each case we have also seen that the criticisms can be answered, at least to some degree. For example:

- While we have to recognize the impossibility of observing facts independently of the theories and concepts that help us interpret what we are looking at, this 'theory-dependency' of observation does not mean that what we see is *determined* by our prior ideas, or that we are free to define what we see in any way we choose. Recognizing that there are no 'raw facts' in social science does not mean that there are no facts at all against which to test our claims to knowledge.
- There are problems in testing theories against factual evidence, for the way we test theories itself assumes that certain other theories are correct, and scientists do not necessarily accept test results when their theories appear to have been falsified. But this does not rule out the possibility of testing theories against evidence. Theory testing may be problematic, but that does not mean it cannot be done at all.
- Attempts to quantify the findings of social research have been attacked by phenomenologists, who suggest that quantification violates the meaning which people

invest in their actions, and by Marxists and feminists, who see the reduction of qualitative differences to a quantitative scale as anti-humanist and oppressive. Recognizing these dangers, we have nevertheless suggested that the use of numbers and statistics in social research need not result in mindless tabulation of data, or in bruising disregard for individual distinctiveness.

Philosophers have been concerned about the problems in positivist social research for a very long time, and they have exposed real difficulties which cannot be ignored. Every time we talk of the 'facts' we have discovered, or claim that some theory has been 'disproved' by our 'evidence', we are likely to be reminded that things are not this simple.

The pragmatism of the social researcher

'However erroneous it may be in philosophical terms, sociological practice does go on ... we [the sociological profession] implicitly accept that the philosophical paradoxes can only be coped with by ignoring them in our own practice ... there *is* a place for systematic empiricism and a kind of generalization and theory which guides sociological analysis of the external world, and which is continuously refined by research, not just by armchair speculation and library critique.'

Geoff Payne, Robert Dingwall, Judy Payne and Mick Carter, *Sociology and Social Research* (London: Routledge & Kegan Paul, 1981), pp. 58–9

All social research is fallible, and social surveys are no exception. It is not easy to do them well, and even when done well, they can never give you foolproof results. But this does not make worthwhile survey research impossible. There are rules and procedures that we can follow that will overcome at least some of the problems and which will improve our chances of producing reasonably reliable, valid and useful data. The rest of this book offers you a guide to these rules and procedures.

DEVELOPING HYPOTHESES

THE LITERATURE SEARCH

The first step in any research project is normally to conduct an in-depth review of the existing literature on the topic. This is done for two main reasons:

- We need to *see what we already know* from previous research. It would be silly to carry out a study in ignorance of the existing store of research findings, so we review the literature to see where the gaps are in our knowledge so that we might attempt to plug them.
- We need to familiarize ourselves with current thinking about the topic so that we can *develop a set of research questions* which are relevant to the problems which the social science community is addressing. We therefore search the literature to find out more about the theories and conjectures which will drive our hypotheses.

The first step in developing our smoking survey is therefore to visit the library:

- We can do *keyword searches* on the library computer to find books and reports that have been written on the subject.
- We can turn to the internet, using *search engines* to locate websites containing relevant information, and then downloading any material that looked useful.
- We can use online *databases* to search for relevant newspapers articles or for papers in academic journals.

We can also try *contacting relevant individuals or organizations* to see what they can give us. When we started work on the Smoking Survey, for example, our students contacted ASH, who campaign in the UK for tighter regulation of smoking, and FOREST, who campaign for the right to smoke, and both organizations proved enormously helpful in providing material.

THE RESEARCH QUESTIONS

Reviewing the various studies they had found, our students identified two main questions around which to base the smoking project:

1 *What are the social factors which lead people to start and continue smoking despite increasing social pressures against it?*

2 *How do people's attitudes and beliefs about smoking relate to their actual smoking behaviour?*

These two basic questions were then elaborated to provide us with ten hypotheses which we wanted to test.

> If you are developing your own survey on smoking, it would be a good idea to include some of these hypotheses as well as developing some others of your own based on the results of your preliminary library research. If you do develop others, try to keep them simple, for this will make it easier to operationalize them (a task we undertake in Chapter 3).

HYPOTHESES ABOUT SOCIAL INFLUENCES ON SMOKING BEHAVIOUR

Hypothesis 1: Parental socialization

Smokers are more likely than non-smokers to have had parents who smoked.

Previous research has reported that parental smoking has little influence on whether people take up smoking when they get older. A study commissioned by the Department of Health and Social Security and published by the office for Population Censuses and Surveys (OPCS) found: 'Smoking by parents during childhood had little association with their smoking behaviour and, moreover, had no effect on intention to give up' (A. Marsh and J. Matheson, *Smoking Attitudes and Behaviour* (London: OPCS, 1983), p. 90). Our first hypothesis aims to replicate this – will we too find no relationship with parental smoking?

Hypothesis 2: Peer group socialization

The more friends they have who smoke, the more likely it is that people will themselves smoke.

J. Krosnick and C. Judd ('Transitions in social influence at adolescence: who induces cigarette smoking?', *Developmental Psychology*, vol. 18 (1982), pp. 359–68) found that peer group pressures are a major factor in people's decisions to start – or quit – smoking. The causation may work both ways – if friends influence our smoking behaviour, it may also be the case that our choice of whether or not to smoke influences our choice of friendship networks. The 1983 OPCS survey found that smokers tended to interact mainly with other smokers, which suggests that continuance of smoking may lead people to seek out positive support or endorsement from others. Equally, non-smokers may prefer not to mix with people who smoke.

Hypothesis 3: Socialization through mass media

Regular exposure to positive media images of smoking and/or to media representations of smoking as 'normal' will positively reinforce the behaviour of smokers.

Much research has been done on the effects of television and other media on people's behaviour and beliefs. Although the results are often mixed, few people doubt that TV in particular can *reinforce* behaviour even if it does not initially *cause* it. Research in the US (reported in the Daily Telegraph, 27 Feb. 2001, p. 8) claims that young people whose favourite movie stars are shown smoking in films are up to three times more likely to smoke themselves, or to have pro-smoking attitudes.

Hypothesis 4: Socialization through subcultures

Membership of a distinct subculture where smoking is common provides smokers with a positive reference group and therefore reinforces their commitment to smoking.

Research on young people's use of tobacco, alcohol and illegal drugs by the Department of Health in 1998 (*Smoking, Drinking and Drug Use among Young Teenagers, Volume I: England* (London: HMSO, 1998) found that those who smoke are also much more likely to drink and use drugs, and this suggests that a distinctive youth lifestyle is associated with smoking. The association between smoking and drinking also seems to persist in older age groups.

Hypothesis 5: Stress

The more stressed people claim to be, the more they are likely to smoke.

The pro-smoking lobby group FOREST points to Australian research which found that smokers suffer less hypertension and lower rates of heart disease than those who have quit. This could indicate that smoking lowers stress levels (and smokers themselves often claim that smoking relieves stress). However, it is unclear whether high stress leads people to smoke, or people who smoke claim to be more stressed. This hypothesis expects to find an association between smoking and stress, but causation may run in both directions.

HYPOTHESES ABOUT THE RELATION BETWEEN ATTITUDES AND SMOKING BEHAVIOUR

Hypothesis 6: Self-interest

Smokers will express greater tolerance of smoking than will non-smokers. Non-smokers will be more supportive of smoking restrictions than smokers.

This hypothesis assumes that we adopt values and opinions which 'fit' our self-interest. Smokers will resist tighter controls while non-smokers will support them. The 1983 OPCS survey found that both groups supported the principle of smoking regulation to protect non-smokers' rights, but they disagreed on outright bans in public places like restaurants and public transport: 'Attitudes to bans on smoking seemed to be guided by self-interest.' This hypothesis will test this claim.

Hypothesis 7: Age effect

Tolerance of smoking declines with age because young people are more inclined than older people to be tolerant of others' behaviour.

Although young people have grown up in a culture which is much less tolerant of smoking than it used to be, we hypothesize that many young people are nevertheless reluctant to be judgemental, and this will influence their attitudes about smoking as it does their attitudes about drug use, sexuality, and many other issues of personal choice and lifestyle (evidence of how permissiveness varies with age can be found in periodic results from the British Social Attitudes Survey).

Hypothesis 8: Social class effect

The higher somebody's social class and level of education, the less likely they are to smoke, and the less tolerant they will be of smoking.

Rates of smoking are lower in the middle classes than in the working class, and middle-class smokers are more likely to quit. There is a class gradient in smoking, both in the proportion of people in each class who smoke, and the amount that they smoke (N. Wald and S. Kiryluk, *UK Smoking Statistics* (Oxford: Oxford University Press, 1988)). The second part of the hypothesis predicts that, irrespective of whether or not they smoke, middle-class people will be more supportive of smoking restrictions because changes in public attitudes usually start at the top of the class system and trickle down.

Hypothesis 9: Zealous converts

Ex-smokers will become increasingly intolerant of smoking the longer they have given up.

This is a hypothesis based in reference group theory. When they first give up, ex-smokers may still identify with the norms and values common among smokers. The more time goes by, however, the more they will come to adopt the values and attitudes characteristic of non-smokers (we leave open the question of whether ex-smokers are ever likely to become as intolerant of smoking as those who have never smoked).

Hypothesis 10: Cognitive dissonance

Smokers will tend to deny that smoking causes harm to themselves or to others and will tend to assert its beneficial effects. These beliefs enable them to continue smoking.

This is another example of a hypothesis where causation runs in both directions – if you smoke, you will want to deny that you are causing harm to yourself and to others, and if you deny that your smoking is harmful, this will enable you to continue smoking. However, a study by Stephen Sutton found that smokers tend to *exaggerate* rather than deny the risks to their health posed by smoking ('Are smokers unrealistically optimistic about the health risks?', *Risk and Human Behaviour Newsletter*, no. 1 (Mar. 1997), pp. 3–5), so we may find that our hypothesis is refuted.

When is a Survey Appropriate?

AIM

This chapter considers the kinds of research questions which may appropriately be addressed by means of a questionnaire survey. Too often, research is carried out using questionnaires without thinking through whether they are the best means of gathering the kind of information required. By the end of the chapter, you should be aware of:

- The limitations of questionnaire surveys as a tool of exploratory research
- The limitations of questionnaires as a means of gathering personal, complex or historical information about people
- The potential usefulness of alternative designs – including archival research, unobtrusive measures, analysis of official statistics, observational methods and unstructured interviewing – which may be considered as alternatives or as complementary to survey-based research strategies
- The kinds of research problems for which a survey design may be appropriate

---

INTRODUCTION

Questionnaires have become familiar instruments for gathering information in the modern world:

- Governments use them to discover a host of things about us from our ethnic background (requested in the national census) to how many crimes get committed each year which are not reported to the police (asked in the British Crime Survey).

- The tax authorities use them each year to find out how much money we have earned so as to calculate how much tax we should pay (the Inland Revenue's annual self-assessment Tax Return form is a questionnaire).
- Market research companies use them to test consumer responses to new products, to evaluate the effectiveness of advertising campaigns, and to monitor changes in popular tastes and lifestyles.
- Political parties make extensive use of them to find out how people intend to vote, to track public opinion on current issues, and to assess the popularity of competing political leaders.
- Popular magazines sometimes invite their readers to complete questionnaires designed to discover what their readers think about drugs, or how many married people have had secret affairs, or whether some royal prince should marry his latest girlfriend.

In addition, questionnaires are also a major tool of inquiry for sociologists and other social scientists.

What is a questionnaire?

Webster's dictionary defines a questionnaire as: 'A prepared set of written questions, for purposes of statistical compilation or comparison of the information gathered; a series of questions.'

It is sometimes assumed that questionnaires are forms which people fill in themselves and then send back to a researcher, but this is too narrow a definition. Some questionnaires are designed for completion by respondents, but others are designed to be administered in an interview situation. Thus:

- Not all questionnaires involve interviewing (for some are designed for self-completion by respondents).
- Not all interviews will involve the use of questionnaires (for some will use a prepared schedule of topics to be explored rather than a prespecified list of questions).

Questionnaires are popular because they appear deceptively easy to construct and relatively cheap to use. They can provide information on the *attributes* of people such as their age, income or race, they can tell us about their *attitudes* and they can document their *activities*. For the price of a bit of photocopying, a pack of envelopes and a few stamps, it is possible to generate a huge amount of information on a wide range of topics.

When approaching a research problem for the first time, people often assume that a questionnaire-based survey is the obvious way of going about it. Yet there are many topics where a questionnaire will *not* be an appropriate research tool, and where we would be better off using some other technique, such as unstructured interviewing or observation. Furthermore, even when a questionnaire *is* appropriate, it is still worth thinking about using some other method in combination with it. Questionnaires are quite limited in the kinds of information they can generate, and the weaknesses of a questionnaire survey can sometimes be complemented by the strengths of some other research technique.

How, then, are we to know whether a questionnaire is likely to be adequate for our particular purposes? There are no hard-and-fast rules on this, but when designing a research strategy, it is worth considering four simple questions:

- Do you know what it is you want to ask?
- Do you need to generate new data?
- Can and will members of your target population tell you what you need to know?
- Are you interested in generalizing about a whole population?

If the answer to all four of these questions is 'yes', a questionnaire survey may be an appropriate research instrument to consider using.

DO YOU KNOW WHAT IT IS YOU WANT TO ASK?

This sounds a daft question, but very often in social scientific research we are very much in the dark about the phenomenon that we are setting out to study. We're not sure what it looks like, we don't have a clue how it might be measured, and we may not even be certain that it exists!

In chapter 1 we distinguished two types of social research:

- *Descriptive research*   The aim here is to measure a phenomenon – to find out how widespread it is, or how it varies across a given population.
- *Analytical (explanatory) research*   This is where we want to go further than just documenting a phenomenon – we want to explain why it takes the form it does.

In both kinds of research, we know what it is that we are looking for. In one case we want to measure it, and in the other we want to explain it, but in both cases we know it exists, and we know how to recognize it.

There is, however, a third type of research where we may not even know this much! In *exploratory research* we have little idea about what a phenomenon looks like or how it might be measured. The purpose of the research is therefore to gather as much relevant information as possible so that we can begin to identify and specify what it is we are studying. Only then can we design studies to measure or analyse it.

It is possible to use survey data for exploratory purposes, but surveys are primarily designed for descriptive and analytical purposes rather than exploratory ones. The reason is obvious – if you are not sure what you should be asking about, it makes questionnaire design almost impossible! In an exploratory study, therefore, you will probably be better off using a less 'structured' method, such as focus group interviews or documentary analysis, where you can allow the themes to evolve as you go along.

Do you really need to generate new data?

The second question to consider when deciding whether a questionnaire is an appropriate instrument for your purposes is whether the information you need already exists in some accessible form.

Historical sources

If your research requires that you gather information on past events, then a questionnaire survey may be inadvisable. Sometimes, the people in whom you are interested may be long dead, in which case questionnaires will obviously be of little use. In these circumstances there are other sources to which you can turn:

What did early capitalists believe? Weber's use of historical sources

The early Calvinists and the pioneer capitalists in whom Weber was interested were all long dead and could not be questioned. Weber's solution was to infer their values and beliefs from their writings. He distilled the 'spirit of capitalism' from the eighteenth-century writings of Benjamin Franklin (a self-made millionaire by the age of 30), while late sixteenth-century Calvinism was interpreted through the work of Calvin's followers such as Richard Baxter.

Max Weber, *The Protestant Ethic and the Spirit of Capitalism* (London: Unwin, 1930)

◆ Diaries, letters and biographies can be useful, provided the people in whom you are interested were literate. One of the classic examples in sociology of a research design using written evidence like this is Max Weber's *The Protestant Ethic and the Spirit of Capitalism*, for Weber relied on written sources for evidence about early Puritan ethics and the values of early capitalist entrepreneurs

---

Were the English always individualistic? Parish records in research

Alan MacFarlane believed that feudalism disappeared much earlier in England than in the rest of Europe, and he set out to demonstrate this by analysing parish records looking for evidence of individualistic values. The records allowed him to calculate how often individuals migrated between different parts of the country, the rate of turnover of land ownership, and patterns of inheritance within families. Without ever having been able to interview them, MacFarlane concluded that: 'The majority of ordinary people in England from at least the thirteenth century were rampant individualists' (p. 163).

A. MacFarlane, *The Origins of English Individualism* (Oxford: Blackwell, 1978)

◆ Old newspapers can provide invaluable contemporary accounts of historic events, and official documents, such as parish records and municipal yearbooks, contain detailed information on things like births and deaths and biographies of local worthies. Local reference libraries, local history societies and county archives often hold both official and unofficial material dating back several hundred years.

Rich men reaching out to heaven: reading signs in the built environment

In one study, researchers were interested in the relation in the past between health and people's social status. To investigate this, they measured the height of tombs in a Glasgow cemetery and compared this with the lifespan of the people buried in them (calculated from the birth and death dates recorded on their graves). Because richer men tended to build taller tombs for themselves and their family members, height offered a good proxy for the wealth of the occupants, and a correlation was demonstrated between people's (imputed) wealth and the length of time they stayed alive.

G. Smith, D. Carroll, S. Rankin and D. Rowan, 'Socio-economic differentials in mortality: evidence from Glasgow graveyards', *British Medical Journal*, vol. 305 (1992), pp. 1554–7

◆ We can also find indicators of social phenomena in the buildings, artefacts and other physical traces that previous generations left behind them. Archaeologists have been able to reconstruct in considerable detail the social, economic and political life of people living thousands of years ago, simply by analysing the tools they used, the way they buried their dead, or even the contents of their stomachs. Similarly, the modern science of semiotics helps us 'read' the symbolism of architecture.

Other unobtrusive measures

All of these examples involve the use of what have been called *unobtrusive measures*, for they make use of information which is already in existence in some form, and do not therefore 'intrude' into people's lives (E. Webb et al., *Unobtrusive Measures: Nonreactive Research in the Social Sciences*, Rand McNally, 1966). Unobtrusive measures are not only used in historical work, for there are plenty of examples where they can be invaluable in telling us about the contemporary world too:

◆ If you want to know which radio stations people listen to, Webb suggests noting the stations to which people's car radios are tuned when they bring their cars into a garage for servicing. People may not know the names of the stations that they listen to, or they may claim to listen to a more 'highbrow' station than is really the case, so analysis of pre-tuned settings on their car radios is probably much more reliable than asking them direct questions.

◆ Alice Coleman's *Utopia on Trial* (Shipman, 1985) used unobtrusive measures to show that insensitive modern housing design produces anti-social behaviour. She measured observable indicators of anti-social behaviour (e.g. graffiti on walls, urine in stairwells) in different kinds of housing developments and correlated her results with features of architectural design such as the height of blocks of flats and the number of exits and entrances.

◆ A lot of work has been done analysing girls' comics and women's magazines for evidence of gender stereotyping, or children's books for evidence of racism. These techniques (known as *content analysis*) have also been applied to film, radio and television – one of the best-known examples in Britain was a series of studies by the Glasgow University Media Group claiming to detect a 'right-wing' bias in television news reporting. Some researchers have combined analysis of media content with interviews with those who consume it to see whether audiences are influenced by the 'hidden biases' revealed by their research (see for example, Greg Philo, *Seeing and Believing: The Influence of Television*, Routledge, 1990).

The great advantage of using 'unobtrusive measures' like documents in archives, articles in magazines, or even (as in Coleman's work) the incidence of dog faeces around tower blocks, is that we make use of information which already exists and which can therefore be analysed and measured without any risk of influencing the way people behave. This kind of research can be *non-reactive* – doing the research doesn't change the situation, and the subjects of the research have no opportunity to shape their answers or change their behaviour to influence the results.

When designing a research project, you should consider whether it is possible to use existing materials as a possible source of data. Some of the most original and enduring contributions to modern social science have been made by researchers who simply made use of information which already existed.

HOW MUCH DO MEMBERS OF THE POPULATION KNOW, AND HOW MUCH ARE THEY WILLING TO TELL YOU?

A common mistake when carrying out surveys is that researchers try to use questionnaires to gather more information than their respondents are capable of providing.

Complexity and level of detail: income and expenditure data

Sometimes people do not have the information that you are trying to collect, or they do not know it in the detail that you require. What you want is too complex to be asked for in a questionnaire. Suppose, for example, you want detailed information on people's income and wealth:

◆ Most of us have a reasonable idea about how much we earn, but if you want full details on a household's income, you will need to ask people about their earnings from employment, deductions on earnings, other earned income, income from property or other assets, money from inheritances, profits from business activities, pension entitlements, endowments, paid holiday entitlements, receipt of welfare benefits, receipt of gifts, cash-in-hand payments, payments in kind, the value of fringe benefits, annual bonuses – the list is almost endless, and many people will be unable to answer your questions without going through a lot of paperwork. You will also need to ask the same questions in respect of every adult in the household.

◆ Inevitably some people will resent your curiosity about their earnings, and some will give you deliberately false answers (we know that self-employed people, in particular, consistently underestimate their earnings when questioned in surveys – if you underreport your earnings to the tax authorities, you are hardly likely to come clean when answering a sociologist's questions).

Collecting information on what people spend is not much easier. Do *you* know how much you spent on alcohol, bus fares, or entertainment last month? Serious surveys of people's spending patterns, such as the government's Household Expenditure Survey, tend not to use questionnaires, but ask people to keep detailed budget diaries instead. Every time survey participants buy something, they enter the expenditure in their diary. Studies of how people spend their time are also generally much better done by a diary method (known as a *time budget diary*) than by questionnaires.

Are you exploited? Marx's *Enquête ouvrière*

Marx devised a questionnaire in 1880 to provide information on the living and working conditions of the French working class. It contained 101 'open-ended' questions (i.e. people were required to write their answers rather than just tick a box), some of which required considerable technical knowledge from respondents, as well as a huge amount of patience and good will:

Q.13: Give details of the division of labour in your industry

Q.16: Describe the sanitary conditions in the workshop; size of the rooms, space assigned to each worker, ventilation, temperature, whitewashing of the walls, lavatories, general cleanliness, noise of machines, metallic dust, humidity, etc.

Q.92: Do you know any instances in which the Government has misused the forces of the State in order to place them at the disposal of employers against their employees?

Marx's questionnaire broke virtually every rule in the methodology book, and not surprisingly, it flopped. The results (if there were any) were never published.

A translation of Marx's questionnaire can be found in T. Bottomore and M. Rubel (eds), *Karl Marx: Selected Writings in Sociology and Social Philosophy* (Harmondsworth: Pelican, 1963)

Information about past events

You will also have problems if you want to use questionnaires to collect accurate information about past events in people's lives, for faulty memories and problems of recall will almost certainly result in some very dubious answers.

◆ Over the years, inflation has wreaked havoc with our memory of incomes and prices, so it is probably not even worth asking people what they were earning ten or twenty years ago.

◆ Many people have trouble remembering dates, and it can be extremely difficult to use questionnaires to reconstruct things like people's job histories, particularly if they have moved around a lot.

◆ Nor does it make much sense asking people about the attitudes they used to hold in the past, for we reconstruct our biographies as we go through our lives, and we always look at our past selves from our present vantage point. An extreme illustration of this is 'false recovered memory syndrome', where adults come to believe that they were abused as children, even when they were not; less dramatic and disturbing examples can probably be found in all our lives.

Reshaping the past to fit the present

'As we remember the past, we reconstruct it in accordance with our present ideas of what is important and what is not . . . the past is malleable and flexible, constantly changing as our recollection reinterprets and re-explains what has happened.'

Peter Berger, *Invitation to Sociology* (Harmondsworth: Pelican, 1966), p. 70

The best solution to this problem of bad memories and selective reinterpretation of past events (what Peter Berger calls biographical 'alternation') is undoubtedly some form of *longitudinal panel design*. This involves recruiting a panel of respondents who are revisited at regular intervals. As time goes by, the researcher can track the major influences on their lives without having to ask them about the past.

Longitudinal designs obviously entail a long-term research commitment, and they can be extremely expensive to set up and keep going. For these reasons, you are unlikely ever to develop such a study yourself, although you may end up using data from one of a number of longitudinal surveys already established in Britain or overseas. We discuss longitudinal survey designs in more detail in Appendix A on our website (www.surveymethods.co.uk).

Reflexivity and awareness

Not only may people have trouble remembering the things that you want to know about – they may not even be aware of them. There are many circumstances where respondents will not know the answers to the sorts of questions you are addressing:

- Much of what we do is so *routinized* that we rarely, if ever, reflect on it. Asked by a sociologist why we continue to smoke, for example, we might quite genuinely have no idea!
- Certain categories of people may not be able to answer questions because of *problems of understanding*. Questionnaires are not generally appropriate in studies of young children, and elderly people also sometimes have problems with them. If you are researching non-English speakers, you may need to translate your questionnaire or perhaps employ multilingual interviewers and coders. In some cases, it may be possible to use *proxy respondents* – parents, for example, can be asked questions about their children, carers can be asked about elderly respondents and English-speaking relatives or friends can answer on behalf of those who do not speak the language. Use of proxies is, however, far from ideal, for the information is being mediated through a third party and may be unreliable.
- Sometimes people have inadequate knowledge about those aspects of their lives that researchers want to find out about. Some health surveys ask people to rate their own health as 'good', 'poor', or whatever, but few of us are medical experts, and we may not know whether aches and pains are serious or not. Similarly, people are unlikely to be aware of how things like advertising influence their behaviour, so there is little point in surveys asking people whether cigarette advertising encouraged them to start smoking.

A pointless survey?

Adverts do have effect, say young smokers

This newspaper headline (from page 6 of the *Daily Telegraph*, 17 June 1998) refers to a survey of 37,000 children, aged 9 to 16, which found that nearly a third of those who smoked said they had been influenced by advertising. However, if people really are influenced by advertising, they are unlikely to be aware of it.

Sensitive issues

Even if people do have the information you want, have reliable memories and are able to tell you about it, there is a fourth reason why a questionnaire may still not be the best method for collecting data – respondents may be reluctant to answer your questions!

This is likely to be a problem where you are after sensitive or personal information. We saw an example of this earlier when discussing income data – people are often quite guarded about what they earn, and they may be reluctant to share this information with you. But this is not the only example where there is likely to be a problem:

♦ Personal questions may cause embarrassment and should only be used with considerable caution and a lot of care.
♦ It can also be difficult to collect information in questionnaire surveys on behaviour which is illegal, shameful or stigmatized. Some 'self-report' crime surveys have found respondents who are happy to divulge details of various nefarious activities in which they have engaged, but even extraverts have their limits, and it is anyway difficult to check the truth of their answers.

In general, 'deviant' behaviour may be better studied by other research techniques than questionnaire surveys. There is, for example, a long and fruitful tradition of participant observer research on gangs, drop-outs and other 'outsiders', and this work has often achieved insights well beyond the scope of most questionnaires.

It is not impossible to use a questionnaire to investigate sensitive, personal or intrusive aspects of people's lives, and in chapter 3 we look at some of the techniques

---

Studying outsiders from the inside

Participant observation involves a researcher joining the group that is being studied and (as far as practicable) doing all the things the other members do so as to understand the way they see their world. It has often been employed in studies of 'deviant subcultures', and is particularly useful as an aid to *exploratory* research.

A classic example is White's *Street Corner Society* which was based on three years spent living in an Italian slum area in Boston in the late 1930s. White learned Italian and became more or less accepted by a gang which was involved in the racketeering and political 'graft' which characterized American 'machine politics' at that time. White explained later: 'As I sat and listened, I learned the answers to questions that I would not even have had the sense to ask if I had been getting my information solely on an interviewing basis' (p. 303).

William Foote White, *Street Corner Society* (Chicago: University of Chicago Press, 1943)

for doing this successfully. Nevertheless, if you need good quality, in-depth, personal information, there are probably better ways of getting it than through a questionnaire survey.

The final issue to consider if you are thinking of carrying out a questionnaire survey concerns the kind of claims you want to make, and the population you are aiming to study.

There are two features of the target population which are pertinent in deciding whether a questionnaire survey is an appropriate research instrument for studying it. One has to do with the units that make up the population; the other relates to its size.

What is a 'population'?

In social research, a *population* refers to all the cases which conform to the specifications which define the object of research. It can therefore refer to individuals, households, groups, organizations, institutions, nation-states, or even inanimate objects such as newspaper reports or gravestones in a Glasgow cemetery. Your population simply consists of all those units which fall into the scope of your research.

Research rarely studies a whole population. As we shall see in chapter 4, we commonly draw a *sample* of cases from a population and concentrate on them.

What is the unit of analysis?

Unlike, say, focus groups or participant observation, questionnaire surveys are individualistic mechanisms for collecting information:

♦ If respondents fill in questionnaires themselves, only one person can tick a box or write in an answer on any one questionnaire at any given time.
♦ If questionnaires are administered face-to-face by an interviewer, this too can only normally be done in a one-to-one situation (we shall see in chapter 5 that interviewing more than one person simultaneously can be very problematic).

It follows that questionnaires are best employed in research where the *unit of analysis* is individual human beings. If your unit of analysis is at a higher level of aggregation than the individual (e.g. families, organizations or whole countries), then to use a survey you are first going to have to identify particular spokespeople within these units who can answer questions on behalf of the group as a whole – and that may well lead to problems.

Suppose we want to compare, say, the quality of relationships enjoyed by married and unmarried cohabiting couples. To research this topic, we need to be able to measure relationship quality: Is it an equal relationship? Is it a stable relationship? Is it a loving relationship? Is it a violent relationship? The relationship, not the individuals, is therefore our unit of analysis, and we aim to compare types of relationships, not types of people. So how do we get at this information using questionnaires?

- One strategy would be to give each couple two questionnaires and ask each partner to complete one. But this is not as simple and neat a solution as it might appear. For a start, it immediately doubles your data collection costs. More importantly, it also means that you have to aggregate *two* sets of answers so that you end up with a *single* measure of relationship quality. What do you do when the answers are inconsistent with one another (e.g. a husband says they go out together socially every week but the wife claims that they haven't been out together in years)? Should you believe one and not the other? Should you take some kind of 'average' of their two answers? Should you simply disregard all answers where they do not agree (in which case you could end up discarding an awful lot of data)?
- An alternative strategy would be to nominate a spokesperson for each couple and let them answer as a 'proxy' on behalf of their partner, as well as for themselves. The problems, however, are likely to be even worse than when you solicit answers from both partners. Whom should you select to answer the questions? And how do you safeguard against the likelihood that one person's view of the relationship is likely to be partial and incomplete?

These sorts of problems become even more intractable as you move to higher and higher levels of aggregation (e.g. from couples to extended families, or from families to whole nations).

How big is the target population?

Questionnaire surveys are most useful when you want to summarize facts about a fairly large population. One of their greatest strengths is the breadth of coverage they can offer, for they provide a standardized instrument which can be applied in the same way to everybody.

Suppose you are doing research on the editors of Britain's national newspapers, or the chairmen of the country's major cigarette companies. You could use a questionnaire, but the small numbers involved will not allow you to do much in the way of generalizing, and you could probably get a lot more from interviewing each individual *in depth* (using an unstructured interviewing technique which is more like a free-flowing conversation) than you could from a rigid questionnaire format.

Unstructured in-depth interviews

In-depth interviews break out of the rigidities imposed by a formal questionnaire format by adopting more of an informal, conversational style. You might draw up a list of the topics you wish to cover (an aide-mémoire), but this should be kept short. Tape recording can be a good idea, but get the informant's permission beforehand (you will also need to make provision for transcribing the tapes, which can be a time-consuming and expensive process).

The secret of a successful in-depth interview is to put the respondent at ease, to pay careful attention to what is being said, and to remain flexible in your questioning. Allow respondents to embellish on their answers, to go off in new directions or even to initiate fresh conversational topics, for you are likely to get richer data in this way.

CONCLUSION: WHEN IS A QUESTIONNAIRE APPROPRIATE?

In the course of this chapter, we have identified a number of criteria which can help gauge the suitability of a questionnaire survey as the basic design for any given research problem. We have identified nine in all.

In concluding, we can summarize each of these nine criteria and illustrate their application by considering whether the hypotheses developed for our research on smoking can all realistically be tested by means of a questionnaire survey.

Look back at each of the ten hypotheses developed in the appendix to chapter 1 (see pp. 37–41), and think about whether they can all be operationalized and tested by means of a social survey. If you have developed some hypotheses of your own, you should also now consider whether all of these can be analysed by means of a survey, or if some of them would be better examined through some other type of research design.

---

1   Questionnaires are not generally suited to exploratory research.

The aims of our smoking study are partly descriptive but are mainly analytical (i.e. to test the ten hypotheses). Our objectives are clear and the categories of analysis are well-defined – this is not a piece of exploratory research. The main objectives appear to be consistent with the use of a questionnaire survey.

2   Questionnaires are usually inappropriate as tools of historical analysis.

The smoking study does not require access to historical data, so this is not a problem.

3   Questionnaires are heavily 'reactive' – respondents know they are being studied and can easily manipulate the information about themselves that is being gathered. If the behaviour being studied is strongly sensitive to context, then it is sensible to adopt a less obtrusive technique.

Hypotheses 6 through 9 all require information on how tolerant or intolerant of smoking people are, but a questionnaire may not be the best way of getting such information:

♦ People may *say* they are tolerant (or intolerant) towards smoking, but in real-life contexts they may behave differently. Expressed attitudes may be poor indicators of actual behaviour.
♦ What people say in a questionnaire survey may not correspond to what they say elsewhere – to friends or family, for example.

Despite these problems, questionnaires are commonly used to ask people about their attitudes. We shall therefore try to operationalize tolerance and intolerance of smoking in our survey, but we shall need to exercise some caution in interpreting the answers we are given.

Context-dependent answers

In a famous study in the US in the 1930s, LaPiere accompanied a young Chinese couple to 66 hotels and 184 restaurants and they were refused service just once. Asked in a subsequent questionnaire whether they would serve Chinese customers, 90 per cent of these same hotels and restaurants said they would not. Johan Galtung, who discusses this example in *Theory and Methods of Social Research* (Allen & Unwin, 1967), concludes rather disarmingly: 'What people say is not what people do.' (p. 127).

---

4   Questionnaires may have problems collecting very complex or detailed information, or where a high level of expertise is required from non-expert informants.

With the possible exception of hypothesis 5 (where we need to develop robust measures of the amount of 'stress' in people's lives), none of our measures requires a high level of expert knowledge by respondents. Nor should we need to go into a lot of detail to achieve usable measures appropriate to testing our various hypotheses.

5   Questionnaires are unreliable as instruments for uncovering information about people's behaviour or attitudes in the past.

There is a possible problem here. To test hypothesis 9 we shall need to know when people first started smoking, and how many times they have tried to give it up. Such information may be shaky when collected by questionnaire survey, for people's recall may not be accurate. In the absence of a longitudinal panel survey, however, there seems no better or more obvious way of gathering this information than by interviewing people.

6   *Questionnaires are poor techniques for analysing influences on behaviour of which people may be largely unaware. They are also unsuitable for use with certain kinds of populations (such as young children).*

This is where we really *do* hit a problem! Hypotheses 3 and 4 refer to the influence of the media and the influence of particular subcultures in reinforcing smoking behaviour. These are important issues to research, but they do not easily lend themselves to a questionnaire survey design. When our students tried to devise suitable questions, they eventually concluded that a short questionnaire administered through street interviewing cannot possibly do justice to either of these hypotheses. They are almost certainly right – hypothesis 3 probably lends itself to an experimental research design, in which an experimental group and a control group are exposed to different media images, and hypothesis 4 would probably best be studied by an observational design.

  We should never stretch any research technique beyond its limitations. These hypotheses are interesting and important but are beyond the capacity of a short questionnaire survey to investigate. Hypotheses 3 and 4 will therefore be dropped from our survey.

7   *Questionnaires need to be used with caution if you are investigating sensitive or personal issues.*

It is unlikely that we shall need to ask any questions which anybody would find intrusive or embarrassing.

8   *Questionnaires are best suited to collecting information on individuals but may prove inappropriate or clumsy tools for gathering information at higher units of analysis.*

Individuals are our units of analysis, for it is individuals who smoke or do not smoke. A questionnaire survey method is therefore appropriate.

9   *Questionnaires are best employed to gather generalizable information on large populations.*

We are interested in differences between smokers and non-smokers *in general*, although time and resource constraints mean we shall have to define our population fairly narrowly to make the survey manageable. In the smoking survey reported in this book, we ended up targeting the population of Brighton (a city in the south of England with a quarter of a million residents). While much of what we find *might* apply to the rest of the country too, we cannot assume this.

Reviewing these nine criteria, a questionnaire survey seems to offer an appropriate research design for our purposes. The next step, therefore, is to develop our questionnaire.

PART II
DATA COLLECTION

PREPARING A QUESTIONNAIRE

AIM

This chapter introduces some basic principles of questionnaire design. By the end of the chapter, you should understand:

- How 'concepts' are operationalized in 'variables' consisting of two or more 'values'
- How a questionnaire is developed by working from research questions and hypotheses to the identification of key concepts, and from there to the identification of the core variables
- The way 'measurement error' arises in the construction of variables, and ways of minimizing it
- Ways of assessing the validity and reliability of questionnaire items
- The difference between self-completed and interview-based questionnaires and the strengths and weaknesses of each
- Why it is important to achieve a good response rate
- The pitfalls which are commonly encountered in designing questions, and ways of avoiding them

An appendix to this chapter explains how the questionnaire used in the smoking survey was developed and finalized.

INTRODUCTION

Questionnaire design is not as simple and obvious as might be imagined. It is true that basic common sense can take you a long way, but there are rules and procedures with which you need to familiarize yourself if you are going to develop a successful questionnaire. If you make mistakes at this stage, they are likely to be catastrophic – the decisions you make now will affect everything that comes later. If your basic instrument of data collection has mistakes in it, all the time, patience and enthusiasm that you put into the later stages of the research will be wasted.

It is surprising just how often questionnaire surveys turn out poorly:

◆ People use questionnaires for purposes for which they are not suited. They 'stretch' the tool beyond its capacities, and they ask questions to which people struggle to give meaningful answers. They still get data, but their results are generally worthless.

◆ Sometimes there is little or no rationale for the questions that get asked, and researchers then have little idea what to do with the answers they get. It is not uncommon for questionnaire surveys to generate much more data than they ever use.

◆ Sometimes the questions are badly framed. Researchers then end up with large numbers of people failing to answer a question, or replying with a 'Don't know.' Or they discover too late that respondents have misinterpreted a question, or that they have all given the same answer to an item intended to tease out variations between them.

In this chapter, we shall negotiate our way through some of the common hazards which you are likely to confront when developing a questionnaire, taking the development of a questionnaire for our Smoking Survey as our example.

RATIONALE: WHAT DO YOU NEED TO ASK?

One of the most common mistakes in the design of questionnaires is that people start developing questions from scratch: 'Surveys always seem to ask people's age and sex and occupation, so we'd better ask that'; 'Yes, and it's interesting to know how people vote, so let's put that in'; 'And don't forget that it's a survey on smoking, so we'd better ask if they smoke or not...'

This is precisely the wrong way to go about things! As we saw in chapter 1, research – whether it is primarily descriptive or analytical – should be *theory-driven*. This means that every item included in a questionnaire should be justified against the theoretical purposes of the research.

The perils of 'abstracted empiricism'

In *The Sociological Imagination*, C. Wright Mills criticized research that has no 'substantive propositions or theories', calling it 'abstracted empiricism'. Much effort is expended on ensuring precise measurement of things, but the rationale for doing the study in the first place gets lost. Mills reminds us: 'Social research of any kind is advanced by ideas; it is only disciplined by fact' (p. 82).

C. Wright Mills *The Sociological Imagination* (New York: Oxford University Press, 1959)

You should resist the temptation to dream up questions simply because they seem like interesting things to ask. If you go down that path, you will end up with a rag-bag of unconnected 'facts' which do not relate to any serious research question. If somebody suggests putting something into a questionnaire, ask them to identify the research question which it is designed to answer. If they cannot tell you, throw the item out!

Step 1: List the hypotheses (or key themes)

The first thing to do when designing a questionnaire is to list the questions your research is trying to answer. If you are doing primarily descriptive research, these will be questions of fact (e.g. what proportion of the population smokes?). If you are trying to test theories in a more analytical study, it will mean listing the hypotheses that the research is seeking to investigate.

Before you go any further, get your list of hypotheses in front of you (if you are replicating our Smoking Survey, these are listed in the appendix to chapter 1 (see pp. 38–41) – remember, though, that hypotheses 3 and 4 have now been dropped).

Step 2: Identify the key concepts

Look at your list. Whether it consists of descriptive questions or hypotheses you will see that your list translates into a series of *concepts*. Concepts are the categories with which we think about things. They enable us to recognize things, sort them into groups and generalize about them. They are the building blocks of our theories.

Table 3.1 identifies the key concepts associated with each of the hypotheses in our Smoking Survey. Some of them seem quite mundane – they are simple nouns or phrases like *age cohort* or *education* or *smoking behaviour*. Others are more technical or complex – *social class*, for example, or *tolerance of smoking*. None of them, however, has a completely self-evident meaning, for the definition of any concept is always open to debate:

♦ *Smoking* is not a difficult concept to understand. Chambers Dictionary defines it as *To take into the mouth and puff out the smoke of tobacco or something similar*, and we can probably go along with that. But which substances other than tobacco should be included? And should inhalation of the smoke be considered a necessary part of the definition (former American President Bill Clinton famously claimed that he had not smoked cannabis as a student because he 'did not inhale')? We must be clear about our definition and its limits.
♦ Other concepts – like *stress* or *social class* – look more complex. There is little agreement among sociologists about how *social class* should be defined, or even

Table 3.1 Concepts and variables in the Smoking Survey

Hypothesis	Key concept/s	Variable/s
Parental socialization	Smoking behaviour (respondent)	Whether smoked cigarette, pipe or tobacco in last week Whether ever smokes Whether ever used to smoke
	Smoking behaviour (parents)	Whether either parent/guardian smoked when respondent was a child
Peer group socialization	Peer group smoking behaviour	Proportion of close family/friends who smoke regularly
Stress	Stress level	Respondent's self-rated stress level
Self-interest	Tolerance of smoking	Eight items measuring attitudes about smoking restrictions
Age effect	Age cohort	Age
Social class effect	Social class	Occupational title Employment status
	Education	Age completed full-time education
Zealous converts	Smoking identity	(Smokers) Number of attempts to quit (Ex-smokers) Time since quit (months)
Cognitive dissonance	Beliefs about harmful effects of smoking	Belief that smoking has benefits for self Denial that passive smoking is harmful to others

whether it is a concept which has outlived its usefulness (see Ray Pahl, 'Is the Emperor naked?', *International Journal of Urban and Regional Research*, vol. 13 (1989), pp. 709–20), and the idea of stress is probably even more hotly contested.

We need to be clear at the outset how each of our key concepts is to be defined and measured, and this means we need theoretical clarity before we start compiling our questionnaire.

Step 3: Identify the variables

The next step is to move from *theory* to *measurement* by translating each of our concepts into one or more variables. Take the concept of *smoking behaviour*. We need to measure this precisely and accurately, for it is pivotal to all of the hypotheses we shall be testing. We have already defined it conceptually – we think we know what it means. But how will we recognize it empirically? How shall we distinguish people who smoke from people who do not?

Concepts and variables

Concepts are mental categories. To test hypotheses, we need to decide how the objects we observe 'correspond' to the conceptual categories derived from our theories. For example, we use a concept like 'dog' to express the *idea* of an object. When we then encounter a real-life snarling furry object on four legs, we apply a set of 'correspondence rules' to determine whether or not it is an object that fits the category. We count its legs, listen to the noise it makes, and see if it chases cats and postmen. So too with social scientific concepts. Our concepts (the concept of 'heavy smoker', for example) entail criteria to determine whether any particular observation fits the category.

Each of the criteria we identify is a potential **variable** in our research. A variable is a quantity of something which has at least two different possible *values*. 'Number of legs', for example, is one of the variables which can help determine whether or not an object fits the category 'dog' (an object will normally only be classified as a 'dog' if the variable 'number of legs' has the value of '4'). Similarly, 'number of cigarettes per day' might be one of the variables used to determine whether somebody belongs to the category 'heavy smoker' (we might decide that people will only be classified as 'heavy smokers' if this variable has a value of '20 or more').

We may need to measure many different variables to *operationalize* a concept – 'number of legs' is not enough to enable us to measure accurately which category of animal a furry object belongs to, and 'number of cigarettes per day' might not be enough to measure which category of smoker a respondent belongs to.

Obviously, we shall need to ask people about their smoking behaviour. But it will not be enough simply to ask whether they smoke or not, for we need to clarify what is to count as smoking for our purposes:

♦ Is somebody who only smokes at parties a 'smoker'? If not, we shall need to gather information on the regularity with which people smoke.
♦ Do we need to know how much people smoke? If so, do we measure the number of cigarettes, the strength of the cigarettes, or the proportion of each cigarette they smoke before discarding it?
♦ What are we going to do about pipe smokers, cigar smokers, and 'roll-your-own' cigarette smokers? Is somebody who smokes five cigarettes a day to be put in the same category (measured at the same value) as someone who puffs their way through five Havana cigars every day? And what about cannabis smokers?

We cannot begin to devise questions until we are clear how we are going to operationalize and measure our key concepts. Even with apparently simple concepts like 'smoking', this needs a lot of careful thought; with more technical and complex concepts, it can be a very taxing task.

> The final column of table 3.1 showed how our students tried to operationalize each of the key concepts in our Smoking Survey. You should similarly now develop a list of variables from the key concepts you have identified for your survey.

There will often be several different ways to operationalize a concept. It may then be sensible when designing a questionnaire to identify several different variables to measure the same concept. Just as surveyors like to take readings from several different vantage points, so too the development of several different variables for the same concept can help achieve precision and minimize *measurement error*.

Measurement error

Nothing in this world can ever be a perfect measure – bathroom scales do not record your *exact* weight, and the police allow a small 'margin of error' if they see you speeding because they know that their equipment is not perfect.

Social survey results also contain 'error'. Just as a speedometer may not precisely record the actual speed at which you are travelling, so too social science variables may not precisely correspond to the phenomena they are meant to be measuring. If this is the case, then the patterns of association that we discover between variables may appear weaker than they really are.

In our Smoking Survey, we measured most of our concepts with just one variable in order to keep the questionnaire as short as possible. For example, we operationalized the concept of *stress* with one simple variable, *self-rated stress level*, but this is the sort of concept which might better have been measured using multiple indicators:

◆   We could have collected information on stressful life events, such as the number of relationship break-ups, house moves or deaths of friends and family experienced by respondents over a given period.
◆   We could have measured behavioural correlates of stress, like how argumentative people are, or how much they allow things to worry them.

Some of the concepts in our Smoking Survey were operationalized by developing more than one variable (see table 3.1 above). For example:

◆   Our key concept, *smoking behaviour*, was measured on three dimensions – the number of cigarettes (or equivalent) smoked in the last week; (if none) whether the respondent ever smokes; and (if not), whether they ever smoked in the past. Answers to these three items will enable us to classify respondents into one of four categories – regular smokers; occasional smokers; ex-smokers; and those who have never smoked.

The 'Global Assessment of Recent Stress' scale

Psychologists have measured stress by identifying various areas of life (work, family, illness, etc.) and asking people how much pressure they have been under in each one. Scoring answers on each item from 0 (No pressure) to 5 (Extreme pressure), an overall stress scale can then be produced by adding all the scores together. This approach was not adopted in our Smoking Survey as it meant asking 14 separate questions (one for each area of life), but it would arguably have produced a more reliable measure than our single-item self-rated stress variable, and if you are replicating this survey, you might consider adding some additional items.

M. W. Linn, 'A global assessment of recent stress (GARS) scale', *International Journal of Psychiatry in Medicine*, vol. 15 (1985), pp. 47–59

◆ Measurement of *social class* was based on two variables – occupation and employment status. Most measures of social class require fairly detailed knowledge of the job that somebody does, and whether they are employed or self-employed (their 'employment status'). In the case of self-employed people and managers, we also need to know how many people they manage or control in their job.

How valid are our measures?

The validity of a measure depends on how accurately it expresses a phenomenon. There are four ways we can assess this:

1   *Face validity*   Does a measure capture what we mean 'on the face of it'? Does it seem sensible and plausible, for example, to measure somebody's 'social class' by finding out what job they do, or to measure their views on smoking by recording what they think about banning smoking in restaurants?
2   *Content validity*   Do our measures cover the range of dimensions entailed in a concept? For example, is our single measure of 'self-rated stress' sufficient to cover all the important aspects of stress?
3   *Internal (construct) validity*   Are people's answers on closely related items logically consistent? For example, if people say they support smoking bans in restaurants we would expect them also to support restricting the sale of tobacco to minors.
4   *External (predictive) validity*   Are our measures consistent with evidence available from 'outside' of the research itself? For example, if somebody tells us they do not smoke, yet they light a cigarette as they leave the interview, the external validity of our measure would be called into question.

♦   To measure people's *'tolerance'* or *'hostility' towards smoking*, we developed no
     fewer than eight variables, each based on responses to a particular statement about
     smoking and smokers. These separate answers will be combined later into a single
     'scale of tolerance'.

Step 4: Distinguish independent, dependent and mediating variables

If we are conducting a piece of *descriptive research*, we are now ready to start devising
items for our questionnaire, but if we are engaged in *analytical research*, one final step
still remains. This involves sorting out our variables to trace the causal relationships
which we expect to find between them.

   Dependent variables are those that our theory predicts will change when other
variables impact upon them. In our Smoking Survey:

♦   The dependent variable in hypotheses 1 and 2 is our respondents' *smoking behav-
     iour*, for our theory suggests that this will vary according to variations in parental
     and peer group smoking behaviour.
♦   In hypotheses 6, 7, 8 and 9, the dependent variable is *attitudes about smoking*, for
     people's tolerance of smoking is predicted to vary with their smoking behaviour,
     their generation, their social class, and their smoking history.
♦   In hypotheses 5 and 10, we predict an interactive relationship between variables. In
     hypothesis 5, stress leads people to smoke but smoking leads people to say they feel
     stress; in hypothesis 10, the belief that smoking is not harmful encourages con-
     tinued smoking but smokers want to believe that smoking is not harmful. In these
     hypotheses, therefore, the relationship between variables is predicted to be *interde-
     pendent*, so there is no dependent variable as such.

   Independent variables are those which our theory says will *cause* a change in
dependent variables. In hypothesis 1, for example, the independent variable is *parental
smoking*, for this (according to the theory) causes a change in the probability that
somebody will smoke.

The role of theory in determining the direction of causation

Note that variables are only 'dependent' or 'independent' in the context of a given
hypothesis. It is our *theory* that tells us what is causing what, and it is therefore
theory that identifies variables as dependent or independent. Thus, an independent variable in one hypothesis may crop up as a dependent variable in another.
This reinforces the point emphasized in chapter 1 – that research is *theory-driven*.
If two variables covary, we look to our theory to tell us which is the causal agent
and which is being acted upon. Evidence of covariation in itself cannot demonstrate that one is causing the shift in the other – to make these judgements, we
look to our initial theory.

Sometimes a hypothesis will link three concepts in a more complex causal chain involving a *mediating variable* (also sometimes called an 'intervening variable' or a 'confounding variable'). A mediating variable influences whether and how an independent variable causes change in a dependent variable.

Patterns of causal relations between variables

Simple causation: X ⟶ Y

The hypothesis suggests that a dependent variable (Y) is influenced by an independent variable (X). For example, people whose parents smoked (X) are more likely to smoke themselves (Y).

Mutual causation: X ⇄ Y

The hypothesis suggests that each variable influences the other – they are self-reinforcing. For example, people will be influenced to keep smoking if they feel stressed (Y causes X); but people who smoke will tend to justify it by claiming that they are stressed (X causes Y).

Multiple causation:

X_1

X_2

Y

The hypothesis suggests that there are two variables, X_1 and X_2 which both independently affect Y, but which also covary with each other. For example, social class (X_1) influences smoking behaviour (Y); education (X_2) also influences smoking behaviour (Y); but social class and education are also associated with each other. For the purposes of the research, it is necessary to acknowledge that X_1 and X_2 covary, but we are not interested in analysing why. We do, however, need to find a way of calculating how much of the change in Y is due to X_1 and how much is due to X_2.

Indirect causation: X ⟶ (Z) ⟶ Y

The hypothesis suggests that X influences the value of Y, but only when some value of Z is present. For example, people whose parents smoked (X) are more likely to smoke themselves (Y), but only if they regularly saw their parents smoking (Z).

Suppose, for example, that some people only smoke when their children are not around. This would mean that their children never see their parents smoke, in which case they may never be influenced to take up the habit themselves. We might then want to amend hypothesis 1 to recognize that the effect of parental smoking (the independent variable) on the child's own smoking behaviour (the dependent variable) may be *mediated* by a third variable – whether or not the child ever saw its parents smoking. The independent variable still exerts its causal effect, but only in certain circumstances.

We need to be clear about the pattern of causation that we expect to find between our variables. This means translating the words and concepts of our original hypotheses into causal 'flow diagrams' mapping the associations we expect to find between observable sets of variables. If you can develop some simple causal diagrams out of your hypotheses, and gather good quality data that support them, then you will end up

---

Spurious correlation

Watching motor racing influences boys to smoke

In November 1997 the press reported on research suggesting that tobacco company sponsorship increases the probability that young boys will start smoking. The research found that boys who watched Grand Prix racing were twice as likely to start smoking as those who did not (i.e. watching GP racing, the independent variable X, causes an increased probability of starting smoking, the dependent variable Y).

But what if the same kinds of boys who are attracted to the excitement and sophistication of Grand Prix racing are also attracted to smoking? This suggests an alternative hypothesis that watching motor racing and smoking are both the outcomes of a common third variable (e.g. personality type) and may not be causally related to each other. In this revised hypothesis, personality is the independent variable (X) and smoking and watching Grand Prix racing are two dependent variables (Y and Z) which covary only because they are both affected by X.

Spurious correlation: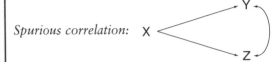

There is an important lesson here. When variables correlate, it does not necessarily mean that they are causally related with each other – the apparent association may be 'spurious'.

explaining a lot more than if you try to develop highly complex flow charts which nobody can follow.

STRATEGIES AND LOGISTICS

Each of our variables needs to be measured by at least one question in the questionnaire. The kinds of questions we ask will depend on what type of survey we intend to carry out.

Self-completed and interviewer-administered questionnaires

Questionnaires can be administered in a number of different environments:

♦ At one extreme you can devise *self-completed* questionnaires. You mail or email questionnaires together with a covering letter explaining the purpose of the research (and a stamped, addressed envelope if you are doing this by post) and you wait for the replies to come back.
♦ At the other extreme, questionnaires can be administered *face-to-face* by an interviewer who asks the questions as they appear on the questionnaire, and fills in the answers. Increasingly nowadays, this is done using a laptop computer, so that people's responses are entered directly into a database.
♦ There are other options between these two extremes. For example, questionnaires can be administered using *telephone interviewing* – this is cheaper than making house calls, but it retains most of the advantages of face-to-face interviewing. Again, telephone interviewing is today often done using computers.

Computer-aided interviewing

Computers can be used in both face-to-face interviewing ('Computer-assisted personal interviewing', or CAPI) and in telephone interviewing ('Computer-assisted telephone interviewing', or CATI). The questionnaire is entered into a software package (e.g. BLAISE) so that questions appear onscreen in the right order, taking account of previous answers, and responses are entered into the computer as the interview progresses, so interviewing and data entry are accomplished simultaneously (we look at data entry in Chapter 6). This has the advantage that inconsistencies and coding errors can also be queried and rectified as the interview is progressing, so we end up with a relatively 'clean' data set.

Self-administered questionnaires

The great advantage of mailing out your questionnaires is *cost*. You only have to pay for postage and photocopying (not even these if you are using the internet). This strategy also has advantages if you are asking intrusive questions, where people might be embarrassed to give an answer face-to-face to an interviewer, or detailed factual questions, where respondents may need time to research their answers.

The disadvantages, however, are daunting, and one of the main drawbacks is the likelihood of a low *response rate*. Postal questionnaires generally achieve low response rates – 20 or even 10 per cent is not uncommon in unsolicited household surveys. With a response rate this low, no reputable social scientist is likely to take your results seriously, for it is unlikely that you will have ended up with a sample that is representative of the population from which it was drawn.

Response rates, and why they are important

The response rate is the proportion of people in your sample who successfully complete a questionnaire. Non-responses occur for three main reasons:

- *Non-contacts* Despite repeated attempts to locate them, you cannot make contact with a sample member to ask them to participate in the survey. They may have moved house, or be away on holiday, or perhaps they work shifts and are never at home when you call.
- *Refusals* People decline to participate.
- *Non-completed interviews* People are contacted, but for some reason (e.g. language difficulties, lack of comprehension due to age of respondent, or inadequate literacy in the case of self-completed questionnaires) the interview cannot be completed.

A high rate of non-response is a problem because you need the people you interview to be *representative* of the wider population from which they have been sampled. People who are difficult to contact, who refuse to participate or who do not understand your questions are likely to be quite distinctive sections of the population, and by failing to recruit them, you are biasing your final achieved sample.

It is very important to keep complete records of non-contacts, refusals or non-completed interviews so that you can calculate your response rate and, if necessary, use the information gathered to help in weighting the sample to make it more representative of the population. The information you record might include the approximate age, gender and ethnicity of the respondent as well as place and time.

There are things you can do to boost response rates from mail questionnaires:

- ◆ Your covering letter is crucial – keep it short, make the survey look relevant and interesting to people, and use an official letterhead and other signs to show that this is not junk mail.
- ◆ Keep the questionnaire short, and make the layout clear and attractive – people may be willing to tick a few boxes on a single sheet of paper and put it back in an

envelope, but few will spend an hour wrestling with pages of densely printed questions.

◆ Try to forewarn people – the local newspaper may be happy to run a report on the survey before questionnaires hit people's doormats, or strategic 'gatekeepers' in organizations may put in a good word for you with their members.

◆ Follow up non-respondents – write to them enclosing another questionnaire and emphasizing how important their answers are to you, or (if feasible) you might try calling on them and waiting while they fill it in.

◆ Reassure people that their answers will be treated as strictly confidential and that it will be impossible for anybody to tell from the final report who said what.

◆ You could consider offering an inducement, such as a prize raffle for all those who return their questionnaires, although you will need to check that you are not transgressing any laws, and that any relevant ethics committee is happy with the arrangements you propose.

Low response rates are not the only problem with self-completed questionnaires. Some of the other problems are intractable:

◆ You can't probe people's answers – what they write is all you get, and if somebody's answer is unclear, then you have to put up with it.

◆ Most people do not like writing, so the use of 'open-ended questions' is normally very restricted.

◆ You cannot control the conditions under which the questionnaire is completed, so respondents may be influenced by other people when they are filling it in, and you can never know whether or not they took it seriously.

Interview-based questionnaires

If your questionnaire is to be administered by an interviewer, then you have more scope as regards its length, its complexity and the use of open-ended questions.

◆ You can probably go for a *longer questionnaire* (once an interview gets going, most people enjoy themselves, and you can often go for an hour or more with people who would not have spent two minutes filling in a questionnaire themselves).

◆ You can certainly go for a *more complex questionnaire*, for a trained interviewer can explain and prompt on difficult questions and will be able to 'jump around' the questionnaire, skipping over questions which do not apply and following instructions which might have bewildered respondents completing it themselves.

◆ You can be more liberal with the use of *open-ended questions*, for you may be able to tape-record interviews and transcribe them later, or you can rely on the interviewer to write down a lengthy answer as a respondent is speaking. Left to themselves, few respondents will be willing to write more than a few words in answer to open-ended questions on a self-completed questionnaire.

◆ In interview-based questionnaires, respondents cannot go back and *change earlier answers* in the light of later questions, as they can if they are completing a questionnaire themselves. This can be important if you are trying to discover how much people know about something that you then go on to discuss in more detail later in the questionnaire.

But there is a downside, for not only does interviewing raise your costs, but it also – potentially – weakens the *reliability* of your results. Precisely because interviewers can prompt and probe and establish a rapport with respondents, they can also distort the answers they get and bias the responses they record (we consider what to do about this in chapter 5).

Reliability and validity

Validity is achieved by using research instruments that measure what they are intended to measure. Reliability is achieved by using research instruments that produce the same results from the same conditions each time they are used.

Questionnaire surveys seek to maximize both validity and reliability, but there may be something of a trade-off between them. For example, if we use interviewers to administer a questionnaire, they may be able to raise the *validity* of the data by probing and checking and building trust with respondents, but the more they do this, the more they threaten the *reliability* of the research, for other interviewers may have probed in different ways and got different results.

Despite possible problems of reliability, however, it is normally better to go for some form of interview (face-to-face or telephone) if you can afford it. You can get reasonable results with a mail-out self-completed questionnaire if you keep it short and simple, and if there is already a fund of goodwill among potential respondents, but interviewing should give you a healthier response rate (ideally, in a general survey of the public, you should probably be looking for 60 per cent or better), and it should also give you a better 'feel' for the data you get back. In developing the questionnaire for our Smoking Survey, we therefore decided that it should be administered face-to-face using interviewers.

Whether you are replicating the smoking survey or carrying out a survey of your own design, you need to decide at this point whether the questionnaire will be self-completed by respondents or administered face-to-face by interviewers, for this decision will certainly influence the sort of questions you put into your questionnaire.

Pre-coded (closed) and open-ended questions

We have seen that variables always have a minimum of two possible values:

◆   A variable like 'gender' will probably only have two values – 'male' and 'female'.

- A variable like 'number of cigarettes smoked in the last seven days' may have many possible values on a continuous range from zero upwards.
- A variable like 'occupation' could have several thousand different values, for there are many different titles for the multitude of different jobs that people do.

When developing questionnaire items, we need to decide for each variable whether we want to specify a predetermined range of values or allow respondents to answer in any way they want. In the first case, we will develop *closed* or *pre-coded* questions; in the second, we will leave our questions *open-ended*.

Closed and open-ended questions

A 'closed' or pre-coded question is one where the respondent is confronted with a pre-set range of possible answers and has to select one. For example:

Q78 Are you ever bothered by other people smoking?
    Frequently   1
    Occasionally   2
    Hardly ever   3
    Never   4

The problem with a pre-coded question like this is that respondents are not allowed to record what they really want to say! For example, somebody with asthma whose life is made a misery by tobacco smoke might respond with an impassioned diatribe about how *intensely* she or he suffers, but their response will simply be recorded as 'frequently' – which hardly does justice to their answer.

An 'open-ended' question, by contrast, is one where the respondent can give any answer, which is then recorded. For example:

Q79 Are there any places or events you regularly avoid because you may be affected by tobacco smoke?
    Yes   1 – *ask (a)*
    No   2 – *go to Q80*

(a) What places or events do you avoid?

The first part of the question is a standard, pre-coded item, but the follow-up is 'open-ended'. Respondents can say whatever they like, and the interviewer will record their answers. The use of an open-ended question here reflects the fact that there is a huge range of possible answers that people could give. The research team therefore decided not to pre-code, but to collect all the answers and classify them later.

Questions taken from Health Education Authority, *Health in England 1995* (London: Office for National Statistics, 1996)

The case for pre-coding

Why bother pre-coding any questions? Why not leave everything open and let respondents say whatever they want to say? There are three good reasons for pre-coding:

- It makes it easier to record information. It is simpler and easier to tick an item than to have to write out an answer.
- It saves time later. In order to analyse the information we collect in a survey, we have at some point to *crunch* people's answers into a relatively small number of manageable categories. There is not much we can do with hundreds of different answers, so we may as well ensure at the outset that people limit their answers to a predetermined range of categories that will prove manageable.
- It ensures you get the sort of data you want. Forcing respondents to restrict their answers to your predetermined categories will lose much of the variety in what they might have said, but it will ensure that everybody gives an answer that can be measured and compared on a common dimension.

Pre-coding responses to attitude statements

In the government's 1995 health survey, respondents were given a series of statements about smoking and were asked to respond to each in turn. The statements included things like:

Q86b   The Government should spend more money to encourage people to stop smoking
Q86d   There is too much fuss being made about the dangers of smoking

After each statement, respondents were asked to select one of five possible answers:

Agree strongly	1
Agree slightly	2
Neither agree nor disagree	3
Disagree slightly	4
Disagree strongly	5

A simple five-point scale like this (often referred to as a *Likert scale*) is commonly used to measure attitudes. We look more closely at scales in chapter 5.

Criteria for choosing between closed and open-ended questions

When should we pre-code, and when should we leave questions open? Here are some 'rules of thumb':

- If a variable can have only a small *number of values*, and these are known in advance, then it is sensible to 'close' the question and pre-code. An obvious example is gender: it is easier to tick one of two pre-coded boxes than to write 'male' or 'female' in an empty space.

◆ If a variable has potentially a large number of values, but you know that you want to analyse it using a *limited set of categories*, then you may decide to pre-code. This is often the case, for example, with attitudinal variables, where we want to limit the range and complexity of people's answers by getting them simply to 'agree' or 'disagree' with various statements.

Prompting in open-ended questions

Open-ended questions can be combined with interviewer *prompts* to ensure respondents address their answers to the particular issues on which you need information. A good example is the following question which has often been used to build up a picture of how people think about the British class system and their own place within it.

Question: People often talk about there being different classes – what do you think?

Interviewer prompts:

   i   How many social classes identified by the respondent
  ii   The terminology used to describe these classes
 iii   What is the major factor determining which class somebody belongs to
 iv   The class position the respondent believes she or he belongs to
   v   Why individuals end up in the class that they do
 vi   How much upward mobility there is in the system
vii   Whether class is inevitable and/or desirable

John Goldthorpe, David Lockwood, Frank Bechhofer and Jennifer Platt, *The Affluent Worker in the Class Structure* (London: Cambridge University Press, 1969), appendix C

◆ If the values of a variable consist of a range of *real numbers*, it is worth trying to record the actual numbers, rather than crunching responses into categories. It takes no more effort to write down a number than to tick a box. For example, if we ask how many cigarettes people have smoked in the last week, then it is sensible to record the actual number they give us, rather than compress their responses into categories such as 'under 50' or '150–199'. Detailed answers can always be 'crunched' later, but if information is only recorded in summary form, the details can never be retrieved later on.

◆ If you are not sure what the *possible range of values* of a given variable might be, then obviously you should not pre-code (you could always try to gauge a likely range of answers by using an open-ended question in the *pilot study* and then pre-coding in the main study).

◆ Sometimes you will be interested in recording *what people say*, rather than simply summarizing it, and in these cases you will obviously want to use an open-ended question.

◆   If the questionnaire is to be completed by respondents, use as many pre-coded items as you can, for people who do not mind ticking boxes can rapidly lose interest if they have to start writing out answers.

The trade-off between validity and reliability – again

The choice between closed and open-ended questions again poses the dilemma that enhancing the reliability of measures can diminish their validity, and vice versa. The more we allow respondents to answer questions in their own words, the more insight we are likely to get into what we are hoping to measure, so validity tends to be greater with open-ended questions. The more we force respondents to address their replies to a pre-set list of possible answers, however, the more we can ensure that each item will be measured in exactly the same way every time it is used, no matter who may be doing the interviewing or who may be responsible for coding. Reliability therefore tends to be enhanced when using pre-coded questions.

Rules for developing codes for closed questions

If you are using closed questions, ensure that the codes that you are using:

◆   make sense to respondents;
◆   are exhaustive (i.e. cover the whole range of possible responses they might give, including 'Don't know');
◆   are mutually exclusive (i.e. do not overlap with each other).

Further guidance on developing coding categories can be found in chapter 5.

DEVELOPING THE QUESTIONS

If you have followed all the steps in this chapter, you will know exactly which variables you need to measure, you will have decided how the questionnaire is to be administered, and you will be alert to the circumstances in which it is appropriate to use closed or open-ended questions. Now all you have to do is to think up clear and unambiguous questions which will provide the information you want in the form that you want it in. When developing your questions, the following ground rules should be born in mind:

Learn from previous research

Look at other people's questionnaires, for many of the things that you want to ask will have been asked before in previous surveys. See how they did it, and if it worked for them and seems appropriate to your purposes, then do what they did. Using other people's questions (modified if necessary, and properly acknowledged in your write-up) carries two huge advantages:

- *Validity* The questions are likely to 'work' – if they have been tried out and found useful in other studies, then they will probably provide you with reasonably valid measures.
- *Reliability* By ensuring some uniformity of measures between your study and earlier work, you will be able to compare your results directly with those reported by others.

An excellent source for questions used in large-scale social surveys is The Question Bank (http://qb.soc.surrey.ac.uk/) held at the University of Surrey, where whole questionnaires, as well as individual questions, can be viewed and downloaded.

Replication in sociology

One good reason for using items that have been used in previous studies is that it allows you to make direct comparisons between your results and theirs. Such replication is rare in sociology, but we should arguably do more of it (see Colin Bell, 'Replication and reality', *Futures* (June 1974), pp. 253–60), for it is a good way of testing the reliability of research findings. This is one reason we encourage you to replicate our Smoking Survey as you work through this book, for in this way you can gauge the reliability of our findings against the ones you get – and vice versa.

Of course, when restudies come up with different results from the original, it may not be because the original study got it wrong. It might also be that things have changed since the first study was done, or that circumstances are different in different places.

Keep it simple

Questions should be worded simply and kept short and unambiguous. A common mistake arises when researchers try to cram more than one dimension of a concept into a single question. For example, a question like: 'Do you think that smoking causes long-term and irreversible damage to people's health?' is two questions, logically requiring two distinct answers: Does it cause long-term damage? Is the damage it causes reversible? Double-barrelled questions like this should be avoided – use a separate question for each item of information you need to collect.

Another common mistake arises when questions are framed in the negative and respondents are then asked to agree or disagree with them, for people rapidly become confused about what disagreeing to a negative statement means. There was an example of this in our Smoking Survey where people were asked to agree or disagree with the statement: 'Government isn't doing enough to discourage smoking.' Our students reported after interviewing that some respondents had become confused when answering this item – does disagreeing with this negative statement mean you want the government to do more or less to discourage smoking? The question would probably have worked better if it had been reworded.

Avoid leading questions...

As a general rule, you should make your questions as 'neutral' as possible. This means:

♦   You should avoid 'loaded' or emotive words in questions.
♦   You should avoid phrasing questions in such a way that a 'correct' or 'preferred' answer is implied in the wording.
♦   You should not ask questions that assume that respondents hold the same sorts of values that you hold.

Leading questions: The end of Harriet Harman

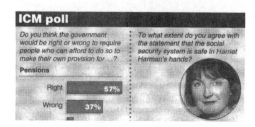

In December 1997, the newly elected Labour government was considering far-reaching changes to the state welfare system. The *Guardian*, which opposed the proposals and was critical of the then Social Security Secretary, Harriet Harman, commissioned a commercial polling company, ICM, to carry out a survey in which voters were asked: *To what extent do you agree with the statement that the social security system is safe in Harriet Harman's hands?* Only 19 per cent of people agreed with the statement, and Harman was sacked by Tony Blair a short while later.

But the question only made sense if you opposed reform of the social security system (as the *Guardian* itself did). It implied that the existing system was a good thing worth preserving – but how are you supposed to respond to this question if you believe that the system *should* be reformed (i.e. that it should not be 'safe' from radical change)? Even more difficult, how can you answer if you believe that the system needs changing but that Harriet Harman is the wrong person to do it? Do you then agree or disagree with the statement?

All of this is easier said than done. We all have biases and our choice of words can unwittingly betray our allegiances. When this happens, it will almost certainly taint the quality of the responses we get back from people.

Doonesbury

BY GARRY TRUDEAU

Getting the results you want: Do you *really* want to pay more tax?

During the 1980s, most surveys found low levels of support for the tax and spending cuts that Conservative governments were pursuing. The 1986 British Social Attitudes Survey, for example, gave respondents three options (the level of support for each is in brackets):

Reduce taxes and spend less on health, education and social benefits   (6%)
Keep taxes and spending on these services at the same level as now   (43%)
Increase taxes and spend more on health, education and social benefits   (45%)

It seemed from this that nearly half the population was willing to pay more tax, but in 1987, two supporters of reduced government spending published a survey showing that only 17 per cent of people were willing to pay more tax to enable higher spending on the health service. This was about two-thirds lower than the proportion recorded in the British Social Attitudes Survey – but Harris and Seldon had asked a very different question! They told their respondents how much the government was spending on the various public services and asked them to choose between different spending priorities (e.g. between health, education and pensions). Only then were they asked if they were willing to pay higher taxes to pay for the increased spending on the service they had prioritized.

Clearly, the way you ask your questions, the sort of information you give people, and the options you allow them to consider can all massively influence the kinds of answers you get back. Neither of these two surveys was 'false', but the results they came up with were completely incompatible with one another.

R. Jowell, S. Witherspoon and L. Brook, *British Social Attitudes: The 1986 Report* (Aldershot: Gower, 1986); R. Harris and A. Seldon, *Welfare without the State* (London: Institute of Economic Affairs, 1987)

It is not unusual for those sponsoring a survey to get the results they hoped to get. This is not because they fiddle their findings, but it may be because, like the *Guardian* in the example above, they ask their questions in such a way that they influence the kind of answers that people are inclined to give.

Take care over question wording. It can be a good idea to get somebody with different values and opinions from yours to look through your draft questions to check for any inadvertent bias or offence that they may contain.

...or use leading questions with care

There are times when it may be acceptable to include leading questions in a survey, but you need to be aware of what you are doing!

◆   Surveys commonly measure people's attitudes and values by asking them to re-spond to a series of statements. Each statement expresses a particular point of view, for there is no point in asking people to agree or disagree with a neutral statement. Because each statement is biased, there is a danger that respondents' answers might be influenced, and to counter this, some researchers try to balance positive state-ments with negative ones (we shall have more to say about this in chapter 5).
◆   Another circumstance where it can be permissible to use leading questions is when people might be too embarrassed to admit to a particular opinion or behaviour unless the researcher signals that he or she has no problem with it.

Asking embarrassing questions

It can help to phrase questions to imply that there is nothing unusual or shameful about the attitudes or behaviour which you are inquiring about. In his famous survey of sexual behaviour in the United States, for example, Alfred Kinsey tried to encourage openness among his respondents by asking not *if* they engaged in certain kinds of behaviour, but rather *how often* they did. However, it seems that the Kinsey report may have overestimated the incidence of certain kinds of sexual behaviour. Perhaps, therefore, some respondents felt awkward about admitting that they had *not* engaged in the various activities that they were being asked about!

Take care that question order does not influence later responses

Value-laden questions are not the only source of bias in a questionnaire. Results can also get skewed by putting questions together in a particular sequence that sets up a specific line of thought in the minds of respondents, thereby narrowing their focus. In this way, the influence of earlier questions 'spills over' to contaminate later answers.

An example of this seems to have happened in a major survey of class inequality in Britain, conducted in the 1980s. In *Social Class in Modern Britain* (Hutchinson, 1988),

Gordon Marshall and his colleagues reported that 'class is still the most common source of social identity' for British people. They found that 60 per cent claimed to belong to a social class, and 79 per cent could think of *no other group* to which they felt a sense of belonging. These were remarkable results, for sociologists and politicians had been suggesting for two or three decades prior to this study that the importance of class was waning, yet here was a major survey claiming that it was still central to people's lives.

There was, however, a problem in the way the questions had been asked. The questionnaire began by taking respondents through a series of questions about industrial conflict, unemployment, government spending cuts and the distribution of income and wealth. It then continued as follows:

Now some questions about social class.

25: In the past there was a dominant class which largely controlled the economic and political system, and a lower class which had no control over economic or political affairs. Some people say that things are still like this, others say it has now changed. What do you think, has it changed or stayed the same? In what ways have things changed?

This is a leading question. Respondents were given no opportunity to disagree with the view that a 'dominant class' controlled everything in the past, but could only say whether this has 'changed'. How were respondents supposed to answer if they did not share the researchers' Marxian view of British history?

26: When you hear someone described as 'upper class' what sort of people do you think of?
27: When you hear someone described as 'middle class' what sort of person do you think of?
28: When you hear someone described as 'working class' what sort of person do you think of?

These three questions provide respondents with the terminology which the researchers use when thinking about class. At question 33, respondents will be asked in an open-ended question which class they think they belong to, and nearly all of them will respond using these three categories – but is this simply because these categories have been planted in their heads earlier?

29a: How is it that people come to belong to the class that they do?
29b: How do you feel about people belonging to a class because of birth, do you approve or disapprove?
29c: Do you think it is easy or hard for a person to go from one social class to another?
29d: Under what circumstances do you think a person could move from one class to another?
30a: Do you think there are any important issues which cause conflicts between social classes?
30b: What conflicts are these?
31: Do you think class is an inevitable feature of modern society?

There is nothing wrong with these questions, except that having worked through them, respondents will have become habituated to using the language of social class, so we need to be very cautious about what we ask next.

> 32: Do you think of yourself as belonging to any particular social class?
> 33: Suppose you were asked to say which class you belonged to, which would you say?

Answers to these questions provide the evidence for the claim that class identity is central for most people in Britain. But after perhaps 15 or 20 minutes of detailed discussion of the class system, it would be difficult for respondents to deny at question 32 that they were part of the system they had been answering questions about! Question 32 should have come at the start of the whole sequence if the research team really wanted to ascertain how many people think in these terms.

> 34: Apart from class, is there any other major group you identify with?

This is where the spillover from previous questions becomes critical. Only one respondent in five could think of any other social identity, but this is almost certainly because the whole of the preceding discussion had focused exclusively on class, so people were not thinking about any other aspect of their lives. Had they been asked to address a sequence of detailed questions about their race, gender, occupation, age or nationality, doubtless similar (or even stronger) findings would have emerged showing the primacy of each of these identities, and class would hardly have got a mention.

Ask specific, concrete questions

Try to ask 'concrete' and specific questions rather than abstract and general ones:

♦   Make your questions sharp (but not rude or aggressive), steer clear of clichés, and avoid questions that almost everybody will answer in the affirmative. Instead of:
Do you think smoking is bad for your health?
ask:
Do you believe that your current smoking behaviour is causing serious damage to your health?

♦   Try to get the most detailed answer you can. Instead of asking 'Do you often...?', try asking 'How often do you...?' or 'When did you last...?' Where it is appropriate, ask for numbers or proportions – not:
Do any of your friends smoke?
but:
How many of your friends smoke?

♦   Questions about people's actual behaviour are usually more reliable than hypothetical questions about what they would do under certain imaginary circumstances. Instead of 'Would you if...', try 'What do you do when...' type questions – not:

Would you smoke in the home of a non-smoker?
but:
When you visit the homes of non-smoking friends, do you smoke inside their house?

Take care over the layout of the questionnaire

Designing a questionnaire means more than developing the questions. You also need to think about blurbs, links, instructions and format:

◆ Give *clear instructions* if respondents are required to answer or ignore particular questions. Most questionnaires include *contingency questions* (where respondents must go to different questions depending on how they have answered earlier ones) and it is vital that they know which questions apply to them and which to ignore.

Contingency questions

In our Smoking Survey, we want to ask some questions to smokers, and others to non-smokers. This means signalling whenever questions are designed for one group or the other. For example:

Q8   *(ask Q8A to smokers, Q8B to non-smokers)*
   A: *To smokers*   When you visit the homes of non-smoking friends or family, do you smoke inside their house?
   B: *To non-smokers*   If friends or family who smoke come to visit you in your home, do you allow them to smoke inside the house?

   Sometimes, a questionnaire will branch into different sections and respondents will be directed to one part or another according to how they answer a filtering question. This requires clear *GO TO* instructions. In the Smoking Survey, for example, the opening question will determine whether or not people have smoked recently. This will be a filter question, for those who have smoked will be asked how much they smoke, while those who have not will be asked if they *ever* smoke. Each group therefore needs directing to different parts of the questionnaire:

Q1   Have you smoked any cigarettes, cigars or pipe tobacco in the last week?
   No *(go to Q3)*
   Yes *(go to Q2)*

Remember that you will also need instructions at the end of a subsection. For example, once they have answered Q2, smokers will need to be told where to go next, for Q3 is for non-smokers only.

◆ *Frame the questions* for the respondents. It is a good idea to have little explanatory 'blurbs' scattered through the questionnaire which explain what is coming next:
I am going to read you some statements. In each case, please tell me whether you strongly agree, agree, have no opinion, disagree, or strongly disagree with the statement...
Finally, some questions about yourself... What is your occupation?

◆ You also need to think about how the questionnaire is to be *introduced and concluded*. If you are using interviewers, what should they say at the start? If the questionnaire is self-completed, do you need an introductory paragraph at the top of the questionnaire? At the end, you should normally give respondents the chance to add anything else they might want to say, and you will need a closing blurb in which you thank them for their participation, tell them how to return the questionnaire (if self-completed), and give them any relevant follow-up information (e.g. how to claim payment if there is any, how to get a summary of the survey results if they are interested, and so on).

◆ If the questionnaire is being administered by interview, think about using interviewer *prompts* and *follow-ups*. With closed questions, you might also consider using *show cards*, where respondents are handed a card with the range of possible answers printed on it and are asked to identify one (this can be useful when there are a lot of answers to choose from, for it is time-consuming for an interviewer to read them all out, and difficult for respondents to remember them all when answering). Cards are also useful when asking personal or potentially embarrassing questions, for respondents can identify their answer by a number or letter on the card, rather than stating it out loud.

◆ The *layout of questions* on the page is important, particularly in self-completed questionnaires. The temptation is to save space by cramming as many items as possible on to one page, but people are put off by dense acres of text. Space your questions out on the page, construct clear boxes where people can check off their answers, use wide margins, and perhaps experiment with the use of colour. Make the questionnaire attractive so that people feel inclined to read it.

Try out your questionnaire with pre-tests, pilot surveys and dummy run analyses

Even if you follow every rule in the book, you are bound to make mistakes when you develop a questionnaire. Questions which you think make sense will get misinterpreted; instructions will prove unclear; questions will not give you the sort of information you are looking for; interviews will take longer than you intended.

   Once you have put your draft questionnaire together, you will therefore need to test it. Do not go straight into data collection, no matter how tempting it is to get started on the fieldwork, for mistakes in questionnaire design cannot be rectified once fieldwork has begun.

◆ The easiest way of testing it out is on friends and colleagues. This *pre-test* will help you judge how long the questionnaire takes to complete and it should throw up any obvious problems in question wording or accompanying instructions.

♦ Following pre-tests, a proper *pilot survey* will normally also be essential. This is where you draw a sample in the same way as you will draw your actual sample, and you administer the questionnaire in the same way as it will be administered in the full survey.

The purpose of a pilot study is not simply to see how the questionnaire works, but is also to ensure that you will be able to analyse the results in the way that you want. This means doing some analysis on the pilot data. You may want to ensure that questions are generating a range of answers, or that attitude statements are all being answered consistently.

By the time you 'go into the field', you should be confident that there are no glitches in the questionnaire, and that the data will be collected in the form that you need. All of this takes time, but it is time well spent, for errors that go undetected now will return to haunt you later.

A NOTE ON ETHICS

Social research is often bound by ethical rules laid down by professional bodies and enforced and interpreted by *ethics committees*. If your work is subject to scrutiny by an ethics committee, they will probably want to look at your questionnaire as well as considering the aims of your study and its overall design. Even if you are not subject to such a committee, it is sensible to ensure that what you are planning to do does not run counter to generally agreed ethical rules and procedures.

As a minimum, you should satisfy yourself on the following points:

♦ *The research is worthwhile and can be justified* – it is unethical to ask people to participate in a study which has no academic or social utility, and you should consider how results of the study can be fed back to participants in an accessible form.
♦ *The research does not harm those who participate in it* – asking sensitive questions can upset people. If there is a possibility that some respondents may be upset, arrangements should be put in place to refer them to appropriate sources of help or advice.
♦ *The principle of informed consent* requires that respondents be given all relevant information about the project prior to their agreement to participate, and that they are aware that they can withdraw at any time.
♦ *Anonymity and confidentiality* are crucial. Participants should normally be given assurances (a) that their identity cannot and will not be divulged, and (b) that their answers will be treated in strictest confidence. Respondents' names and addresses should not be linked to the data set and should never normally appear on a questionnaire. Never discuss particular respondents with other people, and always ensure that no individuals can be identified from patterns of answers in the data.

When people agree to give up their time to participate in your survey, they are trusting you with what are often quite personal and intimate details about their lives. Never betray that trust.

The British Sociological Association ethical guidelines (edited and abridged)

Members must satisfy themselves that a study is necessary for the furtherance of knowledge before embarking upon it.

Sociologists have a responsibility to ensure that the physical, social and psychological well-being of research participants is not adversely affected by the research. They should strive to protect the rights of those they study, their interests, sensitivities and privacy. Members should ... attempt to minimize disturbance to those participating in research.

As far as possible sociological research should be based on the freely given informed consent of those studied. This implies a responsibility on the sociologist to explain as fully as possible, and in terms meaningful to participants, what the research is about, who is undertaking and financing it, why it is being undertaken, and how it is to be promoted. Research participants should be made aware of their right to refuse participation whenever and for whatever reason they wish.

Research participants should understand how far they will be afforded anonymity and confidentiality and should be able to reject the use of data-gathering devices such as tape recorders and video cameras. The anonymity and privacy of those who participate in the research process should be respected. The identities and research records of those participating in research should be kept confidential. Appropriate measures should be taken to store research data in a secure manner. Members should have regard to their obligations under the Data Protection Act. Guarantees of confidentiality and anonymity given to research participants must be honoured.

Special care should be taken where research participants are particularly vulnerable by virtue of factors such as age, social status and powerlessness.

During their research members should avoid, where they can, actions which may have deleterious consequences for sociologists who come after them or which might undermine the reputation of sociology as a discipline.

The full guidelines can be found at www.britsoc.org.uk/about/ethic.htm (email: enquiries@britsoc.org.uk)

CONCLUSION

It takes time and patience to develop a good questionnaire, and mistakes at this stage will blight every succeeding stage of your research. In this chapter we have outlined some simple strategies for developing a successful questionnaire:

- Let your theory drive your selection of the issues to be covered.
- List your key concepts, translate these into variables, identify your independent and dependent variables, and only then develop questions to measure the variables you have identified.
- Consider whether you need to administer your questionnaire in a face-to-face or telephone interview, and take steps to maximize your response rate.
- Think about which questions need to be pre-coded and which can be left open-ended, and give some thought to how you will analyse the open-ended ones.
- When devising questions, look at other people's questionnaires to get ideas for questions that work, keep your questions simple and unambiguous, avoid leading questions (unless you have a good reason for using them), and take care over the order in which questions get asked.
- Spend time on the layout of the questionnaire, and run pre-tests and a full-scale pilot to make sure everything is working as it should.
- Abide by the ethical principles established by professional bodies and your local ethics committee.

In the appendix to this chapter, we outline how our Smoking Survey was developed from first draft to final version, and we see how well the final version meets the various rules and principles which we have set out in this chapter.

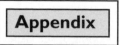

THE SMOKING SURVEY QUESTIONNAIRE

This appendix starts by listing some of the draft questions suggested by our students when devising the questionnaire, and we provide comments on them. We then go on to set out the final version of the questionnaire as it was applied in the study.

A SELECTION OF FIRST DRAFT QUESTIONS (WITH COMMENTARY)

Measures of smoking behaviour (past and present)

Q1 Do you smoke, or did you used to smoke?
Q2 Do you consider yourself a
non-smoker?
occasional smoker?
regular smoker?
social smoker?
chain smoker?
ex-smoker?

Q3 How many cigarettes do/did you smoke on average per day?

Comments

Q1 is a 'double-barrelled' question and should be split into two distinct questions. Also, we need to specify what kind of smoking we are talking about – somehow we have to gather information on consumption of both cigarettes and loose tobacco, and find a way of comparing the two on a common measurement scale.

Q2 raises three issues. First, it fails to use mutually exclusive categories (it is quite possible, for example, to be both an 'occasional smoker' and a 'social smoker'), so the pre-coded answers need rethinking. Secondly, we need to consider whether to provide respondents with these categories, or to leave the question 'open' for them to describe themselves as they wish. Thirdly, we might reflect on whether to classify people's smoking on the basis of their objective behaviour (e.g. how many cigarettes they smoke) rather than their subjective identity (how they think of themselves).

Q3 is another double-barrelled question (we need to distinguish current and past smoking behaviour). And isn't it forgetting about pipe smokers?

History of parental smoking

Q4 Do/did either parent/guardian smoke?

Comment

Q4   is another double-barrelled question which needs splitting into two. The students who devised this question wanted to ask whether parents who used to smoke have subsequently given up, but does it matter for our childhood socialization hypothesis whether people's parents subsequently gave up smoking? Clearly not – we only need to know whether they smoked when the respondent was a child. This is an example of how we can be tempted to think up extra 'interesting' questions when devising a questionnaire, thereby increasing its length without any clear theoretical rationale.

Peer group smoking

Q5   What age were you when you first started smoking regularly?

Q6   Whom were you with when you had your first cigarette?
        Parents
        Peers
        Alone
        Other

Q7   Do most of your friends/peers smoke?

Q8   What situations/environment do/did you smoke in?
        Home
        Work
        Pub/social
        School/college
        Other

Comments

Q5   A host of problems here! How regular is 'regularly'? What do we ask people who do not think of themselves as ever having smoked 'regularly'? And why do we want to ask this question anyway? What are we going to do with the answers we get? There is also a potential problem of selective biographical alteration (or just sheer bad memory) on a question like this. Answers are likely to be extremely unreliable.

Q6   Ditto! Can people remember the circumstances in which they had their first puff on a cigarette? Also, the term 'peers' is too technical – some people will not know what it means. 'Friends' would be better.

Q7   How would this be coded? Presumably a simple 'yes'/'no'. But it would be better to ask something like: 'How many smoke?' – this way we get more detailed information for the same amount of effort.

Q8 Why do we want this? Is it required for any hypothesis? If not, let's drop it – we want to keep the survey as short as possible, and surveys always end up generating huge amounts of material they never use.

Stress

Q9 Do you consider your life stressful? (Code on a scale from 1 = low stress to 5 = high stress)

Q10 'Smoking eases stress levels' Do you agree?
Agree
Disagree
Don't know

Comments

Q9 Measuring stress is a problem. Do we measure it 'objectively' or 'subjectively'? The students are probably right in deciding that all we can realistically do in a short survey like this is to ask how stressed people *think* they are, and the idea of using a scale is a good one. But why limit ourselves to a five-point scale? We could stretch it over ten points, which might help differentiate people better. Of course, people do not ordinarily think of themselves as stressed on a scale of 1 to 5 or 1 to 10, so the answers we get may be somewhat contrived.

Q10 It could be worth asking a question like this (though obviously only to smokers), in which case the quotation would need an introductory blurb, and it may need balancing to avoid leading respondents (e.g. *Some people say that smoking helps relieve stress. Others deny this. What is your view?*). It might also make sense to differentiate degrees of agreement or disagreement (e.g. *Do you strongly agree* (SA), *agree* (A), *have no opinion* (?), *disagree* (D), *strongly disagree* (SD)), since this will help distinguish respondents more clearly.

Tolerance/hostility towards smoking

Q11 Do you agree with banning smoking in public places?
Restaurants   Y/N
Public transport   Y/N
Cinemas   Y/N

Q12 Tick appropriate box (SA, A, ?, D, SD):
(a)   Smoking is socially acceptable
(b)   Smoking should be banned in public places
(c)   Non-smokers should tolerate others smoking in their homes
(d)   There is not enough general propaganda which aims to discourage smoking

Q13   Do you allow people to smoke in your home?

Comments

Q11   The problem with this question is that it emphasizes only one dimension of tolerance – agreement with smoking bans – and then applies it across a range of situations. But attitudes about banning smoking are only one aspect of people's tolerance or intolerance towards smokers. Non-smoking libertarians, for example, may hate smoking yet be opposed to government bans. What we need, therefore, are statements tapping into different aspects of tolerance. Some of these could be phrased positively, others negatively, and they should elicit responses from *Strongly Agree* through *Strongly Disagree* so that we can scale them later (see chapter 5). Banning smoking in public places is certainly one statement we can use, but we need more.

Q12   Here we have four statements to which respondents can respond, and they are balanced (two pro-smoking, two anti). But we need a better introductory blurb, and we need more statements if we want to try to construct a summary scale. We need weak and strong statements, both pro and anti, and we need to ensure they are measuring the 'same' thing (e.g. we want to tap feelings about smoking, not feelings about government telling people what to do). The statements should also be unambiguous – item 12 (a), for example, is an ambiguous measure, for it is unclear whether respondents are being asked if *they* think smoking is acceptable, of if they think that *other people* think it is. In the final questionnaire, we shall raid some earlier smoking surveys for some more attitude items, as well as using some of our students' suggestions.

Q13   This is too vague as it stands – we need to specify it more carefully. Also, we need to ask smokers whether they smoke in the homes of non-smokers.

Generation/cohort; social class; education

Q14   Which age group do you belong to?
Under 21
21–30
31–40
41–50
51–60
Over 60

Q15   What is your occupational status/title?

Q16   What is your highest level of educational qualification?

Comments

Q14   Ideally, we should ask for people's actual age, for this gives us a 'real number' measured on a continuous scale, but we may have to compromise on clustered 'age groups' as some people are sensitive about giving their exact age. If so, we need to ensure that categories do not overlap (e.g. be careful not to have categories such as '55 to 65', '65 and over'), and we should try to keep equal steps between intervals. Both of these conditions have been met in this case.

Q15   When we come to code 'social class', we shall use the categorical schema used in the census and a continuous scale (the Cambridge occupational scale). Appendix B on our website explains both of these schema. You will see from this that both are derived from people's occupational titles, so we must ask for occupational title and employment status. We also need to know the number of people employed or managed by a respondent, so interviewers will have to be told to probe for this information where it is not clear from the initial answer.

Q16   There are three ways we might measure people's education level:

♦   One (adopted in this suggestion) is to ask about their level of qualifications. To do this, you will need to know about national equivalent qualifications (e.g. whether Ordinary National Diplomas are equivalent to GCE 'A' levels), about international qualifications (even Scotland has a different system from England), and about qualifications in the past (e.g. the pre-war 'School Certificate, GCE 'O' levels, CSE Grade 1, and so on). This can make it very complicated to code the answers you get.

♦   A second strategy is to ask about the age at which people completed their full-time education, but there are problems here too. The minimum school-leaving age in England has changed twice since the Second World War – somebody who left school at 16 in 1940 remained at school for two years longer than was normal at that time – and some people return to full-time education later in life, which complicates the answers they give.

♦   A third possibility is to ask about the educational institutions which people have attended – e.g. whether they have completed a college or university course. But this fails to get at qualifications earned since leaving full-time education.

Qualifications are probably the best measure of education, but it can take time for people to list them.

Quitting smoking

Q17   Have you ever seriously attempted to give up smoking?

Q18   (a) (If an ex-smoker): At what age did you stop smoking?
       (b) Which of the following factors influenced your decision to stop?
           health related
           social pressures
           financial reasons

Comments

Q17   This is not a bad question, although it needs pre-coding (yes/no).

Q18   We do need a measure of the length of time since ex-smokers quit (Q18a) but answers may not be very reliable where people stopped a long time ago. As for their reasons for stopping (Q18b), it may be better to leave this open-ended – we do not know what range of answers we might get, and limiting people to just three possible motives is unwise at this stage.

Beliefs about the effects of smoking

Q19   (Smokers only)
        Do you believe that passive smoking is a health risk?

Q20   (Smokers only)
        Do you think that smoking has any positive effects?

Q21   (Smokers only)
        Do you think you have
          (a) the same
          (b) more
          (c) less chance of contracting heart disease, cancer, than someone of your age
          who doesn't smoke?

Comments

Q19   We cannot assume that everybody understands a concept like 'passive smoking', so we need a fuller question which explains it clearly.

Q20   This is simple and straightforward. It will need pre-coding (yes/no), and it should probably have an open-ended follow-up for those who say 'yes' to find out what benefits they think it has.

Q21   The layout of this question is messy, and its 'double-barrelled' character needs sorting out (people may think they have more chance of getting heart disease, but less chance of getting cancer). The students who devised this question anticipated that most smokers will accept that smoking carries health risks – the point is to try to pin down whether they believe it is harming *them*. The problem with the question, however, is that we shall be interviewing in the street. Is it practical or even ethical to confront people with such a blunt question in such a short and impersonal encounter?

THE FINAL QUESTIONNAIRE

The final questionnaire was put together using students' suggestions and items from earlier smoking surveys. It was designed to be administered very quickly in interviews on the street, and in pre-tests it was timed at five minutes. Questions were pre-coded where appropriate, and the first two items (respondent number and gender) were completed by interviewers at the end of the interview. The variable numbers (Var00001, Var00002, etc.) were included to aid later data entry (see chapter 6).

> Electronic copies of this questionnaire can be downloaded from our website and may be printed and distributed without prior permission from the authors. Schools, colleges and universities which attempt to replicate this survey, in whole or in part, are invited to submit their versions of the questionnaire, together with a clean data set and a short explanation of their target population, sampling procedures and hypotheses, and we shall add these to the website (see p. 301 below for details)

Survey on Smoking

Instructions to interviewers:

Introduce yourself, show your identity card, explain that you are a student at Sussex University doing a survey on public opinions about smoking, and ask if they can spare 3 or 4 minutes to answer a few questions. If the respondent seems cautious, give assurances about anonymity (we do not ask for people's names), and explain what will be done with the answers we collect. Do not pressure people who do not want to participate, but make a note of the gender and approximate age of any refusals.

Var00001   Respondent number

Var00002   Gender   0 Female ☐
                          1 Male   ☐

Var00003   **Q1   Have you smoked any cigarettes, cigars or pipe tobacco in the last week?**
                          0 No *(go to Q3)* ☐
                          1 Yes *(go to Q2)* ☐

Var00004   **Q2   Roughly how many cigarettes have you smoked in the last week?**

Var00005   **And roughly how many cigars have you smoked in the last week?**

Var00006   **And roughly how many grams (or ounces) of pipe tobacco have you smoked in the last week?** *(25g = 1 oz)*

Now go to Q5

Var00007   **Q3**   (those who have not smoked in last week) Do you ever smoke nowadays?

> 0 No *(go to Q4)* ☐
> 1 Yes ☐

> *If yes:* **So roughly how much do you smoke in an average week?** *(write in answer)*
> *If normally doesn't smoke in an average week go to Q4; otherwise go to Q5*

Var00008   **Q4 (Non-smokers)   Were you ever a regular smoker?**

> 0 No *(go to Q6)* ☐
> 1 Yes ☐

Var00009   *If yes:* **How long ago did you stop smoking?** *(write in answer)*

Var00010   **Why did you quit?** *(write in answer)*
Now go to Q6

Var00011   **Q5 (Smokers)   Have you ever tried to stop smoking?**

> 0 No *(go to Q6)* ☐
> 1 Yes ☐

Var00012   *If yes:* **Roughly how many times have you tried to stop?** *(write in answer)*

Var00013   **What is the longest period you have stopped for?** *(write in answer)*

Var00014   **Why do you think it is that you haven't managed to stop permanently?** *(write in answer)*

Var00015   **Q6   When you were growing up, did either of your parents (or guardians) smoke?**

> 0 No (neither) ☐
> 1 Yes (mother only) ☐
> 2 Yes (father only) ☐
> 3 Yes (both) ☐
> −1 DK/Can't remember ☐

Var00016   **Q7   Thinking of your close family and friends, how many of them smoke regularly?**

> 1 All or most ☐
> 2 About half ☐
> 3 A few ☐
> 4 Almost none or none ☐
> −1 Don't know ☐

Q8   *(ask Q8A to smokers, Q8B to non-smokers)*

Var00017   A: *To smokers:*

When you visit the homes of non-smoking friends or
family, do you smoke inside their house?

0 No   ☐
1 Yes   ☐
2 Sometimes/it depends ☐
−1 Don't know   ☐

Var00018   B: *To non-smokers:*

If friends or family who smoke come to visit you in your home, do you
allow them to smoke inside the house?

0 No   ☐
1 Yes   ☐
2 Sometimes/it depends ☐
−1 Don't know   ☐

Q9   I am going to read some statements. In each case, please tell me
whether you strongly agree, agree, have no opinion, disagree, or strongly
disagree with the statement

Var00019   Smoking should be banned in places like restaurants

SA   A   ?   D   SD

Var00020   Our society has become too intolerant towards people who smoke

SA   A   ?   D   SD

Var00021   Government isn't doing enough to discourage smoking

SA   A   ?   D   SD

Var00022   Employers should ban all smoking in workplaces

SA   A   ?   D   SD

Var00023   There is too much fuss being made about smoking nowadays

SA   A   ?   D   SD

Var00024   If somebody chooses to smoke, nobody should try to persuade them to
stop

SA   A   ?   D   SD

Var00025   It should be made illegal to smoke in any public space

SA   A   ?   D   SD

Var00026   There are already enough restrictions on where people can smoke

SA   A   ?   D   SD

Var00027   Q10   Some people say that people who don't smoke can still become ill as a result of breathing in other people's tobacco smoke. Do you believe that passive smoking is a serious health risk?

          0 No ☐

          1 Yes ☐

    −1 Don't know ☐

Var00028   Q11   Some people say that smoking can have positive benefits. Do you believe that there are any positive benefits to be had from smoking tobacco?

          0 No ☐

          1 Yes ☐

    −1 Don't know ☐

    If yes: **What kinds of benefits?** (*Write in*)

Var00029   Q12   We all experience a certain amount of stress in our lives nowadays. On a scale from 0 (not at all stressed) to 10 (extremely stressed), how stressful would you say your life is at the moment?

Var00030   Q13   Finally, some questions about yourself. What is your occupation? (*Write in full occupational title – prompt for employment status if necessary*)

Var00031   **Is that full-time or part-time?**   1 Full-time ☐

                                            2 Part-time ☐

Var00032   *If no occupation:* **Are you:**   1 Retired? ☐

                                            2 Unemployed? ☐

                                            3 Housewife/househusband? ☐

                                            4 Permanently sick/disabled? ☐

                                            5 Student? ☐

Var00033   Q14   How old were you when you completed your full-time education?

Var00034   Q15   And which of the following age groups do you belong to?

          1 Under 30 ☐

          2 30–44 ☐

          3 45–60 ☐

          4 Over 60 ☐

Thank you very much for participating in this survey.

DRAWING A SAMPLE

AIM

This chapter considers how to select a representative sample of a target population for inclusion in a survey. It also introduces some simple descriptive statistics. By the end of the chapter, you should:

- Understand the importance of specifying the scope of a survey by clearly defining the criteria for determining people's eligibility for inclusion
- Understand the difference between probability (random) sampling and non-probability (quota) sampling methods, and recognize the strengths and weaknesses of each
- Know how to draw various different kinds of probability samples (simple, stratified and cluster) and how to construct a quota sample
- Understand the basic principles of sample weighting
- Understand and know how to calculate the three basic measures of central tendency (mean, mode, median) and measures of dispersal (variance and standard deviation).

An appendix explains how the sample for our Smoking Survey was drawn.

INTRODUCTION

Some social surveys are conducted on whole populations. Every ten years in the United Kingdom, for example, the entire adult population is required to complete a census form which enables the government to keep a check on how many people are living in the country, how old they are, where they live, and so on.

Surveying 60 million people is a complicated and extremely expensive exercise. If you want to know how big the population is, then you have no choice but to count them in a census, but often we are more interested in finding out things about a population other than its exact size. We might want to know about the distribution of incomes, ethnic composition, or (as in our case) the proportion of the population who smoke. In cases like these, we do not need to contact everybody to develop accurate estimates of the population parameters. We can do it by drawing a *sample* from the population, looking at their characteristics, and making estimates from this sample about the population as a whole.

Estimating population parameters from sample statistics

The characteristics of a population – e.g. its size, or the average income – are called *population parameters*. A parameter is distinct from a *statistic*. Statistics refer to variables in a sample, whereas a parameter refers to the value of a characteristic in the population from which that sample was drawn. When we do surveys, we calculate statistics on samples in order to make estimates about the parameters of populations. For example, we may calculate the mean income of a sample of employees (a *sample statistic*) in order to estimate the average income in the whole population of employees (a *population parameter*).

A sample may consist of only a tiny fraction of the whole target population, but provided it is selected carefully and methodically, it can provide remarkably accurate estimates of the parameters of the whole population.

The rapier and the blunderbuss

During the 1936 US Presidential election campaign, a magazine called the *Literary Digest* contacted 10 million voters and asked whom they were supporting. Two million replies were received, and the magazine forecast from these that Alf Landon would secure a comfortable victory over Franklin Roosevelt, 57 against 43 per cent. Meanwhile, George Gallup interviewed a few thousand voters and forecast from this much smaller sample that Roosevelt would defeat Landon. He was right – Roosevelt secured 61 per cent of the vote and cruised home.

Gallup had demonstrated two things. First, you do not need huge samples in order to get accurate population estimates. Secondly, the way you draw your sample is crucial. The *Literary Digest* had selected names from telephone directories and lists of car owners, but in the 1930s poor people did not have phones or cars. Poorer voters were underrepresented among its 2 million replies and in 1936 the poor voted solidly for Roosevelt. Gallup, by contrast, had ensured that his much smaller sample was *representative* of the whole population – which is why his estimate turned out to be much better.

Of course, estimates of population parameters made from small samples will never be completely accurate, and occasionally they may turn out to be badly wrong. But we rarely need total accuracy – and a fairly accurate estimate derived from a small sample can be achieved much quicker and cheaper than a completely accurate figure based on contacting a whole population.

THE REPRESENTATIVENESS OF SAMPLES

The aim in any sample is that its members should be broadly representative of the population from which they are drawn. How do we achieve this?

Specifying the scope of a survey

The way *not* to do it is to solicit responses from anybody who wants to participate in the survey, yet this is a mistake which is repeated over and over in surveys. Marx's questionnaire aimed at French workers (discussed in chapter 3) provides one example.

Marx's sampling strategy

Marx developed a questionnaire for French workers which he published in the *Revue Socialiste* on 20 April 1880. In addition, 25,000 copies were reprinted and distributed 'to all the workers' societies, to the socialist and democratic groups and circles, to the French newspapers, and to anyone else who asked for it'.

T. Bottomore and M. Rubel (eds), *Karl Marx: Selected Writings in Sociology and Social Philosophy* (Harmondsworth: Penguin, 1963), p. 210

In 1880, there were millions of French workers (the target population). To make reliable estimates of their attitudes and working conditions, it would have been necessary to ensure that those participating in the survey comprised a representative sample of all of these workers. But Marx's approach was almost certain to produce a very *un*representative sample drawn almost exclusively from people who read the *Revue Socialiste*, who had contact with a workers' organization, or who heard about the survey and went to the trouble of asking for a copy of the questionnaire. There were two fundamental flaws in Marx's approach:

- Recruitment of the sample was *selective*, for politically active workers were more likely to receive a copy of the questionnaire than were those who were politically apathetic.
- The scope of the survey was never clearly defined.

Who is 'in scope'?

When setting out on a survey, we need to be clear about two things:

1   What is the target population about which we want to be able to report results?
2   How are we to identify those individuals who are part of this population and who are therefore eligible for inclusion ('in scope') in our sample?

In Marx's case, the target population was the French working class, but the rules for identifying eligible individuals were never thought through. In Marx's own words, 'anybody who asked' could be included in the survey!

The sorts of mistakes Marx made are still made today. Newspapers and magazines often ask their readers to complete questionnaires as a way of gauging public opinion on issues of the day, but the results are often meaningless. In August 2000, for example, an Australian tabloid, the *Herald Sun*, invited readers to telephone in with their views on whether single and lesbian women should get the same free access to fertility treatment which had hitherto been limited to married women. Eight thousand people phoned, and 90 per cent of them were opposed to extending IVF treatment. The paper splashed this 'news' on its front page.

But what did this survey really tell us?

◆   The *population* targeted by this survey was limited to readers of the *Herald Sun*, and it was illegitimate to extrapolate from them to make estimates about the views held by the whole population of Melbourne.
◆   Even within the restricted population of *Herald Sun* readers, moreover, those participating in the survey were a self-selected minority who almost certainly were not representative of the great majority of readers who did not bother to phone in.

What we are left with in a survey like this is a sample statistic – 90 per cent oppose subsidized IVF treatment for single and lesbian women – but we cannot relate it to a population parameter – 90 per cent of *whom* oppose this treatment? Without a clear answer to this question, the whole survey becomes pointless.

In our Smoking Survey, we defined our target population as all people over the age of 16 (the minimum legal age for buying tobacco) who are living in Brighton. Anybody meeting these age and residence criteria was considered 'in scope' for inclusion in our sample.

If you are carrying out your own survey, you should define your eligibility rules before going any further. Be clear about the criteria that determine membership of the population you are interested in studying.

Sydney 2000
Official Partner

Herald Sun

LATE PRICES
PM EDITION

www.news.com.au

THURSDAY, AUGUST 3, 2000 · · · · · N E W S P I C T O R I A L · · · · · TOMORROW: FINE. MAX: 17. PAGE 76 · 99c* (incl. GST)

IVF & SINGLE WOMEN

THE BIG SPLIT

Should single women and lesbians be allowed to use IVF treatment?

NO

"You really have to let the child experience a male and a female influence."
Janine Vitkus and baby Harrison (right)

Premier Steve Bracks

"The issue here is the rights of children."
Prime Minister John Howard (left)

YES

"Cabinet is not listening to Australian women, nor to the men who believe women have a right to fertility treatment."
Federal Sex Discrimination Commissioner Susan Halliday (right)

"The only criteria for having a child is it should be loved."
Roxxy Bent and partner Margie Fischer with baby Ruth (left)

IVF pioneer Carl Wood

Herald Sun **Voteline**

NO 7275 (90%) ▌ 826 (10%) **YES**

AUSTRALIA is divided over the right of single women and lesbians to have IVF babies.

As John Howard stood by his move to limit access, protesters today shredded posters featuring Prime Minister's face.

Angry students stormed Mr Howard's Sydney electorate office before police moved in.

"He's sending a message to the kids of single mums and lesbians that there's something wrong with them," said student Amie Anthony.

By TANYA TAYLOR and ANDREW PROBYN

The issue has split Labor ranks and the churches, with Catholics backing the move to restrict IVF, Anglicans calling for more consultation and the Uniting Church criticising Mr Howard.

Herald Sun readers have also spoken with overwhelming support for Mr Howard in the first poll on the issue. More than 8100 readers called the *Herald Sun* Voteline yesterday.

Ninety per cent said single women should not have access to IVF.

Labor leaders also broke ranks with Premier Steve Bracks, Queensland Premier Peter Beattie and WA Opposition Leader Geoff Gallop backing the IVF ban.

Federal Labor leader Kim Beazley, who initially vowed to fight Mr Howard, yesterday said caucus would decide whether to fight the issue in the Senate.

Medical, community, social and legal figures also were split.

IVF pioneer Carl Wood said les-

bians might make better parents than a traditional nuclear family.

"I think the main emphasis is on a loving, caring couple irrespective of their legal situation," he said.

"There needs to be more study but it's quite possible ... two women may well be better than a man and a woman in rearing children, certainly in some cases."

Monash IVF scientific director Alan Trounson also said IVF was not just for married couples.

But the director of Reproductive Services Albury, the New South

Wales clinic where about 30 single Victorian women seek fertility treatment each year, took a different view.

"I fully endorse John Howard's stance in that sometimes medicine leads social change and that happens very rapidly," Dr Scott Giltrap said.

"We have to take stock of what the general community feels.

"I think Mr Howard has taken a very brave step."

CONTINUED Page 6 EDITORIAL, Page 18

$ **LOAN RATES UP AGAIN: P2** · AFL · **NINE-MATCH BAN FOR AFL STAR: P102**

Two basic sampling strategies

The next question is how we can draw a sample of appropriate size which will accurately reflect the views of our target population. There are two basic strategies available to us:

♦ *probability sampling*, also sometimes called 'random' sampling (although as we shall see, this is a bit misleading, for the procedure of drawing a probability sample is far from 'random');
♦ *non-probability sampling*, generally referred to as 'quota' sampling (this was the strategy used so successfully by George Gallup in the 1936 American Presidential election).

Competing logics: probability and quota sampling

One way to draw a sample that is reasonably representative of a population is to make sure that it resembles the wider population in as many ways as possible. If you know that the population is 50 per cent female, make your sample 50 per cent female; if the population is 10 per cent black, make sure one in ten of your sample members is black; and so on. This method of fixing sample characteristics to reflect population parameters is called *quota sampling* because it involves meeting set quotas of people.

The other way of trying to get a sample that is representative involves exactly the reverse logic. Rather than fixing everything, you fix nothing – you simply ensure that every individual in the population has an equal and known chance of being selected for inclusion in the sample. Provided the sample is big enough, it is likely that its make-up will reflect the make-up of the population from which it is drawn. This is the logic of *probability sampling*.

Probability sampling is normally preferable to quota sampling, but it is not always feasible, and in our Smoking Survey we used a quota sample because it is easier, cheaper and quicker to carry out.

The representativeness of probability samples

The basic principle of probability sampling is that all 'individuals' (be they persons, households, organizations, TV programmes or whatever) in a given 'population' have an equal chance of being selected. This is achieved by ensuring that selection is based on randomness.

Random selection normally generates a reasonably representative sample: a class exercise

When students first encounter probability sampling, they are often sceptical about the claim that random selection of individuals from a population will give you a representative sample. To demonstrate that this is in fact the case, let us work through a simple exercise in which we draw a small sample and attempt to estimate the average age of all the students in the class. When we did this with our undergraduates, there were 32 people in the room – in your case, there may be more or there may be fewer.

The basic principle of probability sampling is that every individual in the population should have an equal chance of being selected. One way of achieving this is to give them all a number, and then draw numbers randomly from a hat, or by some other similar method. Let us therefore begin by giving every individual in the room a unique number (a 'case number'), and note against each number the age of the person. In the example we are working through, there were 32 people in the room, so everybody was given a number between 01 and 32. These numbers were then listed on a whiteboard, and the age of each person was recorded against their number (see table 4.1).

An alternative to putting 32 numbers in a hat, and then drawing them out by hand is to use a table of random numbers to achieve randomized selection. Table 4.2 has been generated by programming a computer to spew out sets of numbers in completely random order. We can use this table to select a small sample of cases, identified by their case numbers. When we did this, we drew a sample of six cases from the 32 individuals in the population, giving us a 6/32 or 18.75 per cent sample. This means that each individual had an 18.75 per cent chance of being selected in our sample. This is called the *sampling fraction*.

There are many different ways in which you could draw your sample using this table of random numbers.

- You could start at row 1, column 1, and work across until you have selected six pairs of digits that fall between 01 and 32: this would select numbers 10, 09, 25, 01, 17, 29 (all the intervening numbers are higher than 32 and are therefore not selected):

  10 09 73 **25** 33   76 52 **01** 35 86   34 67 35 48 76   80 95 90 91 **17**   39 **29** 27 49 45

- Alternatively, you might treat the numbers as single digits, rather than pairs, and read across selecting every pair of adjacent digits which falls within the 01 to 32 range. You would in this case select numbers 10, 09, 32, 20, 13 and 09 again:

  10 09 73 25 33   76 52 **01** 35 86   34 67 35 48 76   80 95 90 91 17   39 29 27 49 45

Table 4.1   Case numbers and ages of 32 undergraduate students

Case no.	Age
1	19
2	19
3	20
4	54
5	38
6	50
7	25
8	62
9	21
10	31
11	19
12	20
13	20
14	26
15	19
16	28
17	33
18	50
19	20
20	21
21	54
22	22
23	26
24	19
25	19
26	19
27	21
28	20
29	19
30	19
31	21
32	47

Mean age of population $(\mu) = 901/32 = 28.156$.

It doesn't really matter how you go about drawing your numbers, provided every person that is in scope has an equal chance of selection.

   Having selected six cases at random, let us see how representative they are of the population from which they were drawn. First, let us see what our sample can tell us about the average age of our students.

Table 4.2   Random numbers

10 09 73 25 33	76 52 01 35 86	34 67 35 48 76	80 95 90 91 17	39 29 27 49 45
37 54 20 48 05	64 89 47 42 96	24 80 52 40 37	20 63 61 04 02	00 82 29 16 65
08 42 26 89 53	19 64 50 93 03	23 20 90 25 60	15 95 33 47 64	35 08 03 36 06
99 01 90 25 29	09 37 67 07 15	38 31 13 11 65	88 67 67 43 97	04 43 62 76 59
12 80 79 99 70	80 15 73 61 47	64 03 23 66 53	98 95 11 68 77	12 17 17 68 33
66 06 57 47 17	34 07 27 68 50	36 69 73 61 70	65 81 33 98 85	11 19 92 91 70
31 06 01 08 05	45 57 18 24 06	35 30 34 26 14	86 79 90 74 39	23 40 30 97 32
85 26 97 76 02	02 05 16 56 92	68 66 57 48 18	73 05 38 52 47	18 62 38 85 79
63 57 33 21 35	05 32 54 70 48	90 55 35 75 48	28 46 82 87 09	83 49 12 56 24
73 79 64 57 53	03 52 96 47 78	35 80 83 42 82	60 93 52 03 44	35 27 38 84 35
98 52 01 77 67	14 90 56 86 07	22 10 94 05 58	60 97 09 34 33	50 50 07 39 98
11 80 50 54 31	39 80 82 77 32	50 72 56 82 48	29 40 52 42 01	52 77 56 78 51
83 45 29 96 34	06 28 89 80 83	13 74 67 00 78	18 47 54 06 10	68 71 17 78 17
88 68 54 02 00	86 50 75 84 01	36 76 66 79 51	90 36 47 64 93	29 60 91 10 62
99 59 46 73 48	87 51 76 49 69	91 82 60 89 28	93 78 56 13 68	23 47 83 41 13
65 48 11 76 74	17 46 85 09 50	58 04 77 69 74	73 03 95 71 86	40 21 81 65 44
80 12 43 56 35	17 72 70 80 15	45 31 82 23 74	21 11 57 82 53	14 38 55 37 63
74 35 09 98 17	77 40 27 72 14	43 23 60 02 10	45 52 16 42 37	96 28 60 26 55
69 91 62 68 03	66 25 22 91 48	36 93 68 72 03	76 62 11 39 90	94 40 05 64 18
09 89 32 05 05	14 22 56 85 14	46 42 75 67 88	96 29 77 88 22	54 38 21 45 98
91 49 91 45 23	68 47 92 76 86	46 16 28 35 54	94 75 08 99 23	37 08 92 00 48
80 33 69 45 98	26 94 03 68 58	70 29 73 41 35	53 14 03 33 40	42 05 08 23 41
44 10 48 19 49	85 15 74 79 54	32 97 92 65 75	57 60 04 08 81	22 22 20 64 13
12 55 07 37 42	11 10 00 20 40	12 86 07 46 97	96 64 48 94 39	28 70 72 58 15
63 60 64 93 29	16 50 53 44 84	40 21 95 25 63	43 65 17 70 82	07 20 73 17 90
61 19 69 04 46	26 45 74 77 74	51 92 43 37 29	65 39 45 95 93	42 58 26 05 27
15 47 44 52 66	95 27 07 99 53	59 36 78 38 48	82 39 61 01 18	33 21 15 94 66
94 55 72 85 73	67 89 75 43 87	54 62 24 44 31	91 19 04 25 92	92 92 74 59 73
42 48 11 62 13	97 34 40 87 21	16 86 84 87 67	03 07 11 20 59	25 70 14 66 70
23 52 37 83 17	73 20 88 98 37	68 93 59 14 16	26 25 22 96 63	05 52 28 25 62
04 49 35 24 94	75 24 63 38 24	45 86 25 10 25	61 96 27 93 35	65 33 71 24 72
00 54 99 76 54	64 05 18 81 59	96 11 96 38 96	54 69 28 23 91	23 28 72 95 29
35 96 31 53 07	26 89 80 93 54	33 35 13 54 62	77 97 45 00 24	90 10 33 93 33
59 80 80 83 91	45 42 72 68 42	83 60 94 97 00	13 02 12 48 92	78 56 52 01 06
46 05 88 52 36	01 39 09 22 86	77 28 14 40 77	93 91 08 36 47	70 61 74 29 41
32 17 90 05 97	87 37 92 52 41	05 56 70 70 07	86 74 31 71 57	85 39 41 18 38
69 23 46 14 06	20 11 74 52 04	15 95 66 00 00	18 74 39 24 23	97 11 89 63 38
19 56 54 14 30	01 75 87 53 79	40 41 92 15 85	66 67 43 68 06	84 96 28 52 07
45 15 51 49 38	19 47 60 72 46	43 66 79 45 43	59 04 79 00 33	20 82 66 95 41
94 86 43 19 94	36 16 81 08 51	34 88 88 15 53	01 54 03 54 56	05 01 45 11 76

Source: H. Blalock, *Social Statistics* (London: McGraw-Hill, 1972), p. 554

Estimating measures of central tendency

The mean

The sample we drew comprised the following six cases:

Case no.	Age
5	38
10	31
25	19
16	28
2	19
30	19

Calculating the mean

The *mean* is the arithmetic average of a set of numbers. To calculate the mean age of six students in a sample, add all six ages together, and divide by six (the total number of cases).

Summing the ages of these six students gives us a total age of 154, and dividing this by six (the number of cases) gives a mean (or average) age of 25.67. The actual mean age of the whole population, given in table 4.1, was 28.16, so if we were to use this sample statistic to estimate the mean age of the whole population of students, we would be two and a half years out. To summarize:

$$\text{Sample mean } (\bar{x}) = 25.67;$$
$$\text{Population mean } (\mu) = 28.16.$$

Greek and Roman symbols

Greek characters are generally used to refer to population parameters, while Roman characters are used to refer to sample statistics (although this 'rule' does not operate in every case).

The Greek character μ (pronounced 'mu') is used to refer to the population mean. The mean of a sample, however, is designated by the Roman character x with a bar above it: $\bar{x}$. There are six basic symbols you will encounter in this book:

μ	mean of population	$\bar{x}$	sample mean
σ	standard deviation of population	s	sample standard deviation
σ^2	population variance	s^2	sample variance

Our sample estimate of 25.67 is wrong, but it is not wildly wrong. This is often the case when estimating population parameters from sample statistics. Occasionally you will be unlucky enough to draw a sample heavily skewed by extreme cases, and if this happens you will obviously end up with some very inaccurate estimates (for example, had we drawn a sample from the cases in table 4.1 consisting of numbers 4, 6, 8, 18, 21 and 32, we would have estimated the average age of the population at nearly 53 – nearly 25 years out). But the likelihood of this happening is very small, and most of the time the samples we draw will more or less approximate the population from which they come.

> To check this, try drawing more samples from your population in the same way that you drew the first one, and in each case, calculate their mean ages. You should find that most of the sample means are fairly close to the actual popula-tion mean. Save all the sample estimates that you get – we shall use them again in chapter 9.

The mode and the median

The mean is one of three statistics known collectively as 'measures of central tendency'. Each gives us a summary of what our sample looks like:

- The mean tells us the average value of all the cases in the sample.
- The mode tells us which value occurs most frequently in the sample.
- The median tells us the middle value in the range of values in our sample.

We have seen that we calculate the *mean* by summing all the individual values and dividing by the number of cases. We calculate the *mode* by identifying which value occurs more than other. In our sample of six students, for example, there are three 19-year-olds, so this is the most frequently occurring value. We calculate the *median* by arranging all the values from lowest to highest and identifying the middle one. When there is an even number of cases (as in a sample of six cases), there is no single middle value, so we take the two cases either side of the middle (in our sample, one of the 19-year olds and the 28-year-old) and average their values to find a median value. In our sample of six students, therefore:

$$\text{sample size (n)} = 6$$
$$\text{mean age } (\bar{x}) = 154/6 = 25.67$$
$$\text{mode} = 19$$
$$\text{median} = (19 + 28)/2 = 23.5$$

We found that the sample mean is about 2 ½ years below the true mean age of the 32 people in our target population. Looking back to table 4.1, we can now calculate the modal and median ages of this population to compare them with our corresponding sample statistics:

♦ Nine of the 32 students are aged 19 – the most common age – so in this case our sample mode corresponds exactly to the population mode.

♦ With a total population size of 32, the middle ranking observation will fall between the 16th and 17th cases. Arranging all 32 cases in age order, we find that both the 16th and 17th positions are occupied by 21-year-olds, so the median age of the population is 21. Our sample median was 23.5, so in this case our sample statistic is 2 ½ years too high.

Our sample of just six students has produced reasonably accurate estimates of three different population parameters. Estimating the mean age, we are 30 months too low; estimating the median we are 30 months too high; and estimating the mode, we are spot on.

Which should we use: mean, mode or median?

The mean is probably the most commonly used of the three measures of central tendency, but it can be misleading in certain circumstances – particularly when a population contains a small number of what statisticians call 'extreme' cases. Our population of 32 students, for example, contained a handful of mature students, and they increase the mean age of the group. Summarizing the typical student's age with reference to the mean would therefore be somewhat misleading. In situations like this, the median may be a better summary statistic.

Measuring dispersal: the standard deviation

We know that our sample of six students has a mean age of 25.67, but this tells us nothing about how spread out or clustered the ages are. A mean age of 25.67 could have been achieved from any of the following samples:

♦ Four people aged 26 and two aged 25 – a range of just one year.
♦ Three 19-year-olds, and three other people aged 28, 31 and 38 (our actual sample) – a range of 19 years.
♦ A one-year-old baby, a toddler of three, a child of eight, a parent of 24, a grandparent of 48 and a great grandparent of 70 – a range of 69 years.

Clearly the *range* of ages in the third sample is much larger than that in the first, but it would be helpful if we could summarize the degree of variation in each of these samples. We do this with a statistic called the *standard deviation*.

Calculating the standard deviation: a worked example

The standard deviation measures the *average amount* by which each case differs from the group mean. To calculate the standard deviation for our sample of six students, we start by working out how far each person's age deviates from the mean age of the sample:

Age	Mean	Deviation from mean
38	25.67	+12.33
31	25.67	+ 5.33
28	25.67	+ 2.33
19	25.67	− 6.67
19	25.67	− 6.67
19	25.67	− 6.67

The total spread within the sample is obviously the sum of these individual differences. However, if we simply add them up as they stand, we end up at zero, because some are negative and some are positive, and they cancel each other out. To add the differences together, we have first to convert them all to positive values, and this is done by *squaring* them.

Squaring numbers

To square a number, you multiply it by itself. The result is always positive, for a negative number multiplied by another negative number gives a positive result.

- For example, 3 squared (written as 3^2) equals +9 (3 multiplied by 3).
- And minus 3 squared (-3^2) also equals +9 (-3 multiplied by -3).

The *square root* of a number is the opposite of its square. Thus, the square root of 9 (written as $\sqrt{9}$) is 3, because 3 multiplied by itself gives you 9. (Equally, of course, -3 is also the square root of 9.)

Thus in this example:

Age	Mean	Deviation from mean	Deviation squared
38	25.67	+12.33	152.03
31	25.67	+ 5.33	28.41
28	25.67	+ 2.33	5.43
19	25.67	− 6.67	44.49
19	25.67	− 6.67	44.49
19	25.67	− 6.67	44.49
			$\sum = 319.42$

Now that we have made all the deviations from the mean into positive numbers, we can add up the differences (the symbol $\sum$ means 'sum' or 'add together', and is pronounced 'sigma'). The sum of all these squared deviations from the mean = 319.42.

What we want to know is the average amount by which each person's age differs from the mean age. The obvious next step, therefore, is to divide the total of the squared deviations by the number of cases to find an average.

There is, however, a slight complication at this point, for this simple average tends slightly to underestimate the degree of spread in the population from which we have drawn our sample. To take account of this, we divide the sum of the squared deviations (319.42) by the number of cases, *minus 1* (i.e. $6 - 1 = 5$). Obviously this correction makes quite a big difference when, as here, we are dealing with a small sample size, but it makes little practical difference when dealing with larger samples.

Doing this calculation, we divide 319.42 by 5 (our sample size minus 1), which gives us an answer of 63.89. This figure is known as the *variance*.

Because earlier we squared all the deviations from the mean before we added them up, the final step in calculating the average deviation from the mean is to take the *square root* of this total to cancel out the effect of having squared all the numbers in the first place. Using a calculator, we find that the square root of 63.89 equals 7.99. This figure is the *standard deviation* of the sample:

$$s = 7.99$$

The variance and the standard deviation

Note that the standard deviation (s) is the square root of the variance $(s^2) = \sqrt{63.89}$; and that the variance is the square of the standard deviation $= 7.99^2$.

The standard deviation tells us the average degree of dispersal within the sample. Our sample standard deviation of 7.99 thus tells us that each of the students in our sample is on average nearly eight years older or younger than the mean sample age of 25.67.

Calculating the standard deviation using a formula

How good an estimate is our sample standard deviation (s) of the actual standard deviation in the target population (σ)? We could calculate the standard deviation of the whole population of 32 students in the same way as we just did it for the sample of six – but we can do it quicker by resorting to algebra.

To use this formula, we need to:

♦   Calculate $\sum x$: we do this by adding up the ages of all 32 students listed in table 4.1. The answer comes to 901.
♦   Calculate $(\sum x)^2$: this is obviously 901 multiplied by itself $= 811,801$.
♦   Calculate $(\sum x)^2/n$: the population size (n) $= 32$, so $(\sum x)^2$ divided by 32 $= 25,369$.
♦   Calculate $\sum x^2$: this means we have first to square each student's age and then add up the results to get the sum of squares. This comes to 30,653.

The formula for calculating the standard deviation

The formula which expresses the procedure we followed in calculating the standard deviation is:

$$\text{Standard deviation } (s) = \sqrt{\frac{\sum (x - \bar{x})^2}{n - 1}}$$

where x is the value of each case, $\bar{x}$ is the sample mean, and n is the sample size. This same formula can be rewritten as:

$$\text{Standard deviation } (s) = \sqrt{\frac{\sum x^2 - \frac{(\sum x)^2}{n}}{n - 1}}$$

which looks more complicated, but actually enables us to work out the standard deviation without having to calculate all the individual deviations first (useful if you have a large sample).

The standard deviation in the ages of the whole population of 32 students can now be calculated as:

$$\sqrt{\frac{30,653 - 25,369}{31}} = \sqrt{170.45} = 13.06$$

This is considerably larger than the standard deviation calculated for our sample of just six students (7.99). It seems that our sample would lead us to underestimate the average scatter of people's ages in the population by about 60 per cent – a big error. So what has gone wrong?

The answer is that our sample size is too small to give us reliable estimates. Looking at the six students we selected, three of them were aged 19 (the youngest age in the population) and nobody was over 40, so the sample failed to pick up the full range of ages in the population, and this is reflected in the underestimated standard deviation. Had our sample included one of the 50-somethings, the scatter of ages would have been greater and the estimated standard deviation would have been that much larger.

There is an important lesson here. The bigger the sample, the more accurate it is likely to be in estimating population parameters. But how big does a sample need to be before we can start to have faith in the accuracy of the estimates we get from it?

How big a sample do you need?

In our class exercise, we drew a sample of just six students from a population of 32. This is fine for the purposes of illustration, but in reality you would never draw a sample as small as this. So how big should a sample be? The answer depends on what your survey is trying to achieve. There are five things to consider.

1   How precise do your estimates need to be?

The accuracy of your sample estimates will be affected by the size of your sample relative to the size of the population from which it is drawn, and by the degree of variation within that population. If the population is fairly homogeneous (e.g. everybody is around the same age), you will be able to get away with a smaller sample than if the variance is larger.

Even with a very large sample, however, you will not end up with completely accurate estimates, so you need to decide how big a *margin of error* you are prepared to accept. Suppose, for example, we want to draw a sample which will allow us to estimate the proportion of smokers in a population. If we are willing to accept a rough estimate – say 10 per cent either way – then we shall be able to make do with a smaller sample than if we want a more accurate estimate – say, within 3 per cent. The bigger the sample, the more accurate we can expect our estimates to be.

2   How much confidence do you want to be able to put in your estimates?

Compare the following claims:

◆   It is fairly likely that the proportion of smokers in the population is between 27 per cent and 33 per cent.
◆   It is almost certainly the case that the proportion of smokers in the population is between 21 per cent and 39 per cent.

The first statement has a tighter margin of error than the second, but the *level of confidence* with which the statement is made is rather weaker. If we are told that it is 'almost certain' that something is true, we will be more inclined to accept it than if we are told it is 'fairly likely'.

Levels of confidence can be expressed in percentage terms. Saying something is 'fairly likely' might translate as saying that there is a 2 in 3 chance that it is true. Saying that something is 'almost certainly' the case is like saying you are almost 100 per cent certain it is true (although we can never be absolutely 100 per cent certain when making estimates from samples).

In chapter 9, we shall see how to calculate confidence levels for estimates with varying margins of error. For now, all we need to understand is that bigger samples will allow us to achieve higher levels of confidence at lower margins of error.

Table 4.3   Sample sizes required to achieve a 95 per cent confidence level for estimates of varying degrees of precision with a heterogeneous population

Sampling error (%)	Sample size
1	10,000
2	2,500
3	1,100
4	625
5	400
10	100

Source: David de Vaus, *Surveys in Social Research* (London: Allen & Unwin, 1993)

We can, in fact, be a little more specific than this. Table 4.3 indicates the size of sample you will need to draw (assuming a heterogeneous population) to achieve a 95 per cent confidence level for estimates with varying margins of error (referred to here as *sampling error*). For example, if you want to be 95 per cent confident that your sample will give you an accurate estimate of a population parameter, plus or minus 3 percentage points, then you will need a sample size of 1,100 to achieve this. With a sample of 1,100, you should be able to make statements based on your survey data like: 'I am 95 per cent confident that the proportion of the population that agrees with banning smoking in pubs is 48 per cent, plus or minus 3 per cent.'

Note that if you are dealing with small samples, a small absolute increase in sample size can pay off quite handsomely by giving you much more accurate estimates. Pushing your sample size up from 100 to 200, for example, will reduce your sampling error from 10 per cent to 7 per cent with a 95 per cent level of confidence that your estimated range will be correct.

Calculating the size of sample you need

If you know the population standard deviation, the degree of sampling error you are prepared to accept and the confidence level you want then the minimum sample size you need can be calculated (but remember also to make additional allowance for non-responses). The calculation requires some understanding of inferential statistics, and for this, you will need to read the first part of chapter 9 up to, and including the section headed 'Calculating sample sizes'. However, if you want to calculate your required sample size without learning the formula then a sample size calculator can be found in section 2 of the website which accompanies this book – www.surveymethods.co.uk.

Conversely, increasing the size of large samples to make them even larger does not appear to be a very efficient use of research resources. For example, to get from a

2 per cent to a 1 per cent level of sampling error, we would need to increase our sample from 2,500 to 10,000, which would be hugely expensive. It is for this reason that most commercial opinion pollsters are quite happy to stick with samples of around one or two thousand, accepting a sampling error of 2 or 3 per cent either way.

The other thing to note about table 4.3 is that these sample sizes assume a high degree of variability in people's responses. Specifically, they assume for any dichotomous variable that half of the population will answer one way, and half another. If this is not the case, and most people fall into one category with only a few in the other, then accurate estimates can be made with much smaller sample sizes. For example, we see from the table that a 50:50 division in answers will require a sample size of 1,100 to give you a 3 per cent margin of error either way, but if people's answers divide in the ratio of 90:10, then the same level of accuracy could be achieved from a sample of just 400.

3 How far do you want to break your analysis down?

A third factor to consider when deciding on sample size is how far you will need to break down your sample into subgroups when you come to analyse your data.

In our Smoking Survey, we are interested in comparing smokers and non-smokers, and we know from other research that smokers make up around one-third of the population. Table 4.3 tells us that a sample of just 300 to 400 will enable us to make a reasonable estimate of the number of smokers in the target population (95% confidence level at 5% margin of error either way), but to test some of our hypotheses, we want to go beyond this. This will mean analysing variations between subgroups in our sample.

Our first hypothesis, for example, predicts that there will be important differences in smoking behaviour based on parental smoking patterns. To test this, we shall need to subdivide our two categories of smokers and non-smokers according to whether their parents smoked. With a sample of 400, and assuming just one-third of people in each generation smoke, we might anticipate ending up with something like the breakdown in figure 4.1.

The smallest subgroup we anticipate finding consists of 44 smokers whose parents also smoke – but a subsample of just 44 people is very small if we want to go any further in analysing the population of smokers whose parents smoke. Breaking this group down by social class, for example, would produce such small numbers in each class category that it would become impossible to make any serious population estimates.

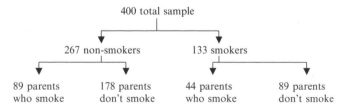

Figure 4.1 Anticipating the size of subgroups in a sample

As a general rule of thumb (and depending on how big you expect the effects to be that you are testing for), around 40 to 50 cases in any single subgroup is reckoned by most researchers to be the minimum you will probably need. Assuming we are dealing with fairly simple variables consisting of just two or three values, this means we could split a sample of 400 twice and still have large enough numbers to work with. But if our variables are more complex than this, and/or we want to do more in-depth analysis than this, then a sample of this size will soon prove inadequate.

4   How big is the non-response rate likely to be?

When calculating your sample size, you will obviously need to anticipate the likely non-response rate. If you realistically expect to achieve, say, a 60 per cent response rate, then to get 400 cases you would need to draw an initial sample of 667 cases to allow for the non-responses.

5   How flexible is your budget?

Inevitably, when determining your final sample size, you will be making trade-offs. Your final decision will depend on the resources you have available to you, and the uses to which you need to put your data:

◆   You may decide that it is crucial to have a large sample, in which case you might sacrifice face-to-face interviewing in favour of a cheaper method of data collection such as telephone interviews or postal questionnaires.
◆   You may try to increase your sample size by reducing the length of the questionnaire, thereby reducing the unit cost of each interview and releasing more money for expanding the number of interviews.
◆   You may decide that you can live with a smaller sample size and accept that this means limiting the depth and complexity of the analysis that you plan to do.

In our Smoking Survey, we decided to aim for a sample of around 400 (although we actually ended up with just 334 cases). We knew that this would restrict the accuracy of the estimates we could make, and that it would limit the extent to which we could analyse subgroups within the sample. Nevertheless, a small sample could be generated quickly and cheaply, and 400 cases would probably suffice for the kinds of analysis that we wanted to do.

Social surveys often aim at larger samples than this – a thousand or two is common – but only rarely do researchers have the resources to generate the sample size they would ideally like. Surveys are inherently expensive things to carry out, and money is always tight, so some sort of compromise normally has to be made.

THE VARIETIES OF PROBABILITY SAMPLING

The essential requirement of probability sampling is that each individual in a population should have a known and equal chance of being selected.

Simple random samples

There is only one method of sampling that fully meets this requirement – namely, *simple probability sampling with replacement*. This was the procedure we used earlier when we drew a sample of six students from the population of 32 students in the class. We used a table of random numbers to ensure that each student had an equal chance of being selected, and allowing the same individual to be selected more than once (sampling 'with replacement') meant that the chance of the second and subsequent people being selected was identical to that of the first.

Don't do as I do, do as I say?

The rules governing probability statistics are very clear – yet in sociological research, they are often bent or broken. One example of this is that very few social surveys use simple random sampling with replacement, yet this is the only pure form of probability sample.

As we go through this book, we shall encounter other examples where the practicalities of doing a research project clash with the requirements laid down by statisticians. It is important that you should know what these requirements are, and that where possible you should strive to meet them. But it is also important to understand that messy compromises are sometimes unavoidable if real research is to get done at all.

Very rarely, however, do social surveys use simple probability sampling with replacement – or, for that matter, without replacement. For all sorts of practical reasons, most surveys end up using some other approach that *more or less* ensures that each member of a given population has a *roughly* equal chance of being selected. Usually, this is good enough.

Systematic random samples

Sometimes, rather than selecting individuals completely at random from a population, it is easier to select every nth case from a list (where n is your 'sampling fraction'). To select 6 out of 32 students in a class, for example, we could work out the sampling fraction ($32/6 = 5.33$) and proceeded to select every 5th student seated around the room.

This sort of approach can be useful when you are drawing a sample from readily available lists like telephone directories, the electoral register, or organizational membership records. It does not strictly meet the condition that every individual should have an equal chance of being selected, for once we have chosen the first person, the selection of the rest is already determined. For most practical purposes, however, systematic random sampling should give you a perfectly usable sample *provided the list is not itself systematically patterned*. Obviously, if you decide to take every second name from a listing of husbands' names followed by their wives' names, then you will end up with a desperately skewed sample consisting entirely of women. But provided you look out for obvious pitfalls like this, there should be no major problem.

Stratified random samples

Stratified random samples allow you to *ensure* that certain key categories of people will be included in your sample in appropriate numbers. They achieve this by dividing the population into different groups on the basis of known parameters such as their sex or age, and then drawing random samples from within each group.

For example, if you *know* that 6 per cent of the population belongs to an ethnic minority group, and if it is crucial to your survey that you pick up the right proportion of ethnic minority respondents, then you could split the population into 'ethnic minority' and 'white' categories and then sample the same proportion from each category.

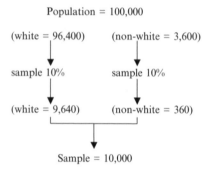

Figure 4.2   Stratifying a sample by ethnicity

If your sample is large enough, it should not really be necessary to stratify it to ensure that it will pick up this or that group in the right proportions. If 6 per cent of the population is non-white, you should find in a simple random sample that about 6 per cent are non-white. So why would you ever choose to stratify?

◆ One reason is if your sample size is small, in which case you may not want to run the risk of failing to pick up the correct proportion of people from minority groups. Stratifying ensures that you will.
◆ A second reason is that you may want deliberately to *overrepresent* some groups within your sample.

Let us consider this second reason in more detail. If you deliberately oversample one group, and undersample another, then you are flagrantly breaking the principle that every individual should have an equal chance of being selected. This does not matter, however, provided:

◆ *either* you analyse the two groups separately (i.e. effectively you treat them as two distinct samples) as in figure 4.3a;
◆ *or* you *re-weight* them before combining them into a single sample where they can be analysed together, as in figure 4.3b.

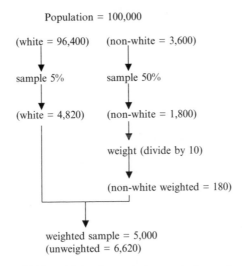

(a) Weighting and analysing samples separately

(b) Re-weighting for analysis as a single sample

Figure 4.3   Weighting stratified samples

A note on weighting

Suppose, as in figure 4.3b, you have sampled every 20th white resident and every 2nd non-white resident in a population. Each non-white person has had 10 times the chance of being selected than each white person. You can rectify this when you analyse your data by applying *weights* to each of these groups. This will give you accurate estimates for the whole population.

Furthermore, weights can also be used to correct for unintentional biases arising in the process of sampling itself. For example, you may find after drawing a simple probability sample that the sample underrepresents ethnic minorities. One solution to this is to weight ethnic minority respondents' answers by an appropriate multiplier to restore the balance.

Multistage cluster samples

How would you go about drawing a random sample of 1,000 UK citizens? There are around 60 million people in the UK of whom perhaps 50 million are of an age where

---

National random samples using telephone interviewing

If you are doing a *telephone survey*, you could plan something close to a simple probability sample by taking the electronic telephone directory as your sampling frame and randomly selecting numbers. However, you will miss people who have no phone (e.g. the very poor), or who only have a mobile phone (e.g. young people) or whose numbers are unlisted (e.g. more affluent people).

Alternatively, you could use random-digit-dialling, where a computer is programmed to call up any possible telephone number. This will catch unlisted and mobile phone numbers, but will generate a large number of void calls (e.g. to business numbers or telephone boxes), and you cannot calculate a response rate since you will not know whether unanswered calls were to people who were out or away, or were to void numbers.

---

they might be interviewed. Our sampling fraction is therefore 50,000,000 ÷ 1,000 = 1/50,000. So you need to select 1 person in 50,000 for inclusion in your sample. But how are you going to do it?

One problem is finding a suitable sampling frame. There is no easily accessible list of all the names and addresses of everybody living in the country. But even if there were,

---

Peter Townsend's sample of the United Kingdom population

To carry out his survey of poverty, Townsend first divided the UK into nine regions. Each region was then divided into 'urban' and 'rural' parliamentary constituencies, and the 'urban' constituencies were further stratified into 'rich', 'medium' and 'poor' clusters. Two constituencies were then randomly selected from each cluster in each of the nine regions with the probability of selection being adjusted for population size.

At this stage, 52 constituencies across nine regions of the UK had been selected. The next task was to select smaller study areas within each of these constituencies. The wards in each constituency were divided into 'rich' and 'poor' (based on the proportion of their population who left school at the minimum leaving age) and each stratum was randomly sampled to get about 130 wards. Townsend then used electoral registers and domestic rating records to draw a random sample of approximately 2,000 household addresses from among the residents of these wards.

The sample closely approximated the whole UK population in age, sex, country of birth, household size, household type, housing tenure and receipt of various state pensions and benefits.

See Peter Townsend, *Poverty in the United Kingdom* (Harmondsworth: Penguin, 1979), appendices 2 and 3

are you really going to select 50,000 people at random from all over the country? This might not be a problem if you are planning to use a postal questionnaire or telephone or email interviewing, but face-to-face interviewing would be a daunting prospect given the distances between each interview.

The solution is to use multistage cluster sampling. This means that you *first* organize the population into geographical clusters, and *then* you sample individuals randomly from within the clusters you have selected. Peter Townsend's survey of UK poverty was a good example of such a strategy.

Multistage cluster samples do not give every individual in the population an equal chance of being selected so they breach the pure rule of probability sampling. But carefully organized and administered, this kind of strategy can work perfectly adequately to give you a representative sample of a large and scattered population without incurring huge travel costs in interviewing.

QUOTA SAMPLING

We saw at the start of this chapter that two different logics may be applied when setting out to draw a representative sample from a population:

◆ You can leave the selection of individuals to chance, knowing that random selection will usually give you a representative sample. This is the logic of probability sampling.
◆ You can select individuals to match some particular characteristics of your sample with those of the whole population. This is the logic of non-probability quota sampling.

Quota sampling is extensively used in commercial opinion polling and consumer research, but in academic social science probability samples are generally preferred.

How to draw a quota sample

The procedure for drawing a quota sample is very simple.

◆ First you identify some basic characteristics on which to match your sample to the population. You may decide, for example, that the sample must reflect the population on its gender composition, its age structure, its socio-economic status and its regional distribution.
◆ Next, you find accurate information about these population parameters to enable you to construct your quotas. This means finding out what the gender balance is, what the age distribution is, and so on.
◆ Thirdly, you decide on your target sample size, and you break this down into its constituent quotas. If half of the population is male and half female, for example, then a target sample size of 1,000 would require that you select 500 males and 500

females. If one-quarter of the men in the target population are aged under 30, then you will need 125 of the men you select to be under 30. And so on.

♦   Finally, you go out and find people who are members of your target population and who fit one of the profiles (quotas) you need to fill.

Advantages of quota sampling

Compared with probability samples, quota samples are *quick* and *cheap*. This is why commercial survey agencies like them. Once you have constructed your quotas, all you have to do is find appropriate respondents to fill them. This might involve hanging around on street corners, in shopping precincts or in other public places and approaching people for interviews until you have filled the quotas.

This is obviously much easier than drawing a probability sample of names and addresses, travelling to meet respondents, waiting around for appointments, making repeated call-backs to those who are out, and wasting travelling time calling on those who refuse to participate.

An added advantage of quota samples is that you *do not need a sampling frame*. If there is no list of names and addresses of the individuals who make up a given population, there may be no way of constructing a reliable sampling frame from which to draw a probability sample. In such a situation, quota sampling might be used instead.

Disadvantages of quota sampling

Notwithstanding their obvious attractions, quota samples have some major disadvantages.

The use of probability statistics is invalid with a non-probability sample

One drawback is that selection of respondents in a quota sample is not based on chance, which means that, strictly speaking, probability statistics will not be appropriate for making population estimates from the data you collect. With no sampling frame, we cannot know what the chances were of any single person being selected, so the core assumptions of probability theory are violated.

Having said that, people do use probability statistics to analyse quota sample data, and we shall be doing so ourselves in our analysis of the Smoking Survey. But statisticians shudder when we do this, for in quota sampling, rather than allowing people an equal chance of being selected, we actually go out and pick them according to the particular attributes that they happen to have.

Questions of representativeness beyond the quota parameters

If you fix the proportions of your sample on three or four key criteria, such as gender, age and socio-economic status, then you can be certain that your sample will reflect the population from which it is drawn *on these attributes*. In this sense, a quota sample is a bit like a stratified random sample – you make sure that the sample is representative on certain key characteristics.

Unlike a stratified random sample, however, you have absolutely no grounds for assuming that the sample is representative on any other characteristics. By fixing a few things, and leaving nothing to chance, you have suspended the 'laws of probability' which random designs rely on to generate what they hope will be representative samples. Ensuring representativeness on a few characteristics brings no guarantee that you will end up with representativeness on any others.

Biased selection of respondents

A related problem concerns the way we choose the people who fill our quotas. In a probability sample, introverts are just as likely to be selected as extroverts, hermits as party animals, stay-at-homes as gadabouts. This is not true in a quota sample, for you will only select from the people that you happen to come across.

This makes the choice of *sampling sites* and the *timing* of interviews very important:

◆ If you stand outside a train station at 8 a.m., you are likely to end up with a sample that overrepresents commuters.
◆ If you draw a sample of students by standing outside your university library shortly after it opens, you are likely to overrepresent those who take their studies seriously while underrepresenting those who stay in bed nursing a hangover.

What is needed is sites where *anybody* might go at whatever time of day you are there with your clipboard, but this is not easy. Almost any time and place you select will tend to favour the chances of some groups ending up in your sample and reduce the chances of others. Given that you are trying to recruit a representative sample, this is a major problem.

No proper measure of response rates

With a probability sample you can calculate the proportion of people who refuse to participate or who are not successfully contacted. This then allows you to calculate a response rate which gives you an important indicator of the reliability of your study.

In a quota sample, you can note how many of the people you approach refuse to be interviewed, and you can make a note of their sex and approximate age, so that you can check later whether there was an obvious pattern to the refusals. What you cannot do, however, is calculate a proper response rate, for you never had a finite sample size to begin with.

When you draw a quota sample, you can always achieve the sample size you want, because you keep on approaching potential respondents until all your quotas are full. But you have no way of knowing how many people you might have 'missed' (e.g. people away on holiday, people who work shifts, people who never go out of the house). When you carry out a survey based on a quota sample, therefore, you never really know how representative the sample is likely to be.

Inefficiencies and impracticalities

Although quota sampling is generally quicker and cheaper than probability sampling, it does have its own inefficiencies, not the least of which is that you will often interview more people than you need. Suppose, for example, you have interviewed all the women in your 50 to 59 age quota, but you are still looking for more women aged 60 to 69. You keep approaching women who appear to be in the age range you want, only to find (when you eventually ask their age) that they are in the wrong age group. The whole interview will then be surplus to requirements.

It can also be difficult to find the information you need to construct quotas. Quota samples require that you have reliable information on several key population parameters. It is an irony of quota sampling that you have to know something in advance about the population before you can start to find out anything about it.

The second-best option?

Because of their limitations, quota samples can go badly wrong, and *you should consider using probability sampling wherever this is feasible.* However, we should not exaggerate the problems with quota sampling – most of the time, surveys based on quota samples turn out to be fairly reliable. If your survey aims are modest and your resources are tight, you might get away with a quota sample without any major mishaps. But probability samples are the generally preferred option. Quota sampling is second best, but sometimes second best is all that is possible or is the only option you can afford.

If you are developing your own group survey, then you must decide at this point whether to draw a probability or a quota sample.

If you go for a *probability sample*, you might select at random a few wards in the local authority area where you live, sample electoral districts within these wards, and draw a sample of households from these electoral districts using the electoral register (the reference library will have a copy, or you can buy the sections you need from the Town Hall).

If you go for a *quota sample*, as we have done, you will need to gather some basic population information, probably using small area census data. Detailed information on local areas based on the decennial census is available in reference libraries, and probably also in your local university library. If you are working through this book using our Smoking Survey data you will not need to draw a sample of your own, but you should still read the appendix to this chapter to see how we drew our sample.

CONCLUSION

Sampling is a technically sophisticated business. Get it wrong, and the rest of your survey becomes worthless.

The aim when drawing any sample is to identify a group of cases which are representative of the wider population from which they are drawn. Normally, the best way to do this is by using some version of a probability, or random, sampling procedure. Provided it is large enough, a probability sample should not only give you a reasonably representative group of cases, but it will also enable you to make predictions about population parameters within clearly defined confidence levels.

Non-probability, quota sampling is generally the second-best option, but its cost and time advantages mean that it can sometimes make sense to go for this rather than for a probability sample design. In our Smoking Survey, we opted for a quota sample for precisely these reasons, and the appendix to this chapter takes you through the procedure that we followed.

DRAWING A QUOTA SAMPLE FOR THE SMOKING SURVEY

The target population for our survey consisted of all adults over the age of 16 who are ordinarily resident in Brighton. Inspecting the data from the most recent census (1991), we collected various demographic and employment statistics, some of which are reproduced in table 4.4. These data were already quite old at the time of the survey (1997), and figures on unemployment in particular will certainly have changed.

In drawing our quotas, we decided to keep things simple by using just two population parameters – age and sex. These are characteristics which can be determined visually in the street, so our interviewers would know without stopping people whether or not they were eligible for a particular quota. In a more serious and elaborate survey, we would probably include several other criteria (e.g. occupation and level of education), for the more parameters we fix, the less likely we are to end up with a badly skewed sample.

Table 4.4 Selected statistics from the 1991 census for Brighton (percentages)

Gender	
Male	47.8
Female	52.2
Age	
Under 18	18.4
18–29	20.8
30–44	21.3
45–pensionable age	17.7
Over pensionable age	21.8
Economic activity, males 16–64	
Full-time employed	52.8
Part-time employed	3.0
Self-employed	16.6
Unemployed/govt scheme	13.5
Not economically active	14.1
Economic activity, females 16–59	
Full-time employed	38.2
Part-time employed	20.5
Self-employed	4.9
Unemployed/govt scheme	6.3
Not economically active	30.2

How big should each quota be?

One problem in constructing our quotas was that the census categories did not always conform to our categories. We needed a lowest age cut-off of 16 (the age at which people in Britain may legally buy tobacco), but the census used an age 18 cut-off. At the other end of the age distribution, the census used an age cut-off of 65 for men and 60 for women, but we needed a common age point for both, which we set at 60. Problems like these are not uncommon when constructing quota samples – you are at the mercy of whatever data are available – although in this case the effects are small.

Classifying the population into four age groups for men and four for women gave us eight quotas to fill. Using the figures in table 4.4, we decided that all eight should be roughly equal in size, meaning that each quota should contribute about 50 cases (12.5 per cent of the total sample):

Males, aged 16–29:	50	Females, aged 16–29:	50
Males, aged 30–44:	50	Females, aged 30–44:	50
Males, aged 45–60:	50	Females, aged 45–60:	50
Males, aged over 60:	50	Females, aged over 60:	50

Setting equal quotas will slightly underrepresent women (especially those over pensionable age) in our sample and will slightly overrepresent the 45 to 60 age group. This slight skew in the sample will hopefully not distort the results too badly – if it does, we could make a slight correction by weighting.

Where do you find your respondents?

Student interviewers went out into Brighton with instructions to fill their quotas. But where, and when, should they interview?

◆ We agreed that interviewers should avoid function-specific areas or times of day, such as mainline stations during the rush hour, or football grounds on a Saturday afternoon, for the sample could be badly biased if quotas were filled from among specific types of people such as commuters or football fans.

◆ We also agreed that interviewers should approach the first available person to minimize interviewer selectivity. It would be 'natural' for interviewers to avoid people who look threatening or unfriendly, and to wait for a friendly (or attractive!) looking person to come along, but this could seriously bias the sample.

In the event, most interviews were conducted in busy streets in central parts of the town, and they were spread over different times of day, and over weekdays and weekends.

In a serious survey, it is important to recruit experienced interviewers, to spend time training them in the specific requirements of your survey and to monitor them closely to ensure that they are doing what they are supposed to be doing (e.g. you need to check that interviewers actually carry out the interviews allotted to them). In our survey, however, interviewers were inexperienced, untrained and unpaid. Perhaps it was not surprising, therefore, that some failed to complete their allotted interviews. In the end, we completed only 334 of the 400 planned interviews.

FAILURE TO STICK BY THE QUOTA

This shortfall in sample size might not have mattered too much were it not for the fact that some quotas were filled more successfully than others. Whether it was because older people were harder to find, or because young student interviewers did not try very hard to find them, it was the older age categories where we undershot the most seriously.

Compounding this problem was the difficulty that interviewers had in judging people's ages. In the questionnaire, people were not asked their age until the end of the interview, but for quota purposes our interviewers needed to gauge people's ages before approaching them. The result was that interviews got conducted with respondents who were believed to fit one quota category, but who turned out in the end to belong to another.

The combined effect of the failure to complete quotas and the underestimation of respondents' ages resulted in a sample with too many younger people, and not enough older ones (table 4.5). The youngest age group was overrepresented, and the oldest age group was underrepresented, by about 25 per cent – a bad skew which should not happen in a properly managed quota sample. The gender quotas were, however, met successfully.

One response to this problem could be to apply weights to rectify the distortion – i.e. we could deflate all answers of the youngest age group by 25 per cent and inflate all answers of the oldest age group by 25 per cent. But in a serious survey, you should really ensure that this sort of bias does not occur in the first place.

TESTING FOR REPRESENTATIVENESS

A good test of a quota sample is to compare its features against some characteristics in the population which are known but which were not controlled for when developing the quotas. We can evaluate the representativeness of our sample by looking at men's and women's employment status. We know from table 4.4 that 53 per cent of men

Table 4.5   Age distribution and gender in the achieved quota sample (percentages)

	16–29	30–44	45–60	Over 60	Total
Female	16.3	12.0	12.3	9.2	49.7
Male	14.7	13.8	11.7	10.1	50.3
Total	31.0	25.8	23.9	19.3	100.0

Target quota for each cell = 12.5%.

Table 4.6 Employment status of men and women, comparing the Smoking Survey sample with the target population of Brighton

	Census 1991 (%)	Sample 1997 (%)
Males aged 18–64[a]		
In full-time job[b]	71	62
In part-time job	3	10
Females aged 18–59[a]		
In full-time job[b]	44	47
In part-time job	20	20

[a] Sample = males and females aged 16–59.
[b] Census full-time figures comprise full-time employees plus self-employed.

under retirement age had full-time employment, while another 3 per cent had part-time jobs and 17 per cent were self-employed. For women the proportions were 38, 21 and 5 per cent respectively. How close did our sample come in reproducing these patterns?

Table 4.6 compares our sample statistics with the Census data looking at the proportions of men and women below retirement age who had full-time or part-time jobs, whether as employees or self-employed. The results are reasonably heartening. The statistics on female respondents are close to the true population proportions, and the males are not too far out. Of course, we cannot know whether the sample is representative of the population on all the other characteristics we cannot test for, but at least we can feel some confidence that it is not wildly out of line on those we can check.

INTERVIEWING, CODING AND SCALING

AIM

This chapter looks at how we collect and classify data. We cover some basic rules of interviewing and see how to record answers in a codified form that a computer can read. We also consider how to combine answers to different questions to create single indexes and scales. By the end of the chapter, you should:

- Understand the negotiation of meaning at the heart of interviewing and coding
- Be aware of common sources of interview bias and how to minimize it
- Develop your understanding of coding (including procedures for coding missing data and multiple answers)
- Know the four different levels at which data may be measured
- Be familiar with the basic principles involved in constructing indexes and scales

There is an appendix which reflects on the use of the Smoking Survey questionnaire in interview situations. In addition, appendix B on the website (www.surveymethods.co.uk) explains how to code occupational data to various social class schema.

INTRODUCTION

There are many different ways in which interviews can be conducted, but interview design varies along two basic dimensions. The first is the distinction between *structured* and *unstructured* (or perhaps semi-structured) interviewing:

♦   In structured interviews, the interviewer works through a predetermined list
    of questions in a set order and enjoys little freedom to depart from the
    questionnaire.
♦   In unstructured interviews, the interviewer engages respondents in a more conver-
    sational style, often dispensing with a formal questionnaire and referring instead to
    a list of key themes (an aide-memoire), or even allowing the conversation to flow
    with no fixed agenda.

The second dimension entails the distinction between *individual* and *group* interviewing. Most interviews are conducted one-on-one, but focus groups have become
increasingly popular in recent years:

♦   In a focus group, the researcher ('facilitator') leads the discussion and tries to get a
    sense of what the group as a whole thinks by encouraging participants to exchange
    ideas and discuss issues among themselves.
♦   This contrasts with individual interviews where it is important that respondents
    should not be influenced in what they say by the presence of others.

In this chapter, we shall be concerned only with structured interviews in one-to-one
situations, for this is the normal pattern in surveys.

DOING AN INTERVIEW

Just as you can bias survey results by developing a shoddy questionnaire, or by drawing
an unrepresentative sample, so a further potential source of bias arises when you ask
people questions in interviews.

Negotiating reality

We often refer to social surveys as 'collecting' data as if the facts simply have to be
'gathered' from people. This implies a simple 'stimulus–response' model of interaction
between the interviewer's questions and the interviewee's responses, but we saw in
chapter 1 that this is not how interaction takes place. Between the stimulus and the
response is a process of *interpretation*. The respondent has to 'make sense of' the
question, and the interviewer has in turn to 'make sense of' the answer.

This is obvious in situations where interviewer and respondent encounter problems
understanding each other – where an interviewee is hard of hearing, perhaps, or has a
poor understanding of English. In cases like these, the problematic nature of interper-
sonal communication is explicit, but mutual understanding is a problem inherent to *all*
interviewing. The meaning of an interviewer's question or a respondent's answer is
rarely unambiguous, even though each party assumes they know what the other means.
The interviewer assumes that the interviewee understands the question in the way that
she or he intended, and assumes again that she or he has interpreted and recorded the
answer in the way the interviewee intended.

The phenomenologists' warning (1): Interviewing

'The existence of grammatically correct sentences in a language and their use in social research do not ensure that subjects being interviewed will perceive and interpret the questions in the same way as the interviewer.'

Aaron Cicourel, *Method and Measurement in Sociology* (Glencoe: Free Press, 1964), p. 125

What the interviewer records is, therefore, what the interviewer believes the respondent means to say, but this judgement is mediated through a thick cloud of our own 'common sense'. Because we impose our own structures of meaning on to the responses that we record in interviews, our data are not so much 'collected' as 'constructed' in the course of the interaction.

We should not exaggerate these difficulties, for interviewers and interviewees from similar cultural backgrounds will normally share a broad area of understanding, and there are in any case some simple steps we can take to minimize the problems. Nevertheless, we should remain alert to the ways in which the interview context itself might influence the way 'data' come to be recorded.

Impression management

Interviewees' responses can be influenced by the impression they form of the interviewer:

◆ If you are interviewing people about illicit drug use, for example, they are unlikely to admit to much if you dress like an authority figure.
◆ If you are interested in older people's views about the 'youth of today', you may not get a totally frank answer if you are an adolescent with a nose stud.

Respondents usually want to be 'helpful', and they normally seek to avoid embarrassment or confrontation, but this can make them reluctant to say what they really think if they sense that the interviewer will not agree. They may also make up an answer rather than admit that they do not know (for people do not like to appear ignorant or unhelpful).

How the interview context can influence what respondents say

In the US in the 1960s, William Labov tested the claim that the 'non-standard English' used by inner city black children inhibited abstract reasoning. He showed that when interviewed by a black adult, black children who had previously appeared uncomprehending proved perfectly capable of expressing complex and abstract ideas. The children's 'ability' thus depended crucially on the context of the interview.

William Labov, 'The logic of non-standard English', in P. Giglioli (ed.), *Language and Social Context* (Harmondsworth: Penguin, 1972)

These problems can be countered by helping respondents feel at ease (so that they will not feel pressured in the answers they give) and by ensuring that interviewers do not give any inadvertent signals about 'appropriate' or 'inappropriate' answers. This means paying attention to the interviewer *role*:

- Your 'basic roles' – your race, gender or age – may influence the responses you get. Men interviewing women or whites interviewing blacks will probably pick up different kinds of answers than if people of the same race or sex are used. One way of countering this problem may be to use mixed teams of interviewers.
- Your 'achieved roles' – the kind of person you appear to be – can be actively managed by the way you dress, how you speak, how formally or informally you behave.

Managing first impressions

'When an individual enters the presence of others, they commonly seek to acquire information about him ... If unacquainted with the individual, observers can glean clues from his conduct and appearance which allow them to apply ... stereotypes to him ... The individual will have to act so that he intentionally or unintentionally *expresses* himself, and the others in turn will have to be *impressed* in some way by him.'

Erving Goffman, *The Presentation of Self in Everyday Life* (New York: Doubleday, 1959), pp. 1–2

Usually the aim in an interview is to establish rapport with informants, and this might mean dressing and behaving in ways that will be familiar to them and help them feel comfortable and relaxed. This is not always the best strategy, however, for informality and a good rapport can sometimes undermine an interview. You want people to take the interview seriously, and the 'role of interviewer' might require a suit, a clipboard and a little social distance if this is what people expect from you.

Interviewer bias and the use of discretion

Interviewer bias can arise when interviewers lie about their results (or even make them up), or when respondents hold back on what they say, or when interviewers are selective about what they record and how they record it. Some selectivity is inevitable, however, for a lot of words get spoken in an interview which will never be recorded on the questionnaire.

This raises the possibility that interviewer bias may occur unconsciously – things get missed or overlooked because they do not seem interesting, or because the interviewer expects to hear something else. This will be less of a problem in tightly focused interviews using many pre-coded items than in less structured interviews with mainly open-ended questions where the interviewer enjoys much more discretion in recording answers. But even in tightly structured surveys, interviewers enjoy some discretion.

A major source of interviewer discretion is the freedom to probe answers and follow up responses:

- Most interviews involve use of *prompts* (where the question includes follow-ups which clarify what is wanted and focus respondents on particular themes or issues).
- Some also use *probes* (where the interviewer is permitted or instructed to delve deeper into an informant's initial answer to get richer information).

Prompts and probes can be valuable in improving the quality of the data you collect, but the more freedom you give interviewers to diverge from set questions, the greater will be the potential problems of interviewer bias.

Minimizing interview bias

A number of strategies are available to reduce the risk of bias in interviews:

- Interviewers can be matched to interviewees on characteristics like age, gender and ethnicity so as to maximize mutual understanding. Alternatively, they can be randomly mixed so as to cancel out biases arising from respondent reactions to particular kinds of interviewers. When interviewing people for whom English is not a first language, try to use interviewers who are fluent in the interviewees' native tongue.
- Train interviewers thoroughly so that they understand the purposes of the questions, arrange practice in group sessions before fieldwork begins, and keep close supervision of the interviewing process while it is going on. Check up periodically on your interviewers by going back to a sample of informants to ask how it went and to establish that they really were interviewed.
- Keep questions simple, for this reduces the temptation by interviewers to rephrase or skip wordy or difficult items. Ensure that questions are asked exactly as they are written and that any elaboration is done using pre-prepared prompts and probes. Have the same question asked in several different ways during an interview and check the consistency of responses to ensure that respondents are answering them consistently.
- Pay attention to dress and demeanour (try out different kinds of roles during piloting to see which are the most successful in encouraging respondents to open up).
- Interviewers should emphasize to respondents that there are no 'right' and 'wrong' answers, and be careful not to react to their answers. Respondents will sometimes ask what their view is on an issue they are questioning them about – they should maintain a polite and friendly manner, but should not accede to such requests!

If you are replicating our Smoking Survey, or if you are part of a group carrying out a survey of your own, you should now carry out your interviews before going on to the remainder of the chapter. If you are reading the book on your own, you could still do a few interviews at this point using our Smoking Survey questionnaire (downloaded and printed out from our website).

There is no substitute for real life experience of interviewing members of the public (don't use people you know!). A commentary on our students' experience of interviewing people for the Smoking Survey can be found in the appendix to this chapter on pp. 153–4.

CODING QUESTIONNAIRES

When the interviews have been completed, you need to prepare the answers so that they can be analysed using a computer. To do this, we develop different number 'codes' to represent different kinds of answers, and these are recorded in a 'code book'. Take question 1 in the Smoking Survey as an example:

Q1 Have you smoked any cigarettes, cigars or pipe tobacco in the last week?

We coded all the 'no' answers as '0' and all the 'yes' answers as '1'. These codes were then recorded in a code book so that anybody using our data set will know what the numbers mean.

Coding answers to pre-coded questions

We saw in chapter 3 that questions may be 'pre-coded' or left open-ended.

♦ With questions that are pre-coded, the interviewer has to code answers on the spot by ticking one (or more) of a series of answers that are already listed on the question-naire.
♦ With open-ended questions, the interviewer has to note down what the respondent says, and code the answer later.

Problems can arise in coding both type of questions.

'Crunching' people's answers

You may think that there should be no problem in coding people's answers to pre-coded questions, for all you have to do is read out the question and tick the appropriate answer. The problem, however, is that respondents do not always answer according to the categories that we have on our questionnaire. For example, in our Smoking Survey we asked the following pre-coded question:

Q7 Thinking of your close family and friends, how many of them smoke regularly?
    1 All or most
    2 About half
    3 A few
    4 Almost none or none
    −1 Don't know

If the question is read out without telling the respondents the range of possible answers, they may not give one of these answers. If, on the other hand, we read these categories out to them (a common strategy, albeit one that can make interviewing a bit tedious), respondents may be reluctant to trim their reply to fit our categories.

Consider how we are to code somebody who tells us in answer to question 7:

'Well, my mum used to smoke, but she only has the occasional one now, because my dad doesn't like it. Quite a lot of my friends smoke, but my mum's the only one in the family who smokes – apart from my brother-in-law, he smokes like a chimney, but we rarely see him nowadays.'

We may try to 'guide' this respondent back towards the range of 'permissible' categories from which they have to choose. Perhaps we read the pre-coded answers out one by one as prompts and force our respondent to select just one. Or we might try to reinterpret what they have said in an impromptu follow-up of our own that draws on our system of categories rather than theirs:

'So, would you say that this means that "about half" of your family and friends smoke regularly, or would it only be fewer than that, just "a few" of them?'

Whichever strategy we employ to 'crunch' the respondent's spontaneous answer into one of our pre-coded categories, it is clear that we are at this point back to the problem of *negotiating meanings* in interviewing. What we end up with is not what the respondent wanted to tell us, but a negotiated compromise between the respondent's answer and our requirements. Two obvious problems arise in this process of negotiating an 'acceptable' answer:

♦ The detail and subtlety of the respondent's original answer has been lost – the recorded answer may still represent 'the truth' (e.g. about half of their friends and family do smoke), but it is far from 'the whole truth'.

♦ We may end up with a completely *different* answer from the one they wanted to give us – their response has effectively been fabricated by us.

Forced responses in attitude questions

When measuring people's attitudes, respondents may be asked to state how strongly they agree or disagree with a series of statements. Consider, for example, question 9 from the Smoking Survey which consists of eight statements (p. 96). Each statement was read out in turn, and informants were asked to respond using one of five possible answers:

1 'strongly agree'
2 'agree'
3 'no opinion' (i.e. neither agree nor disagree)
4 'disagree'
5 'strongly disagree'

When we debriefed the students who had conducted these interviews, everybody had succeeded in recording people's answers using this pre-coded scale, but some felt uneasy about the way this had been achieved:

♦ Some respondents had wanted to give a qualified answer to some statements, but this had been ruled out in the structure of the questions. For example, responding to the statement 'It should be made illegal to smoke in any public place', some people wanted to distinguish places that are 'outside' from those which are enclosed. The question, however, demands that they give a view on banning smoking *both* indoors and outside.

♦ Other respondents had queried what 'strongly' means (as in 'strongly agree' and 'strongly disagree'). What one person thinks of as 'strong disagreement', another might report as mere 'disagreement'. Some studies using attitudinal statements have found that respondents are reluctant to select 'strong' answers, although this does not seem to have happened in this case (the proportion of respondents who gave a 'strong agree/disagree' response varied from 16 per cent, on the 6th and 8th items, to 30 per cent, on the first item).

- Some respondents could not (or did not wish to) answer in terms of any of our five categories. They did not have opinions that could be summarized adequately by means of these categories, or their arguments were more complex than that. Some people insisted on explaining their thoughts at length and they were reluctant to see the complexity and sophistication of their argument boiled down to a simple 'agree' or 'disagree' category.

These kinds of questions have many critics, and their use in surveys has prompted some very uncomfortable questions to be asked of researchers. For example:

- What are the 'attitudes' that we are measuring? Did our respondents already hold these opinions before we put our statements to them, or have we created an opinion by demanding that people express a view?
- Do the answers *mean* anything when they are divorced from any social context? In real life, our attitudes are embedded in specific social contexts, and they can vary as situations change, yet these answers are treated as if they were attributes of people.
- What do attitudes tell us about how people actually behave? People might tell us they 'strongly agree' with some statement yet their everyday actions may contradict what they say.
- Are all answers equivalent? Attitudinal questions suffer from a 'democratic bias', for everybody's answers count equally. Somebody who has thought long and hard about an issue and somebody who gives an off-the-cuff answer without really thinking about it are treated in exactly the same way.
- What does a 'middle' answer tell us? It is defined as 'having no opinion', or 'neither agreeing nor disagreeing', but it could equally be that people are ambivalent. Surely, though, ambivalence is not the same as indifference?

Coding open-ended questions

The kinds of problems which occur in coding answers to pre-coded questions arise even more sharply when it comes to coding 'open-ended' ones where respondents have been free to say what they like, and interviewers have written down their answers verbatim. People answering open-ended questions are not forced at the time of the interview to adjust their answers to our categories – but later, those doing the coding will still have to 'crunch' their answers into a limited range of categories.

One example of an open-ended question in the Smoking Survey occurs in question 4 where ex-smokers were asked:

Why did you quit?

This question was not pre-coded because we had little idea about the range of different reasons that people might come up with. People were therefore left free to say whatever they wanted, but how do we now code their answers? Take an answer like:

'Well, it was costing a lot of money that I couldn't very well afford – maybe 25 quid a week – and that's just money up in smoke, and then the price went up again in the Budget, and I just thought "That's it, I've got to stop!" And a friend of mine had stopped, and I thought, "If he can do it, then so can I". So I stopped. But it wasn't easy.'

With an answer like this, coders must decide what the *key points* are in what is being said – but the respondent is no longer present to argue with your interpretation!

The phenomenologists' warning (2): Coding

As an experiment, Aaron Cicourel asked a group of experienced coders to code American criminal files. There were constant arguments about how the information should be coded: 'The entire set of procedures for coding police and probation records constituted a continuous improvised set of decisions, whose primary purpose was to achieve practical solutions to problems whose outcomes or resolutions could not be decided according to explicit criteria based upon an explicit theoretical position vis-à-vis the intended meaning of the data.' Coders had to resort to 'common sense' to get the job done because the data themselves had no clear meaning.

A. Cicourel, *The Social Organization of Juvenile Justice* (London: Heinemann, 1976), pp. 106–7

Deriving the categories

We start by reading through all the verbatim recorded responses to a question and abstracting from them the basic points that we think respondents were making. For example, taking the answer to question 4 that we just considered, we might decide that this respondent is giving two main reasons why he or she stopped smoking:

◆ There was a financial motive: 'it was costing a lot of money...'
◆ There was the example set by a friend: 'a friend of mine had stopped...'

Obviously the answer contains more information than just these two points, but arguably the rest of what is being said simply elaborates on these two themes and does not introduce a third. Now consider another answer to the same question:

'Well, it's money down the drain, isn't it? And it's bad for you – lung cancer and that. I used to get this really bad cough in the mornings, a smoker's cough. And then when I got pregnant I thought: "That's it! I've got to stop for the sake of the baby."'

Again we find a financial motive. But this respondent is also introducing two other reasons that we did not come across in the first answer:

◆ A concern with her health: 'it's bad for you...'
◆ Pregnancy: 'then when I got pregnant...'

Gradually, as we sift through people's answers, we begin to compile a list of codes that reflects the main themes in what they told us. In the case of question 4, for example, we went through all the answers we had collected and ended up with 13 categories of responses. Each of these was allocated its own numerical code:

 1 Finance
 2 Health
 3 Pregnancy
 4 Lifestyle/image
 5 Don't like being addicted
 6 Don't like being exploited by tobacco companies
 7 Influence of friends
 8 Anti-social habit
 9 Parental or other family pressure to stop
10 Didn't enjoy it/grew out of it
11 No longer stressed so didn't need it
12 Other reasons
-1 Don't know

As the phenomenologists remind us, however, none of this is unproblematic. Different people may devise different sets of categories from reading the same interview transcripts, and when this happens, there is no objective set of criteria which can be applied to resolve the disagreement. Coding question 4, for example, we argued about whether people who quit smoking because they no longer enjoyed it could be included in the same category (code 10) as those who stopped because it was behaviour they had 'grown out of'. These are different kinds of answers, but in the end we felt that they shared a common theme (smoking is something that was no longer attractive), so we put them together. Such decisions are always contentious – we just have to argue them out.

When to crunch?

Decisions about crunching answers or keeping them distinct as separate coding categories are never easy.

- In favour of crunching, you should remember that you are looking for patterns and generalizations in your data. If you end up with dozens of different categories of answers to a question, you will find it difficult to detect any pattern at all.
- In favour of keeping answers distinct, you do not want to combine responses which have very little in common, for you will end up riding roughshod over what your respondents intended to convey to you by their answers.

If in doubt, go for discrimination rather than crunching. You can always combine different coding categories later, but you can never unpack a category without going back to the original questionnaires and recoding them.

Trouble in the census

In 1991, the UK government included a question on ethnicity in the national census for the first time. People were asked to tick one of the following boxes:

0. White
1. Black-Caribbean
2. Black-African
   Black – Other (*please describe*)
3. Indian
4. Pakistani
5. Bangladeshi
6. Chinese
   Any other ethnic group (*please describe*)

This system of coding was hopelessly confused for it mixed up *ethnicity* (cultural identity) with *race* (white/black) and *nationality* (Indian, Pakistani, etc.). Some respondents could legitimately have ticked several different boxes (e.g. white Indian passport holders) while others (e.g. people of mixed race) seemed to be overlooked. This census question broke the most basic rule of coding, for its categories were not *discrete*.

The 2001 census had another go. Ethnicity, race, nationality and 'cultural background' still all got mixed up in the same question, but the response categories were more carefully differentiated:

What is your ethnic group? Choose ONE section from A to E, then tick the appropriate box to indicate your cultural background

A. White:

   British

   Irish

   Any other white background

B. Mixed:

    White and Black Caribbean

    White and Black African

    White and Asian

    Any other mixed background

C. Asian or Asian British:

    Indian

    Pakistani

    Bangladeshi

    Any other Asian background

D. Black or Black British:

    Caribbean

    African

    Any other Black background

E. Chinese or other ethnic group

    Chinese

    Any other

This more cumbersome system of coding probably overcame most of the problems in the 1991 version, although a letter-writer in *The Times* still complained: 'the confused and barbarian creators of this form regard "ethnic group" and "cultural background" as synonymous…I do not recognise myself as falling within any of the designated "cultural backgrounds"' (24 Mar. 2001). Can you think of any way in which this coding scheme might be further improved?

Allocating answers to the coding categories

Once you have devised a set of codes, all the respondents' answers have to be coded to the categories you have developed. But this too raises problems. Consider the following answer to question 4, for example:

'My clothes smelt. I felt bad. You'd go to people's houses and have to go out into the garden to have a cigarette. I just felt stupid in the end – weak.'

How would *you* code this, using the 13 categories listed on p. 139?

♦ There seems to be a concern about being anti-social in the presence of friends (having to go out into the garden), so perhaps codes 7 and 8 are relevant?
♦ The respondent 'felt bad' about himself or herself, so perhaps code 4 (self-image) is appropriate.
♦ Alternatively, 'feeling bad' could be a reference to his or her state of health at the time, in which case code 2 would be more appropriate than code 4.
♦ And what are we to make of 'feeling stupid and weak'? Is this indicative of a desire to change his or her self-image (code 4), is it indicative of a dislike of being addicted (code 5), or is it simply a different kind of answer altogether (in which case it should be coded 12 – 'other')?
♦ How are 'smelly clothes' to be coded? Does this indicate a concern about other people's reactions, a concern with self-image, or a distinct category of reason?

Inevitably, the process of coding open-ended questions is to some extent arbitrary. One way to reduce this problem is to do the coding twice, using different, independent coders each time. Where they agree, you can be reasonably confident about the way respondents' answers have been classified; where they disagree, you can at least discuss it and try to reach an agreement if you can.

Basic rules of coding

There are a few general guidelines to follow when constructing coding schema:

♦ *Discrete categories*   Codes must be defined clearly so that no single answer could be coded to more than one category. Take care when devising numerical categories such as age groups that you do not overlap any of the categories (e.g. 20–30, 30–40) – a common mistake.
♦ *Exhaustive categories*   The full set of codes must cover all possible answers to the question. Remember to include a code for 'other responses', for this gives you a code for quirky answers (but make sure you do not end up with a large number of answers coded 'other', for there is not much you can do with them). You should also always include a code for those who say they do not know (in the Smoking Survey, we gave 'Don't know' answers a code of −1 throughout the questionnaire).
♦ *Discriminatory categories*   It is a good idea to code all variations of answers separately and to 'crunch' similar responses together later on rather than to combine different kinds of responses into a single code at the outset.

+ *Consistency of codes*   It is sensible to keep the same codes for common answers (such as 'yes', 'no' and 'don't know') through all questions. If you code 'no' as 1 on one question and as 0 on another you will almost certainly get coding errors creeping in.
+ *Levels of measurement*   In general you should code to the highest possible level of measurement (we explain 'levels of measurement' later in this chapter). If the data exist as real numbers, keep them in this form – if you know people's exact ages, incomes, or whatever, then code their age or income rather than crunching the answers into age groups or income bands.

Coding questions with multiple answers

Sometimes it is possible for respondents to give more than one answer to a question. We have seen, for example, that ex-smokers often had several reasons for having quit. When people can give several responses to a single question, we can code their answers in one of two ways.

Creating several new variables using the same codes

The simplest way to code multiple answers is to treat the question as if it had been asked several times over, rather than just once. Whereas in question 4 we actually asked ex-smokers why they had quit, we can analyse their multiple answers *as if* we had asked the question several times and had received a different answer on each occasion:

Give me one reason why you quit
Now give me a second reason why you quit
Now give me a third reason why you quit...

When it comes to coding, each different answer is then treated as if it were a response to a different variable (which means we have to create some additional variables to add to our code book) This was the solution we adopted in the Smoking Survey, where we ended up creating three different variables for why people stopped smoking (the final part of question 4). Because we only allowed for one (var 00010) when we originally devised the questionnaire, we added two new ones at the end (var 00035 and var 00036). Similarly, we created three variables for answers to the final part of question 5 (var00014 plus var00037 and var00038), and three for the follow-up at question 11 (the benefits of smoking), which became var00039, var00040 and var00041).

Creating a series of dichotomous variables

The other way in which we could code multiple answers is by treating each possible answer as a variable with just two values:

1 Mentioned by respondent
0 Not mentioned by respondent

Thus, the final part of question 4 generated 13 different reasons why people stopped smoking, so each of these could be treated as a variable in its own right. This means we analyse people's multiple answers *as if* we had asked 13 different questions:

Did you quit for financial reasons?	0 = no 1 = yes
Did you quit for health reasons?	0 = no 1 = yes
Did you quit because you were pregnant?	0 = no 1 = yes

...and so on. This procedure can get quite cumbersome – in this example we would end up with 13 new dichotomous variables which for most cases are coded 0 (not mentioned). It is, however, useful to code multiple answers in this way if you are interested in further analysing particular answers (e.g. if you want to know whether men are more inclined than women to give up smoking for health reasons).

Coding missing data

Sometimes there is no information for you to code – the respondent's answer is missing. There are several reasons why an answer to a question might be missing:

- *A skip* The question was not relevant to this respondent and therefore was not asked. In the Smoking Survey, for example, people who answered 'no' to question 1 were not asked question 2, for it was not relevant to ask those who had not smoked in the last week how much they had smoked.
- *An oversight* The question should have been asked and answered, but for some reason it was not. This can happen if an interview has to be terminated before all the questions have been completed, and it occurs in postal questionnaires when respondents miss some questions.
- *A refusal* The question was asked, but the respondent refused to answer it.

When data are missing, they must still be coded, and it can be a good idea to use different codes for different kinds of missing values. Commonly researchers define missing values as minus numbers, blanks, zeros or nines, but these are only conventions.

Coding conventions for missing values

There is no one set way to code missing responses but some conventions do exist. The following is the list of coding conventions used in the longitudinal British Household Panel Survey:

- −1   a respondent response of 'Don't Know'
- −2   a respondent response refusal
- −3/−4   reserved for situations where invalid data are given
- −7   indicates the interview was not completed
- −8   represents data missing because it is not applicable
- −9   represents data missing in error, with no other explanation

---

Every answer has a number: developing a code book

Most of the questions on the Smoking Survey questionnaire were pre-coded, and those that were not (the open-ended questions) have now been given codes (appendix B on the website explains how we coded the occupational data to get social class categories). The next step is to produce clear documentation so that anybody using our data set will know what all these numbers mean.

Whether you do it using the computer (the SPSS program that we shall be learning has a 'Display Dictionary' command which will prepare the basic rudiments of a code book for you) or manually, you will need to ensure that you have a *code book* which tells users:

♦ the full and original wording of each question on the questionnaire;
♦ how each item on the questionnaire corresponds to a variable in the data set, and the column in the spreadsheet where this variable can be found;
♦ how the responses to each question have been coded (i.e. the values of each variable);
♦ how any new variables have been created (we shall see in chapter 7 how to create new variables – called *derived variables* – by recombining data).

> The code book for the Smoking Survey is available on our website in section 2. If you intend using this data set when following the chapters on data analysis, you will need to print a hard copy of this code book. If you have generated your own data set with your own survey, then you will need to create a detailed and well-documented code book of your own and keep it updated as you transform variables and create new ones.

LEVELS OF MEASUREMENT

We have seen that in coding, each value of a variable is assigned a number. On the Smoking Survey, for example, females were coded 0 and males were coded 1 on the variable 'gender'.

In this example, these numbers are just arbitrary labels – they have no significance arithmetically. It makes no sense, for example, to say that if women are coded 0 and men are coded 1, then men are infinitely greater than women, or that a man and a woman together add up to $(0 + 1) = 1$, or that the average of a man and a woman = $(0 + 1) \div 2 = 0.5$. The numbers 0 and 1 are just labels which help the computer to process our data. We could code females 7 and males -300 if we wanted to – it would make no difference.

Some variables, however, do have codes which are real numbers. Look at Question 2 on the Smoking Survey:

Roughly how many cigarettes have you smoked in the last week?

The answer is a real number. If somebody says they have smoked 200 cigarettes then the number 200 is entered as the value of the variable. The different values recorded for different cases can then be subjected to all the usual arithmetical procedures (e.g. someone coded 400 smokes twice as many cigarettes as someone coded 200, and taken together, these two individuals account for 600 cigarettes between them).

Clearly, we are using numbers in different ways when we code different kinds of questions. Put more precisely, we code different kinds of variables at different *levels of measurement*.

The four levels of measurement

Nominal measures are the lowest level of measurement. They use numbers simply as names (the word 'nominal' comes from the Latin word for 'name') or as labels for different values, and no mathematical significance attaches to the numbers themselves. There are many examples of nominal level variables in the Smoking Survey. Gender is one of them, for the codes 0 and 1 merely label the two genders, female and male.

Ordinal measures are one level up from nominal ones. They too use numbers as labels, but the numbers form a rank order of ascending or descending size. On an ordinal scale, something coded zero is less than something coded 1, which is in turn less than something coded 2, but we do not know how much less, and the gaps between each point on the scale are not necessarily equal. Question 7 on the Smoking Survey provides an example:

Thinking of your close family and friends, how many of them smoke regularly?
1   All or most
2   About half
3   A few
4   Almost none or none

As the number codes increase from 1 to 4, so the proportion of friends and family who smoke falls. However, the gaps between each of the four categories are not the same, e.g. the mathematical difference between *all* your friends smoking and *half* your friends smoking is greater than that between *half* of them smoking and *a few* smoking.

Interval measures also use numbers to represent a rank order, but unlike ordinal measures they ensure that the intervals between each value on the scale are equal. Question 15 on the Smoking Survey comes close to being measured at an interval scale (although the top and bottom categories are open-ended, which means the four categories are not spaced at exactly equal intervals):

Which of the following age groups do you belong to?
1   Under 30
2   30–44
3   45–60
4   Over 60

Ratio measures are the highest level of measurement. Here numbers form part of a continuous scale with equal intervals and a base of zero such that they can be expressed in proportion to one another. They are, in other words, real numbers. Question 2 is an example:

Roughly how many cigarettes have you smoked in the last week?

It is crucial that you fully understand and remember the differences between these four levels of measurement, for when we start analysing data you will see that some statistical procedures are designed only for data measured at higher (interval or ratio) levels. Indeed, you already know this! In chapter 4, we encountered three 'measures of central tendency' used for summarizing distributions – the mean, the median and the mode. Now that you understand the differences between different levels of measurement, try to work out the lowest level of measurement at which each of these measures of central tendency can sensibly be used (the answers are given at the bottom of this page).*

Continuous and discrete variables

Variables measured at nominal and ordinal levels are sometimes referred to as 'categorical'. This is because they distinguish different groupings, or categories, of people (men and women, people whose friends smoke and those with no friends who smoke, and so on). These categories are sharply demarcated from each other (i.e. they are discrete).

Variables measured at a ratio scale are not like this. They consist of a continuous sequence of numbers rather than a set of categories, and for this reason they are called 'continuous variables'.

Variables measured at an interval level may be discrete (categorical) or continuous, although in social science they are nearly always categorical. Our 'age groups' variable, for example, consists of four clearly demarcated categories with an equal 'distance' between each of them. This constitutes an interval scale, but it is not a continuous measure, for there is a 'jump' from one category to the next.

To see why all this matters, consider the following (hypothetical) age distribution of individuals:

1	0–9 years:	53
2	10–19 years:	43
3	20–29 years:	71
4	30–39 years:	48

This is an interval scale, but because the variable consists of discrete categories, there are limits to the mathematical procedures we can perform:

- We can calculate the modal age group – the group with the most members is the 20–29-year-olds – but we cannot calculate the modal age, for we have no idea which age between 0 and 40 is the most common in this population.
- We can calculate in which age group the median falls – with a total of 215 cases, the middle observation is the 108th, and this person is in the 20–29 age group. But we cannot know what age the median person is.
- We cannot calculate a mean at all, for to do this would require a continuous scale. All that we can do is take the mid-points of the four age categories and estimate a very approximate mean by treating the first 53 cases as if they were all 4 ½ years old, the next 43 as if they were all 14 ½, and so on.

---

* The lowest level at which the *mean* can be measured is the interval level (it is the arithmetic average and therefore can only be calculated on real numbers). The lowest level at which the *median* can be measured is the ordinal level (as the middle-ranking observation on an ascending or descending scale, the median requires as a minimum that the data be rank ordered). The lowest level at which the *mode* can be measured is the nominal level (the mode is simply the observation which occurs most frequently in a distribution).

We can see from this that our use of statistics depends both on the level at which our variables are measured, and on the way they are measured, as continuous or discrete scales.

Attitudinal questions and levels of measurement

In the Smoking Survey, at question 9, we used eight different attitude statements, each of which was coded on a simple five-point scale, from 'strongly agree' to 'strongly disagree'. These questions will give us eight categorical variables measured at no higher than an ordinal level:

♦ They will be categorical variables because respondents selected answers from one of five distinct categories.
♦ The scale on each variable is ordinal because there is a rank order ('strongly agree' ranks above 'agree' which ranks above 'no opinion' which ranks above 'disagree' which ranks above 'strongly disagree'), but the intervals between each value cannot be assumed to be 'equal' (it makes no sense to claim that, say, the gap between 'strong agreement' and 'agreement' is the same as that between 'no opinion' and 'disagreement').

Sometimes, questionnaires measure people's attitudes in a rather different way, by asking respondents to select a point on a continuous scale rather than selecting a particular category of answer. For example, we might ask people to respond to a statement by giving a number between 0 and 7, where 0 indicates strong disagreement and 7 means strong agreement. Some researchers prefer this strategy for it recognizes that there are 'shades of opinion' (a continuous gradation of views) and that people are not differentiated into sharply defined opinion categories. It also has the advantage of producing variables that are continuous rather than categorical – although the level of measurement is still ordinal.

If we collect attitude data in this way, we *appear* to end up with variables measured at a higher, interval, level, for each attitude is measured by a real number scale. However, the phenomena we are measuring have not changed – no matter how we record their attitudes, it will never make sense to say that somebody is twice as opposed to banning smoking in public parks as they are to banning it in restaurants. Coding people's attitudes by using a numerical scale does not therefore transform them from ordinal to interval measures, even though some researchers do treat numerical attitude scores *as if* they were interval measures.

MEASURING ATTITUDES BY SCALING

Creating indexes from multiple indicators

In our Smoking Survey, we used eight attitudinal items intended to measure people's tolerance or intolerance towards smoking. Answers to any *one* of these eight items, taken alone, were not of any particular interest to us – what mattered was the overall measure of tolerance or intolerance that we hoped to derive from taking all the responses *together*.

The obvious way to put all these answers together is to give each answer a score and then sum the eight scores to make a single *index*.

Summing indicator scores in a simple index

Each of our eight items has five possible responses, from 'strongly agree' to 'strongly disagree'. In four of these items, a respondent's agreement indicates intolerance towards smoking:

'Smoking should be banned in places like restaurants' (var00019)
'Government isn't doing enough to discourage smoking' (var00021)
'Employers should ban all smoking in workplaces' (var00022)
'It should be made illegal to smoke in any public space' (var00025)

Why use more than one indicator?

When a doctor checks on your overall level of health and fitness, she or he will gather information on a variety of indicators such as blood pressure, cholesterol count, urine acidity, diet, frequency of exercise, smoking, drinking, and so on. Although each of these items of information has some importance on its own, what really matters is the way they build up into a pattern when looked at together. No sensible doctor would judge your overall level of health and fitness from data relating to only one of these indicators.

The same logic applies in social science when measuring a phenomenon like 'tolerance'. One indicator alone might not be reliable, but several all pointing in the same direction will give us a more robust composite measure of the phenomenon.

In these cases, we can score every 'strongly agree' answer as 1, every 'agree' answer as 2, and so on through to 5 for every 'strongly disagree' answer. Low scores thus indicate high intolerance.

In the other four items, agreement indicates tolerance towards smoking:

'Our society has become too intolerant towards people who smoke' (var00020)
'There is too much fuss being made about smoking nowadays' (var00023)
'If somebody chooses to smoke, nobody should try to persuade them to stop' (var00024)
'There are already enough restrictions on where people can smoke' (var00026)

In these cases we shall need to score people's answers the other way around, assigning a score of 1 for every 'strongly disagree' answer through to 5 for every 'strongly agree' answer. Low scores thus again indicate high intolerance.

With eight items in all, summing respondents' scores will give everybody a total score on a range between 8 (indicating extreme intolerance towards smoking) and 40 (indicating extreme tolerance). This summary score gives us a simple index of people's tolerance – the lower your score, the more you object to smoking.

Balancing biases in attitude scales

When we were constructing the Smoking Survey questionnaire, we tried to avoid biasing responses with leading questions by dividing our attitude statements into four that were supportive of smoking, and four that were hostile to it. Splitting statements in this way is a common strategy, although some researchers believe it can cause more problems than it avoids. This is because respondents tend to react differently to positive and negative statements, so we end up with varying patterns of response caused purely by the way we asked the questions. There is no consensus in the research community on which is the better strategy. (We return to this issue in our discussion of factor analysis in appendix F included on our website).

Summary scores as ordinal-level measures

An index like this is still an *ordinal* measure (just as the eight indicators that make it up are ordinal measures). Somebody with a higher score on the index is less tolerant of smoking than somebody with a lower score, but we have no basis for claiming that each extra point on the range indicates an equal increment in the degree of intolerance displayed.

It is, however, not uncommon for researchers to use such index scores as if they were *interval* measures, for this enables them to use more powerful statistics when analysing them. They know that these statistics may not be accurate, because the statistical procedures assume equal intervals between each value of the index when no such assumption can in fact be made. Nevertheless, they make the pragmatic judgement to live with this element of error rather than abstain from analysis altogether. They reason that it is better to have an unreliable result than no result at all.

We are not going to try to justify this – we simply alert you to the fact that in 'real research' it often happens, and that the result is not necessarily disastrous. Here again, we see that empirical research is a rather messy business that does not always follow the rules precisely as laid down in the methods textbooks. When in doubt, though, the best advice is to err on the side of caution and stick by the rules.

Likert scales

The index we have created is very crude. It assumes that all eight of our indicators are equally good measures of people's tolerance towards smoking, but this may not be the case. If some indicators are better than others, then simply adding them all together will give us an overall measure with a lot of error in it. Clearly we need to check (a) whether all the items are good measures of tolerance, and (b) whether they are consistent with each other. The process of making these checks is called *scaling*.

Table 5.1   Testing the composite attitudinal
index score on the Smoking Survey

Variable	Correlation
var00019	0.75
var00020	0.61
var00021	0.58
var00022	0.70
var00023	0.70
var00024	0.59
var00025	0.76
var00026	0.81

Testing the strength of individual items

A simple way of testing whether all eight items in our index are needed is to look at the strength of association between each of the individual items and the summed index scores. Any items which correlate weakly with the index are probably poor measures and should therefore be deleted.

We shall see in chapter 8 that the strength of association between two interval or ratio level variables can be analysed using a statistic called a *correlation coefficient*. Correlation coefficients measure strength of association on a scale from 0 (which indicates that there is no association between two variables) to 1 (complete association). The higher the number, therefore, the stronger the relationship between two variables.

The column of numbers in table 5.1 consists of the correlation coefficients between each of the individual items in our index and the overall index score (do not worry for now about how all these statistics are computed). The weakest coefficient is 0.58; the strongest is 0.81. As a rough rule of thumb, any item in an index which correlates with the total index score at below about 0.3 is deemed to be a poor indicator and is dropped from the index. This clearly does not apply to any of these eight items, all of which therefore seem to have 'worked' quite well as measures of tolerance to smoking.

From indexes to scales

An index which has been tested both for construct validity (it measures what it is supposed to be measuring) and for reliability (the individual item responses are consistent) can be called a scale.

Indexes and scales

An 'index' is a number derived from putting together the scores from a series of indicators. A 'scale' is an index in which the constituent measures can be shown to be 'structured' or patterned in relation to each other (e.g. scores correlate and are consistent).

A Likert scale is one of the simplest examples of scaling in social science. To achieve adequacy, a Likert scale requires only that people's answers to the different indicators should be consistent. Other scaling procedures are much more sophisticated and elaborate (a Guttsman scale, for example, would also require of our tolerance index that each of the eight items should occupy a distinctive place on a rising scale of tolerance, and that all respondents' answers should be consistent in relation to the positions of the items on this scale – a condition called 'multidimensionality').

We can also go further in checking whether all the items in an index are equally good indicators of the same phenomenon by using a technique called *factor analysis*. This is explained in detail in appendix F on our website.

CONCLUSION

We have seen in this chapter that we do not so much *collect* survey data as *construct* it.

- When we interview people, we do not simply *report* what they tell us, but we *select* from (and actively *interpret*) what they say.
- When we process this information by coding it, we force it into categories which make sense to *us* and which derive from *our* theoretical and practical frame of reference.
- When we create indexes and scales to summarize and measure the way our respondents feel and behave, we end up with scores and coefficients which make sense in terms of *our* analytical objectives, but which our respondents would scarcely recognize.

In the terminology of the phenomenologists, we are in the business of creating our own 'second-order accounts' out of the 'first-order accounting practices' of our respondents.

Because survey research cannot exactly reproduce social reality as it is lived and experienced by those we are studying, critics of survey methods often claim that such research is fundamentally flawed and essentially misconceived. But in our view, this is an overreaction.

It is true that interviewing, coding and the development of measurement scales and indicators are always problematic. We end up with fuzzy compromises, and (if we are good researchers) we will always be worrying about the way we have collected and processed our data. But we have also seen in this chapter that the process of collecting, coding and measuring survey data is grounded in quite rigorous safeguards. While it is true that we construct our data, the way we do it is not capricious or arbitrary. Constructing data is not the same thing as making it up, and provided we are careful and methodical, the results that we get from surveys can and do provide us with reliable information and insights about the social world.

INTERVIEWING ON THE SMOKING SURVEY

Our students reported very few problems in getting people to agree to be interviewed – there were fewer than 20 refusals to generate a final sample size of 334. The feeling among most interviewers was that people had been willing to do the survey (most were friendly and helpful), but few had been particularly engaged by it. Four minutes was as long as it was reasonable to keep people standing in the street. Older people were slightly more likely to refuse than younger ones, and some of the younger male students thought that some older women may have been slightly wary of them.

The questionnaire contained no formal prompts or probes, but many interviewers admitted that they had not always stuck rigidly to the question wording and that when respondents hesitated, they had often tried to phrase the question in a different way. On reflection, perhaps we should have included some prompts and probes to help out our interviewers.

The questionnaire itself seemed to work quite well, although there were some glitches. Going through the questions in a debriefing session, the following points were raised (see the questions again on pp. 96–7):

On Q1: There was some confusion over the wording 'in the last week': 'in the last seven days' would have been less ambiguous.

On Q2: Smokers do not think of their consumption in weekly terms – it might have been better to have asked for daily consumption. Also, those smoking hand-rolled cigarettes were uncertain as to whether they should answer the first or third parts of the question (some answered the first part by counting cigarettes; others answered the third part by calculating weight of tobacco).

On Q3: The follow-up question for those answering 'yes' was too vague – because it failed to distinguish cigarettes, cigars and tobacco, it failed to collect information in a common format.

On Q4–6: No problems reported.

On Q7: There were several problems here! What is meant by 'close family' (there are no instructions to guide interviewers on this)? Similarly, how is 'regular' smoking being defined here? And, perhaps most problematic, the question runs two different questions into one (do your friends smoke? Do your family smoke?) – some respondents had friends who smoked but family who did not, and for them the question became confused. (We discussed this issue of 'double-barrelled' questions in chapter 3.)

On Q8: There was some difficulty when *our* definition of somebody as a 'smoker' or 'non-smoker' did not correspond with their self-identity. Instructions to interviewers were that part A should be asked to those who answered 'Yes' at Q1 or Q3; part B should be asked to everybody else. However, there were a few cases where this did not make sense (e.g. somebody who has one or two cigarettes at the occasional party may not think of themselves as a smoker, but they were treated as such in the survey).

On Q9: The attitude questions have already been discussed in the main text of this chapter.

On Q10: A report on passive smoking was published just a few days before interviewing, and this may have influenced answers on this question.

On Q11: Some respondents were unsure whether this question referred to the personal benefits of smoking (e.g. it aids relaxation) or benefits to the wider society (e.g. it generates tax revenues). This is not really a problem, though – the question wanted to see if smokers were rationalizing their behaviour to themselves (a test of hypothesis 10 on cognitive dissonance), and in this sense the distinction between personal and social benefits is unimportant.

On Q12: Most people answered the 'stress scale' without difficulty, although some did take a long time to decide on an answer (which suggests that the question was not consistent with everyday thinking and experience). The question is susceptible to daily fluctuations in people's lives (e.g. one respondent had just been dismissed from his job and was therefore 'highly stressed'), but it was intended as a measure of longer-term, relatively stable stress levels.

On Q13: No problems, although the items would have worked more smoothly if we had started by asking people's employment status rather than implicitly assuming that they had an occupation.

On Q14: Problems arose with respondents who had returned to full-time education at a mature age – some gave as their answer their age when they left school; others gave their age when they completed college as a mature student. Some had been in and out of full-time education several times. This question clearly did not work well.

On Q15: No problem (despite our worries that age may be a sensitive question for some people).

If this survey had been a serious piece of research, rather than a learning exercise, we would have collected this sort of feedback from interviewers at the *pilot* stage, and we could then have used it to make various changes to the questionnaire, and to issue more precise instructions to interviewers. As it is, we did not conduct a full pilot before going on to do the survey, and the problems that interviewers encountered could not therefore be rectified.

PREPARING A DATA FILE

AIM

In this chapter we learn how to enter data from a survey on to a computer using the SPSS for Windows software package. By the end of the chapter you will:

- Understand how to access different procedures in SPSS
- Know how to enter data in SPSS, to save the data as a file, and to retrieve the file on subsequent occasions
- Understand the procedures for defining variable names, specifying labels for variables and values, and identifying codes for missing data
- Be familiar with copying output from SPSS into Word for Windows files

INTRODUCTION

Before we can analyse the data we have collected from our Smoking Survey, they need to be entered into a computer software package called SPSS for Windows.

SPSS stands for Statistical Package for the Social Sciences. It is a powerful data analysis and statistics program specially tailored to the requirements of social science researchers and widely used by social researchers in universities, government agencies and the private and voluntary sectors. SPSS is not the only computer software package available for the analysis of quantitative data but it is one of the most popular. In subsequent chapters we will be using it to analyse our data and to present our results.

Statistical packages such as SPSS do not do the analysis for you; their role is to allow you to do your analysis much faster than you could if you had to analyse the data manually. The speed of computers enables us to use complex statistical techniques on large data sets in a way that would not be practicable if the data had to be analysed by hand. But if you input poor quality data or run inappropriate commands, SPSS will give you meaningless results. The computer will not do your thinking for you – it is your responsibility to ensure that the data you put into SPSS and the commands you ask it to run make sense.

Versions of SPSS

There are a number of different versions of SPSS for Windows commonly in use and you might find yourself using any of the versions from 9 upwards. In the following chapters, we shall be using version 11.

For the most part, differences between versions are small. The main difference that you should be aware of is that version 9 differs from later versions in the way that the data set is labelled (rather than labelling through the Variable View pane in the Data Editor this job is done using dialog boxes to specify the variable details). If you are running version 9 then you can go to section 7 of our website (www.surveymethods.co.uk) for detailed instructions on how data are labelled.

GETTING STARTED USING SPSS

SPSS runs on the Microsoft Windows operating system. With Windows running on your computer, you may find that there is an icon for SPSS on the Desktop. If so, start SPSS by double-clicking the icon. Alternatively, start SPSS by opening it under programs in the Start menu.

Starting an SPSS session

If you are familiar with other Windows applications, you will find it simple to navigate around SPSS. There are three kinds of operations you are going to want to carry out:

♦   Enter data into an SPSS data file.
♦   Manipulate and transform the data to get it into the form that you want to analyse.
♦   Generate results.

SPSS reflects these distinct processes in the way the application is organized. It consists of two core windows:

♦   The Data Editor window is where you enter new data or modify an existing data file.
♦   The Viewer window displays the results of your analysis.

To manipulate and transform the data we use the drop-down menus in the Data Editor window.

At the start of an SPSS session, a dialog box opens asking you what you want to do. Since we want to enter new data from our questionnaires, we click the radio button beside 'Type in Data' and then click 'OK'. The dialog box will close to reveal the Data Editor window. This is the window into which our data will be entered.

The menu bar

Each window in SPSS contains its own menu bar with a number of menu selections. Most of the tasks we shall be carrying out can be performed through the menu bar. The Data Editor window contains ten menu items including:

- *File* This allows us to create a new SPSS file, to open a file created in a previous session, to save or print a file, and to 'exit' from SPSS.
- *Window* This allows us to change the active window and it tells us which window is currently active by placing a tick against it. It also allows us to minimize all the windows.
- *Transform* We use items in this menu when we want to crunch data or to create a new summary variable out of several existing ones.
- *Analyze* Every time we want to do some analysis on our data, we shall do it by selecting an item from this menu. For example, we select 'Frequencies' when we want to generate a simple frequency count (such as a count of how many males and females there are in our sample).
- *Graphs* This menu allows us to create graphical output such as bar charts and pie charts.
- *Help* This offers the 'Topics' option (which provides guidance on all the procedures in SPSS) as well as a step-by-step Tutorial.

Note that some of the drop-down menu choices which appear when you click on the menu items have a right-facing arrow head next to them ($>$), and that some have dots trailing after them (...). If you highlight an item with an arrowhead, a submenu of further items will appear from which you must select one. If you highlight an item followed by dots, you will open a dialog box which enables you to input commands.

The toolbar

Each window has its own toolbar with its own tools which you will find below the menu bar. The toolbar buttons are shortcuts for commonly used operations. For example, to go immediately into the dialog box which allows you to open a data file, click on

You can go through the menus to start up any of these procedures, but the toolbar allows them to be accessed more quickly. To find out what a tool does, point the cursor at it and a brief description will pop up.

The status bar

The status bar at the bottom of each window provides information about what is currently happening within the window. If you look at the status bar in the Data Editor window you will see 'SPSS Processor is ready'. This informs you that SPSS is not currently occupied doing computations. When you run a procedure the message will change to tell you what computation is being processed and how far through the cases the computer has gone.

ENTERING DATA IN THE DATA EDITOR WINDOW

Having coded the questionnaires from the Smoking Survey, we have a list of *variables* corresponding to different items on the questionnaire (as well as some additional 'derived' variables), and for each variable there is a set of *values*. For example, the variable 'gender' has three possible values: '0' (for females); '1' (for males); and 'blank' (where information on the respondent's gender has not been recorded – SPSS automatically reads blanks as missing). To put this information into SPSS, we enter the code for each case into the relevant cell of the grid (or 'spreadsheet') in the Data Editor window (figure 6.1).

The Data Editor consists of two panes, Data View and Variable View. By default only the Data View pane can be seen when SPSS is started and this is the pane we will be working in at the moment. The Data View spreadsheet consists of columns, each of which represents a variable, and rows, each of which represents a case (i.e. one of your respondents). To enter data into any given cell of this grid, put the mouse pointer into the cell, click on it to highlight it, and type the number that is to go into that cell (the number you type appears in the cell editor above the grid). Press the 'Enter' key on your keyboard and the number is transferred to the cell that you highlighted.

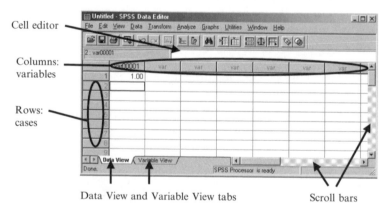

Data View and Variable View tabs   Scroll bars

Figure 6.1   Entering data in the Data View pane of Data Editor

After you press Enter, three things happen:

♦   The number you typed appears in the designated cell.
♦   The column containing that cell is given a default variable name by SPSS (e.g. 'var00001').
♦   The cell immediately below it in the same column is highlighted.

You can now proceed to enter the next code. To complete data entry you must enter the values for all of the variables in respect of every respondent. When we entered the data from the smoking survey we ended up with 334 rows (one for each completed questionnaire) and 42 columns (one for each variable).

Moving around the grid in the Data View pane in Data Editor

To move around in the grid, you can use the vertical and horizontal 'scroll bars' to the right and at the bottom of the grid (see figure 6.1). When you arrive at the cell where you wish to enter data, highlight the cell by clicking on it. Alternatively, you can use the cursor keys to navigate around the grid.

You can also use the menus to move around in the grid. If you want to go to a particular variable, click on the Utilities menu, select 'Variables . . .', highlight the variable you want to go to in the dialog box, and click on 'Go To'. If you want to go to a particular case, click on the Data menu, select 'Go to case . . .', type in the case number in the dialog box, and click on 'OK'.

When you have entered the data from all your questionnaires, you will end up with a completed spreadsheet with variables along the top and cases down the side. The variables will all have the default names given to them by SPSS (var00001, var00002, etc.); we shall see in a moment how we can create more meaningful variable names or attach labels to these default variable names.

EDITING AND DELETING DATA

Once you have entered the data it is important to check through it to look for inputting errors. If you find that a value has been entered incorrectly, use the cursor keys or the mouse to highlight the cell with the error in it. Then enter the correct value and press the enter key.

If you need to delete a case or row then use your mouse to click on the row number corresponding to the row you wish to delete. This will highlight the entire row. Click on the delete key on your keyboard or go to the Edit menu and click on 'Clear' in the drop-down menu to delete the row. In a similar way, if you need to delete a variable or column then click on the variable name heading the column and you can then delete the highlighted column using the delete key or 'Clear' in the Edit menu.

SAVING AND ACCESSING DATA FILES

To save the data file you have just created, ensure you are working in the Data Editor, then click on the File menu at the top of the screen and select 'Save As...' to open a dialog box in which you specify file and drive details. By default SPSS may try to save your data files to a folder named 'Spss11' which is probably on the computer's 'C' drive. If you wish to save your data in a different drive then click on the downward arrow in the upper part of the dialog box and select the drive you want in the drop-down menu that opens. Select the correct folder by double-clicking on the relevant folder in the large box in the centre of the dialog box.

You must tell SPSS the type of file you are saving. The default option in the 'Save as type' box is 'sav' and is the one you want, for SPSS data files are called *save files* and are always designated by the .sav suffix. You also need to choose a file name by clicking in the box next to 'File name' and typing the name under which you want the file to be saved. When all this is done, click on the 'Save' button (note that the title bar in the Data Editor changes from 'Untitled' to the name you have given this file).

If you intend working with our Smoking Survey data, you should at this point download from our website the file **dirtydat.sav**. This is the first, 'uncleaned', version of the data set containing the coded responses of the 334 people who were interviewed for this survey. Nothing has been done to this file – it is in the form in which our students compiled it. It is riddled with coding errors (and we need to learn how to deal with these), and it contains no 'derived' variables other than those created when the questionnaires were first coded. Instructions on how to download files from our website can be found on p. 298.

If you have collected your own data, then you should work from now on with your own data file. Simply follow what we do with our Smoking Survey data set, and repeat each step with your own data file. (If you have been working in a group and each individual enters their own interview data into SPSS, your tutor will need to merge all these individual files into a single data file that everybody can use. Instructions on merging files can be found in the SPSS Help menu.)

To retrieve a data file, click on 'File' on the menu bar, 'Open' in the drop-down menu and then 'Data'. A dialog box will open which allows you to select the data file to be opened. The file you want to open may be in the dialog box, ready to open. If not, you must browse the drives and folders to find the location of the file. Once you have located the file, click on it once and then click on 'Open'.

DEFINING AND LABELLING VARIABLES AND VALUES

It may be obvious to you at the moment what each variable and value means but come back to the data set after some weeks or pass it on to someone else and lack of labelling of the data will make the data set very difficult to make sense of. Therefore, it is important to take some time to relabel and define the data.

Redefining variable names

SPSS creates default names for each variable but you can create new ones. Any name you create:

- must begin with a letter of the alphabet;
- may be no longer than eight characters;
- must not contain blanks, question marks (?), exclamation marks (!), apostrophes (') asterisks (∗) or full stops (.);
- must be unique (no two variables can have the same name).

Within these rules it is up to you what names you give to the variables. Some people like to give variables explicit names like 'gender', 'age' or 'smoker', while others prefer to name them by the questionnaire numbers to which they refer (e.g. 'q1', 'q2a' 'q2b'). Some simply stick with the SPSS default names – it is up to you.

To change the default variable name click on the Variable View tab at the bottom left of the Data Editor. This will bring to the front the Variable View pane (figure 6.2). The format of the Variable View grid is different from the format of the Data View grid in that each row corresponds to a single variable. So, for example, because the Smoking Survey data set contains 42 variables there are 42 rows. Each of the columns contains information about an aspect of the variables such as their names or what their missing values are. For example, the first column headed 'Name' presents the name for each of the 42 variables and the first row of the first column relates to the first variable that we created which was given the default variable name 'var00001'.

Let's start by renaming the first variable. Click on the top left cell with 'var00001' in it, simply type the new variable name you wish to give followed by the 'Enter' key on your keyboard. Our first variable is the respondent number so let's rename this variable

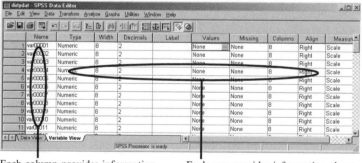

Each column provides information on an aspect of the variables (e.g the *Name* of each variable)

Each row provides information about a variable across a number of aspects

Figure 6.2   The Variable View pane in Data Editor

'respno'. Since we are limited to just eight characters the variable names are likely to be rather cryptic. However, we can also add a detailed label for each variable.

Variable labels

You do not *have* to give your variables descriptive labels – SPSS will run quite happily without them – but you will probably find it helpful to do so, especially where the variable name is not self-explanatory.

Adding variable labels allows you to provide a more detailed description of the variable. Variable labels can be up to 120 characters long and can include blanks, but long labels may not be fully printed out on output, so it is a good idea to limit them to a maximum of about 30 characters. The labels you specify will appear at the head of all the tables of output you produce.

To label the variable, simply click on the cell corresponding to the variable you wish to label in the 'Label' column and type in the description. For example, to label our first variable, 'respno', click on the cell in the top row in the column headed 'Label', type in 'Respondent number' and press the 'Enter' key on your keyboard.

A common way of labelling the variables is to type in a shortened version of the question. For example, 'var0003' records the responses to question 1, 'Have you smoked any cigarettes, cigars or pipe tobacco in the last week?', and we might label this variable 'Smoked in last week?'

Value labels

Labelling the different *values* of each categorical variable is also important. For example, if 'female' is coded '0' and 'male' is '1', analysis of the 'Gender' variable will simply tell you how many respondents are zeros and how many are ones, unless you tell SPSS what '0' and '1' refer to.

To label the values, click on the cell under the column headed 'Values' which relates to the variable you wish to work on. Within the cell a small box with three dots will appear. Click on this and a dialog box will open which allows you to label each value (figure 6.3). Type the value number in the 'Value' box, type its corresponding label in the 'Value Label' box, then click on the 'Add' button. It then appears in the box at the bottom. Repeat for each value. Finally, click the 'OK' button.

It is rarely necessary to label values measured at the interval or ratio level since the numbers are usually self-explanatory. For example, in the case of 'var0004', which records the number of cigarettes the respondent has smoked in the last week, it would be pointless to label every possible value from, say, 1 cigarette to 250 cigarettes because it is already obvious what an answer of '1' or '250' means without a label.

Defining missing values

When information is missing on any given variable for a particular respondent, it is important to define it as such so that SPSS knows that this case should be ignored when performing statistical calculations.

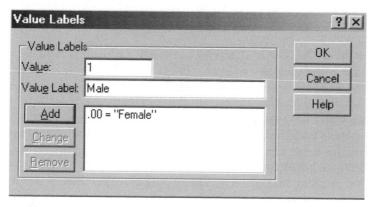

Figure 6.3 Defining labels

There are two ways of defining missing responses in SPSS. We can leave the appropriate cell blank (what SPSS calls *system-missing*), or we can assign a code (called a *user-missing* value). In the Smoking Survey, we used blanks for missing cases, and SPSS will automatically read these as missing without being told. However, on some variables we might also want to ignore 'Don't know' answers (which we coded as '−1'), so we could define these as 'missing' so that SPSS will ignore them when it comes to the data analysis stage.

To define a value as user-missing, click on the cell under the column headed 'Missing' which relates to the variable you wish to work on. Within the cell a small box with three dots will appear. Click on this and a dialog box will open which allows you to define missing values. To define '−1' as missing, click on the radio button next to 'Discrete missing values' and type −1 into the first box. SPSS allows us to specify up to three values as missing. Click on 'OK' to close the dialog box.

Specifying the level of measurement

To specify the level of measurement of a variable, click on the cell under the column headed 'Measure' which relates to the variable you wish to work on. Within the cell a small box with a downward arrow will appear. Click on this and a drop-down menu will appear with three options: scale, ordinal or nominal. If the variable is measured at the ratio or interval level then click on 'Scale'. If the variable is measured at the ordinal level or nominal level then click on whichever applies. If you cannot remember the level your data are measured at then you should refer back to chapter 5 for a recap on the four levels of measurement.

A reminder...

Once you have entered and labelled all the data it is important to save the data file so that your inputs are not lost. If the computer is your own you will probably want to save your data file to your computer's hard disk. If it is someone else's computer then you will probably want to save the data to a floppy disk or CD, or to a network server.

Changing SPSS default settings

When you come to the stage of data analysis you will probably find it easiest to select the variables you wish to analyse from a list of variable *names*. However, by default SPSS expects you to select the variables from the list of variable *labels*. It is therefore a good idea to change the way SPSS lists variables. To do this, click on 'Edit' on the menu bar and then 'Options' in the drop-down menu. A dialog box will open. Click on the radio button next to 'Display names' and then click on the radio button next to 'Alphabetical'. Click on 'OK'.

The changes you have made to the way that the variables are listed for selection will not take effect until the next time you open a data file. Therefore, if you wish to move on to chapter 7 and start some data analysis in this session, you should save your data file and reopen it.

Handling output

We have now input and labelled all of our cases in a data file, which means we are ready to do some analysis. If you are impatient to get going, you can move directly to chapter 7 and return to the remainder of this chapter when you start to generate some output. Alternatively, you may prefer to get acquainted with the basic procedures for handling output before you start, in which case, read on.

Exploring the Viewer

When we run an SPSS procedure, the results are sent to the *Viewer* window. From here, output can be saved to a file and can then be printed.

The Viewer window opens automatically when you run any analysis, but you can also open a new Viewer window at any time by selecting 'New' followed by 'Output' within the File menu. All of your output during a session is sent to the same Viewer window unless you open a new one and tell SPSS to start sending output there instead. Every time you run a job, output gets tacked on to the end of all the other output from all the other jobs you have run, unless you instruct SPSS otherwise. The output is displayed in the pane on the right (see figure 6.4).

The pane on the left lists the procedures that you have run. To move to different parts of the output (contained in the right pane), click on the relevant icon in the left pane (alternatively, you can scroll up or down to the output you want using the scroll bars). A small arrow beside the icon indicates that the corresponding output is currently being displayed in the right pane.

Printing from the Viewer window

To select specific parts of your output to print, click either on the icon in the left pane corresponding to the output you want, or on the output itself in the right pane. Then go to the menu bar, click on 'File' and then 'Print . . .', and a dialog box will open. Check

Clicking on an item will display the corresponding output in the right pane

A red arrow indicates that the corresponding output is being displayed in the right pane

Adjust width of panes by moving this bar

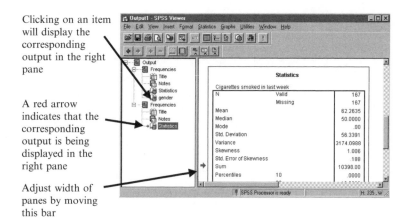

Figure 6.4   Output in the SPSS Viewer window

under 'Print range' that the button beside 'Selection' has been chosen (this is to ensure that only the selected output is printed), and click 'OK'. The selected output will be sent to the printer.

Managing output

During an SPSS session you may create a great deal of output, much of which you may not want to save or print. One way of keeping things manageable is to open a new window called the *Draft Viewer* and send your output there first. Output sent to the Draft Viewer is not of presentation quality, but this means it is less elaborate. To open the Draft Viewer, click on 'File' (in either the Data Editor or Viewer window), move the mouse down to 'New' and select 'Draft Output'.

Another way of managing output is simply to open a series of different Viewer windows to receive output from different stages of your analysis. This organizes your output in a coherent way and reduces the amount of output in each Viewer window.

Designating the output window

Simply opening a new Viewer or Draft Viewer window is not enough to ensure that your next output will be sent there. This is because SPSS sends output to whichever is the *designated output window*, and until you tell it otherwise it assumes that the designated output window is the one which was opened when you began your session. To designate a new Viewer window or Draft Viewer window as the one to which new output should be sent, you must click on the red exclamation mark in the toolbar (in Figure 6.4 it is the last button on the right – if this button is greyed out it indicates that the output window you are in is already the designated window). To confirm that it has become the designated window, look for the same red icon on the status bar at the bottom of the window.

Saving output

If you want to close a Viewer or Draft Viewer window, you do it in exactly the same way as in any other Windows application – by clicking on the X button in the top right corner. Remember, though, that *your results are not automatically saved*. If you want to save your output, you need to do it by saving the contents of the window as a new file.

To save the contents of an output window (either the Viewer or Draft Viewer window), go to the File menu and select 'Save As...' This will open a dialog box which will ask you the name of the file you want to create as well as the drive to which it should be sent.

A file containing the results of a job is called an *output file*. As with all file names, the name you give to your output file is limited to eight characters, followed by a full stop, followed by a three-character suffix which tells you (and SPSS) what kind of file it is. In SPSS, Viewer output files have the suffix '.spo' and Draft Viewer output files have the suffix '.rtf'.

Opening saved output files

To look at or edit an existing output file which was created and saved in a previous session, click on 'File' on the menu bar of the Data Editor or Viewer window, then 'Open' and then 'Output...'. This opens a dialog box in which you can select the folder where the file is located (a list of files will appear in the centre section of the dialog box, and you highlight the one you want).

Copying and pasting output to Word for Windows

When you come to write up your results you will probably want to splice SPSS output into your text. If you are using a word processor application such as Microsoft Word, output can be 'cut' from SPSS and 'pasted' into the word processor application. To do this, click on the output (e.g. table, chart, etc.) that you wish to copy, go to 'Edit' on the menu bar and click on 'Copy'. You can then switch to Word for Windows by clicking on its icon in the taskbar at the bottom of the screen (if Word is not open then you will

---

Taking things further: the Syntax Editor window

Although the most important procedures you are likely to want to carry out can be accessed through the drop-down menus in the menu bar, as you become more experienced in data analysis and data transformation, and as you want to run more complex procedures, you will find it useful to learn how to enter commands in the *Syntax Editor*. This is a separate window which allows you to write and then run your own commands in a 'language' known as Syntax.

A guide to using Syntax for the transformation of data, running data analysis commands and running sequences of commands can be found in section 7 of our website.

need to open it now). Place the cursor at the point in your text where you want the copied item to appear, and click on 'Paste Special . . . ' (*not* 'Paste') in the 'Edit' menu to bring up a dialog box. Click on 'Picture' and then 'OK', and the copied item will then be pasted into your Word document.

Once SPSS output has been copied into Word for Windows there is only a very restricted amount of editing that can be done on it. If you want to edit the output item (for example, you wish to change the font or change the colour of a pie chart) then this is best done in SPSS before you paste it into Word for Windows.

CONCLUSION

Having worked through this chapter, you should know how to open and close SPSS, switch between windows, and use the menu bar and manipulate the scroll bars. You should understand the purposes of the Data Editor window and the Viewer window and know how to enter data in the Data Editor window in order to create or amend a data file.

Having created a data file, you should also know how to tailor it to your purposes. This means naming and labelling variables, labelling values of variables, and specifying missing values. You should know how to do this using drop-down menus and dialog boxes.

You should also acquaint yourself with the different kinds of files created in SPSS – the .sav data files and the .spo and .rtf output files. You should know how to open and save existing data and output files, how to send output to a designated Viewer window, how to print output and how to paste it from SPSS into a Word for Windows file.

You are now ready to start analysing your data!

PART III
DATA ANALYSIS

Describing and Exploring Data

AIM

In this chapter we see how to generate and interpret some simple procedures and statistics for summarizing and exploring data. You will learn to:

- Run and interpret one-way frequency counts and associated summary statistics (you will also learn what a 'normal distribution' is)
- Present one-way frequency counts visually using bar charts, pie charts and histograms
- Search for possible problems in a data set, using boxplots, and what to do when you find them

An appendix explains how to clean a data set by identifying and rectifying coding errors, and how to create new 'derived' variables using the SPSS 'Recode' and 'Compute' commands.

INTRODUCTION

In chapter 1 we drew a distinction between 'descriptive' research (which aims to discover facts) and 'analytical' or 'explanatory' research (which tries to test theories about why things happen as they do). In this chapter, the focus is on the former, for we shall be describing and counting responses to our Smoking Survey. In chapter 8 we shall see how to start testing hypotheses about the causal associations between variables.

The statistics we shall be using in both of these chapters are appropriate for analysing sample data or data gathered on whole populations. These statistics can be used on all sorts of data sets – not just those generated by means of surveys, but also records such as official registers of births and deaths, immigration files or Inland Revenue data. Survey researchers use these statistics to describe, summarize and analyse their findings, but their uses are not limited to surveys.

The analysis in this and all the following chapters uses data from our Smoking Survey. There are two versions of this data set:

- **dirtydat.sav** is the original version. It has not been checked for coding errors and contains no derived variables other than those created when the questionaires were first coded (e.g. the Registrar-General 'Social class' variable that was created when the occupational data were coded).
- **cleandat.sav** has been checked and cleaned of coding errors and contains a number of new, derived variables created in the course of our analysis in later chapters.

Both files can be obtained from our website at www.surveymethods.co.uk (details on p. 298). Unless you are working with your own data set, you should open file **dirtydat.sav** now.

Running one-way frequency counts

One of the first things we want to look at is the frequency counts for our main variables, to see how people answered our questions. Let us start with the variable 'gender', to see how many men and how many women there are in our final sample.

Obtaining a frequency count

To examine the gender distribution using the 'Frequencies' command:

- Click on 'Analyze' in the menu bar of the Data Editor window.
- In the menu list that opens highlight 'Descriptive Statistics' and then click on 'Frequencies...'. This opens a dialog box (figure 7.1).
- On the left-hand side of the dialog box is the source box listing all the variables in the data file. Only some are visible, but you can scroll up and down to find the rest. Select 'gender', using the mouse to highlight it.
- Click on the right-facing arrow button in the centre of the dialog box to transfer 'gender' to the 'Variable(s)' box on the right-hand side (while it is highlighted there the arrow will become left-facing). Ignore the buttons near the bottom of the dialog box for the moment, and just click on 'OK'.

SPSS now produces a table of frequency counts for the variable you have selected. This output is sent to the designated Viewer window where you can look at it.

Select variable(s) from the source box

Use the arrow button to move the selected variable(s) to the target box

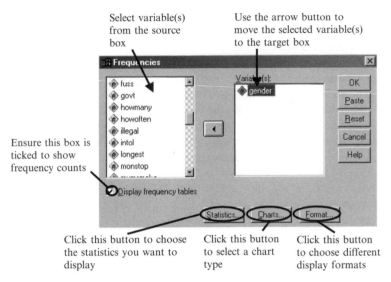

Ensure this box is ticked to show frequency counts

Click this button to choose the statistics you want to display

Click this button to select a chart type

Click this button to choose different display formats

Figure 7.1   Running a frequency count

Interpreting the frequency output

Your output will look something like that in figure 7.2. The first part of the output gives the total valid and missing cases. In our example it shows that we have 333 valid cases and one missing case. (Given that we knew the gender of all of our respondents, there should not be any missing cases, so in due course we shall have to investigate what has gone wrong here. For the moment, however, let us ignore this anomaly.)

Statistics

gender

N	Valid	333
	Missing	1

gender

		Frequency	Percent	Valid Percent	Cumulative Percent
Valid	female	165	49.4	49.5	49.5
	male	166	49.7	49.8	99.4
	2.00	2	.6	.6	100.0
	Total	333	99.7	100.0	
Missing	System	1	.3		
Total		334	100.0		

Figure 7.2   Output from the 'Frequencies' command run on the variable 'gender'

The main part of the output gives the frequency counts. We can see that there were 165 females and 166 males, and that two cases were coded '2'. (This must be an error in the coding of the data since the only valid codes for gender are '0' for female and '1' for male). The third column – Percent – expresses the frequency count for each value as a percentage and the fourth – Valid Percent – does the same but excludes the missing cases from the calculation (percentages are expressed to one decimal place; they may not sum to 100 due to rounding). The final column – Cumulative Percent – adds up the valid percentages as it moves down the column.

If you want to keep this output, you should copy and paste it into a Word for Windows file, from which you can also print it out (the procedures were explained in chapter 6).

Coding errors, missing cases and data cleaning

The frequency run on 'gender' has brought two possible errors to light that will need to be investigated. The first is a missing value when there should be no missing cases, and the second involves the two cases coded incorrectly as '2'.

Errors like these are common in a new data set (they usually creep in at the data inputting stage). If we fail to correct them, all our subsequent analysis will obviously be contaminated. And if there are errors on this variable, it is likely that we shall find errors on other variables too. In the appendix to this chapter, we explain how to search for errors in the Smoking Survey data set, and what to do when you find them.

> If you are working with our Smoking Survey data set, you will need to work through the appendix at some point using the **dirtydat.sav** file. If you prefer to leave this until later, and to proceed with the rest of this chapter first, then you should now access the cleaned version of the data in the file on our website named **cleandat.sav**. But make sure you work through the appendix at some point, for knowing how to clean up a data set is an essential skill.
>
> If you are working from data that you have collected yourself, then you should follow the procedures on data cleaning outlined in the appendix on p. 190 before proceeding further with your analysis.

Running a one-way frequency count with summary statistics

Let us run another 'Frequencies' job using the clean data set. This time we shall ask for some statistics. Call up the 'Frequencies' dialog box again as outlined earlier. If the previously selected variable ('gender') is still selected, move it back into the left-hand box by highlighting it and clicking on the arrow (which is now left-facing). This leaves the right-hand side 'Variables' box empty. You can now select a different variable to analyse.

Select a variable which is measured at an *interval* or *ratio* level of measurement. In our Smoking Survey, we asked in question 2:

(a) how many cigarettes people had smoked in the last week (var00004);
(b) how many cigars they had smoked (var00005);
(c) how many grams (or ounces) of tobacco they had smoked (var00006).

In order to get an overall measure of how much people smoke, we have combined these three items of information into a new variable, 'comsmoke'. This provides a summary measure of cigarettes, or cigarette equivalents (cigars/pipe tobacco/hand-rolling to-bacco) smoked each week (basically, we treat one cigar as the equivalent of five cigarettes, and one gram of loose tobacco as the equivalent of two cigarettes). The appendix to this chapter explains how this new variable was created, but do not worry about that for the moment.

> If you are working from the Smoking Survey with the data file **cleandat.sav** open, select the variable 'comsmoke' from the list in the left window of the 'Frequen-cies' dialog box.
>
>   If you are working with your own data set, select one of your existing variables that is measured at interval or ratio level.

After selecting the variable to be analysed, click on the 'Statistics ...' button at the bottom of the dialog box (see figure 7.1 again). This opens the 'Statistics' dialog box (figure 7.3).

Measures of central tendency

In the frequency statistics dialog box we can request the three measures of central tendency that we encountered in chapter 4:

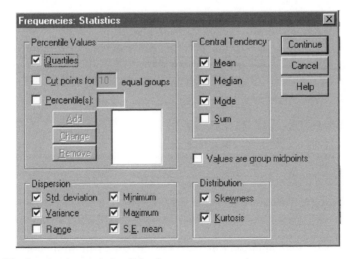

Figure 7.3   The frequencies statistics dialog box

- The *mean* is the arithmetic average. The actual mean can only be calculated if you are dealing with a continuous scale, but you can estimate a mean from grouped data by taking the mid-points in each category, and SPSS offers you this option by clicking on the 'Values are group midpoints' check box. We see from the output in figure 7.5 below that the smokers we interviewed got through an average of 77 cigarettes (or the equivalent in cigars and tobacco) per week.
- The *median* is the value below which half the cases fall. It can be used at any level of measurement from ordinal upwards. In the Smoking Survey, the results in figure 7.5 (p. 179) show that the median smoker got through 70 cigarettes (or the equivalent in cigars and tobacco) per week.
- The *mode* is the value which occurs most frequently, and it can be used at any level of measurement. In the Smoking Survey, the most common number of cigarettes (or equivalent) smoked per week was 100.

Because we are dealing with a variable measured at the ratio level, we can request all three measures of central tendency, so click on the check boxes by the mean, the median and the mode.

Percentiles

Next, look at the area of the dialog box entitled 'Percentile Values'. The options here allow us to split our sample into various categories. We have three options:

- *Quartiles* will divide the sample into four equally sized groups. If we look at the output in figure 7.5 below, we can see where the cut-off point comes for the lightest smokers (25 per cent smoked 30 cigarettes or less per week) and the heaviest smokers (25 per cent smoked 100 or more per week).
- The *Cut points* option is similar, but here we can decide for ourselves how many equally sized groups we want the sample divided into. For example, if we are interested in knowing the cut-off points for the lightest one-third and heaviest one-third of smokers, we can divide the sample into three equal groups and find the base number of cigarettes smoked for each group.
- *Percentile(s)* is similar again, but here we can specify group sizes in terms of any percentage we want. For example, if we want to know about the cut-off point for the heaviest 15 per cent of smokers in the sample, we can click on Percentiles, type 85 into the box, and click on 'Add'.

We chose quartiles, but decide for yourself which of these various options you want to request and click on the relevant check boxes.

Measures of dispersion

Now look at the area of the dialog box at the bottom left labelled 'Dispersion'. Here we can request statistics that will tell us how clustered or spread out our data are:

- *Minimum, maximum and range* are self-explanatory. Minimum tells you the lowest value in the sample (in figure 7.5 below, we see that the lowest number of cigarettes, or cigarette equivalents, smoked is 1 per week), maximum tells you the highest (in this case, 375 per week), and range will tell you the distance between them.

♦ *Standard deviation and variance* are measures of how far all the cases in our sample vary on average from the mean (see chapter 4 for an explanation of these two statistics). We know from figure 7.5 that the mean number of cigarettes (or equivalent) smoked by smokers in the survey was 77 and we can see that the standard deviation was 60.5. This tells us that on average, smokers' weekly consumption was 60 cigarettes above or below the sample mean figure of 77.

♦ *S.E. mean* refers to a statistic called the Standard Error of the Mean, which we shall not be concerned about until we look at inferential statistics in chapter 9, although you can request it now, for we shall be using it then.

Distribution

The final set of statistics we can request tells us about the shape of the distribution of tobacco consumption in our sample.

What is a 'normal distribution'?

Sometimes the values of a variable cluster towards the lower or upper end of the distribution – income distributions in most societies, for example, are commonly clustered towards the lower end, for many people have lower-than-average incomes while only a few have very high ones. Such a distribution is said to be 'positively skewed', and it is represented graphically in figure 7.4c.

Sometimes, though, most cases will cluster around the middle of a distribution, and the number of observations falls away on either side of the mid-point, as in figure 7.4a. Where such a distribution forms a perfectly symmetrical graph, with each side of the mid-point a perfect mirror image of the other, it is called a *normal distribution*.

When data are normally distributed, the mid-point (the median) will coincide with both the mean and the mode. Furthermore, in a normal distribution we always find that one standard deviation either side of the mean encompasses 68% of all the cases, two either side take in 95%, and three either side cover 99%.

Some of the statistics we shall use later require that the phenomenon they are measuring should be (roughly) normally distributed. This is not as unusual in social science as might be imagined, for on many of the things about human populations that we might try to measure – intelligence, sociability, honesty, attractiveness – most of us are somewhere around the middle point and numbers trail off fairly evenly towards the extremes.

♦ *Skewness* tells us whether the data are 'skewed' towards one end or other of the distribution (i.e. if there is a long trail of cases of people with 'extreme' patterns of cigarette consumption), or whether the distribution is roughly symmetrical (i.e. most people's consumption is clustered around the mean). If the mean and median

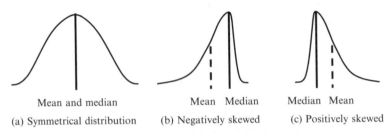

Figure 7.4   The mean and the median in normal and skewed distributions

are very different, this is a sign that the distribution is skewed. The skewness statistic will be close to zero if the distribution is symmetrical, but if there is a trail of extreme cases below the mean, it will be negative, and if there is a trail of extreme cases falling above the mean, it will be positive. In the Smoking Survey, the skew statistic (1.394) is positive, but not very large.

Suppressing the frequency table

When you have made all your selections, click on the 'Continue' button to return to the main 'Frequencies' dialog box.

We have selected a lot of summary statistics about people's cigarette consumption, but we do not particularly want to know the frequency counts for each value of this variable (how many people smoke 1 per week, how many smoke 2, and so on). To avoid getting a long and rather uninteresting frequency table, click on the 'Display frequency tables' check box to remove the tick (i.e. to disable the display command), and then click on 'OK'.

The results will appear in the Viewer window. Check them over, make sure everything seems to have run properly, and save the output if you want to use it later.

Frequencies and Descriptives

Summary statistics can also be achieved using the 'Descriptives' command (which, like 'Frequencies', is found under the 'Descriptive Statistics' item in the Analyze menu of the Data Editor window). You get exactly the same results and it is quicker, but you cannot request the mode or the median with 'Descriptives.'

REPRESENTING DATA VISUALLY USING CHARTS

So far the frequency counts have appeared in the form of tables, but sometimes such data are better presented visually:

Statistics

cigs + cigars*5 + grams*2

N	Valid	160
	Missing	174
Mean		77.2531
Std. Error of Mean		4.78699
Median		70.0000
Mode		100.00
Std. Deviation		60.55119
Variance		3666.447
Skewness		1.394
Std. Error of Skewness		.192
Minimum		1.00
maximum		375.00
Percentiles	25	30.0000
	50	70.0000
	75	100.0000

Figure 7.5 Summary statistics output from 'Frequencies' command examining weekly tobacco consumption (in 'cigarette equivalents'), suppressing the frequency table. 'Cigarette equivalents' calculated as the number of cigarettes smoked, plus (the number of cigars × 5) plus (grams of tobacco × 2)

♦ Data can sometimes be more clearly expressed visually than by tables of numbers, and reports can look more accessible (and professional) if they have charts and diagrams to break up the text.
♦ Charts can also help us explore our data before we move on to more complex procedures, and this can be important if the statistics we hope to use make certain assumptions about what the data look like.

Choosing a chart type

There are three main types of chart used to display a frequency distribution:

♦ *Bar charts*   These are used to display nominal data (or ordinal data if the number of categories is few). Along the horizontal axis lie the categories while the vertical axis measures the frequency or proportion of cases for each category.
♦ *Pie charts*   These display a frequency distribution as a 'pie' which is divided into 'slices'. Each segment of the pie represents the proportion of the total cases in each category. There should not be too many categories or it can become difficult to grasp what the chart is showing you.
♦ *Histograms*   These look a bit like bar charts but they are used to represent interval-level data. As with bar charts the vertical axis represents the frequency of each value, the horizontal axis represents the scale on which the variable is measured. The histogram facility in SPSS allows you to fit a normal distribution curve to the histogram so that you can check for normality and skew.

Creating a bar chart from the 'Frequencies' command

We start by creating a bar chart using the 'Charts' option within the 'Frequencies' command. We need a variable which has only a few values and which is measured at the nominal or ordinal level. When we coded the occupational data on the Smoking Survey, we created a new variable (var 00042) corresponding to the Registrar-General's measure of 'social class.' This variable has six values – classes I and II correspond to professional, managerial and administrative positions in the 'middle class', IIIN designates skilled white collar workers, IIIM is skilled manual workers, and classes IV and V refer to the semi- and unskilled 'working class'. These six social class categories are ranked ordinally (further details can be found in appendix B on our website).

To create a bar chart displaying the size of these six social classes in our sample, go into the 'Frequencies' dialog box (from the Analyze menu), select var00042 from the variables list, click on the 'Charts...' button to open the 'Frequencies: Charts' dialog box, and select the 'Bar charts' option from the list of chart types you are offered. The bar chart will appear in the right pane of the Viewer window.

Editing the bar chart

SPSS produces perfectly reasonable charts on its default settings but you may wish to customize the chart you produce. To do this, double-click on the chart in the right pane of the Viewer window and another window opens called the *Chart Editor*. The menu bar in this window has a number of options which allow you to modify various features of the chart. You can change the colour, the style (e.g. to create a three-dimensional effect), the size and font of the text and the labelling.

For example, to change the heading of your chart, double-click on the title in the Chart Editor and the 'Titles' dialog box opens. You can now delete the original title and type in the new one. Similarly, to edit the category axis title or value labels, double-click on one or the other to open the 'Category Axis' dialog box where you can make the amendments you want.

Figure 7.6 illustrates some of the modifications that can be made. We have changed the title and category labels, added frequency counts to each bar, and selected the 3-D option.

Creating a pie chart using the graphs menu

You created your bar chart by selecting 'Charts...' in the 'Frequencies' dialog box, but you may have noticed that there is a *Graphs* menu in the menu bar. You could have created your bar chart using this and without going through the Frequencies procedure.

The charts options under 'Frequencies' are very limited, offering just bar charts and histograms. To produce a pie chart, we must use the Graphs menu. Click on the Graphs menu and select 'Pie...'. A dialog box will open offering you three options:

1   'Summaries for groups of cases' will produce a chart in which each 'slice' represents one value of a single variable.

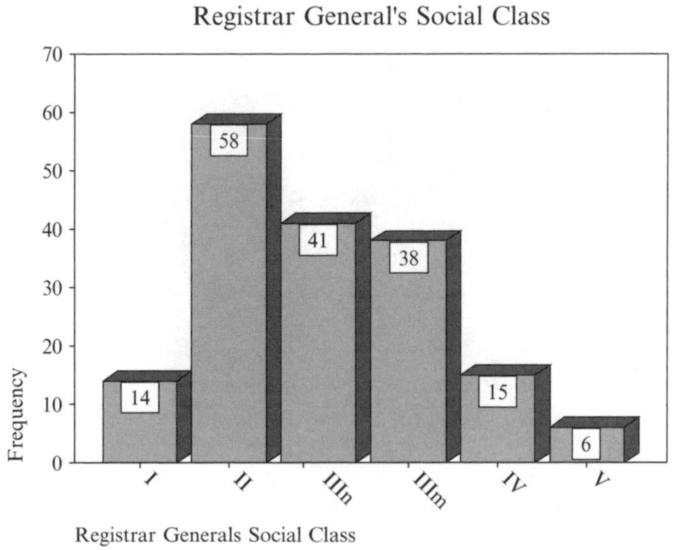

Registrar General's Social Class

Registrar Generals Social Class

Figure 7.6   A customized bar chart showing social class frequencies in the Smoking Survey sample

2   'Summaries of separate variables' will create a chart based on several variables in which each slice represents a different variable.
3   'Values of individual cases' will create a chart in which each slice represents a single case (i.e. a single respondent).

To produce a pie chart representing the six categories of the social class variable, we want the first of these options. Select it and click on 'Define' to open the 'Define Pie' dialog box. Decide on what you wish each slice to represent (the most likely choice will be number of cases or percentage of cases) by clicking on the relevant radio button. Select the variable you want from the variable list and transfer it to the 'Define slices by:' box, then click on 'OK'.

The pie chart appears in the Viewer window. This can then be modified in exactly the same way as you modified your bar chart, by clicking on the parts you want to edit. In Figure 7.7, missing cases have been omitted, the colours of the slices have been changed (to ensure clarity on a non-colour printer), and labels have been placed inside the slices.

Creating a histogram using the graphs menu

A histogram is used to summarize the distribution of interval data. It is particularly useful for examining the shape of a distribution (for example, seeing whether it is skewed). For our example, we can use our created variable, 'comsmoke', which measures people's smoking consumption in terms of cigarettes or 'cigarette equivalents' smoked in the last week.

We can create a histogram through the Graphs menu by selecting the 'Histogram . . .' option. Note that in the dialog box that opens there is an option to 'Display normal

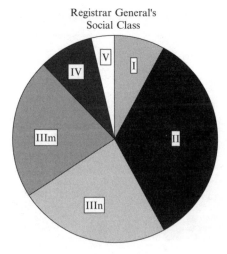

Figure 7.7 Example of a customized pie chart showing social class frequencies

curve'. Ticking this will generate a histogram with a superimposed normal curve in the Viewer window. Double-clicking on the chart will open the Chart Editor which allows you to edit the histogram in the same way that you edited the bar chart and the pie chart.

The distribution revealed by the histogram confirms the results obtained for this variable earlier in this chapter when we inspected the summary statistics. The superimposed normal curve shows that the distribution deviates markedly from normality (it is positively skewed due mainly to a long trail of relatively heavy smokers). But it also shows that the distribution has a number of peaks and troughs. It seems there are three fairly distinct groups among the smokers in our sample: a big majority who are relatively light smokers (0–100 cigarettes a week), a smaller band of heavier smokers (150–200 cigarettes a week) and finally, a small cluster of very heavy smokers (250 or more cigarettes per week).

Creating charts interactively

SPSS offers an alternative method of producing charts which allows you to customize them to a greater extent than we have been able to do so far. You can modify the style of a chart quite radically (e.g. by altering the shape of the bars) and you can produce complex graphs encompassing second and third variables. All of this is done within the Graphs menu by highlighting 'Interactive' before selecting the type of chart you want to create. We leave you to experiment with your own artistic creations – but don't let your ingenuity get in the way of producing clear and readily intelligible output.

CHECKING FOR PROBLEMS USING BOXPLOTS

Graphs and charts are not only used to make our results more attractive and accessible for the people who read them. Sometimes we produce visual output for our own

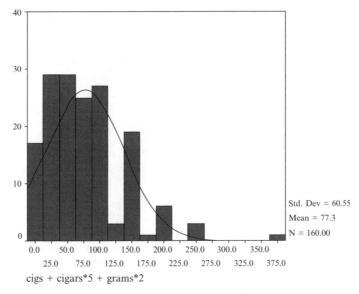

Figure 7.8   A histogram showing the distribution of cigarettes (or cigarette equivalents) smoked in the last week

purposes so that we can inspect our data in more detail and pick up any problems that may be hidden in all those numbers. Indeed, we have already begun to do this, for the histogram in figure 7.8 allowed us to check to see whether the distribution of weekly cigarette consumption approximates normality or is skewed.

Exploring data using boxplots

Boxplots are particularly helpful when we want to explore what our data look like. This procedure is used to explore distributions measured at an interval level or higher, for like the histogram or a simple line graph, it involves plotting data on an axis and therefore assumes equal intervals on the axis. The 'stress' variable on our Smoking Survey will provide a good illustration, for this is measured on a continuous numerical scale from 0 (indicating that somebody feels under no stress at all) to 10 (indicating extremely high stress).

We obtain the boxplot via the SPSS 'Explore' command which you will find under 'Descriptive Statistics' in the Analyze menu. Highlight the variable you want and transfer it to the 'Dependent list' box. SPSS gives us the option of displaying only the plots, only the statistics, or both, and we shall select 'Both'. Then click on the 'Plots . . .' button to open a second dialog box called 'Explore: Plots'.

By default, SPSS expects you to request both a boxplot and a stem-and-leaf plot (both items are already selected). Deselect the stem-and-leaf option by clicking on the radio button (a stem-and-leaf plot does much the same job as a boxplot, but we shall not discuss it here). You are also asked for details about the boxplot you want. The default setting is the one we want (i.e. 'Factor levels together'), for in this example there is only one factor ('stress') that we are exploring. Click on 'Continue' to go back to the original dialog box, and then on 'OK' to run the job.

The first part of the output (labelled 'Descriptives') contains summary descriptive statistics for the variable you selected including the mean, median, standard error, standard deviation, variance, minimum, maximum and range. These are followed by the boxplot. Any or all of this output can be saved as an SPSS output file, printed directly from the Viewer window, or copied into a word processing package such as Word.

What does the box designate?

At the centre of the boxplot is a shaded box. This represents half the cases in the sample – those between the 25th and 75th percentiles. The length of the box tells you how clustered or dispersed our observations are (the longer the box, the more dispersed the data).

The line through the box is the median value (in figure 7.9, the line is drawn at 5, which is the median level of reported stress). If it is closer to the bottom than the top, it indicates that your data are positively skewed, and vice versa if it is nearer the top than the bottom. In this example, the line is close to the middle which indicates that the skew is very small.

By looking at the scale down the left-hand side of the chart, you can see the values between which the middle half of your distribution of stress scores varies. In the example in Figure 7.9, half of all the cases cluster in a range between 3 and 7.

Extending vertically above and below the box are two lines (known as whiskers). The points at which these lines stop indicate the lowest and highest values which are not 'outliers' in the distribution.

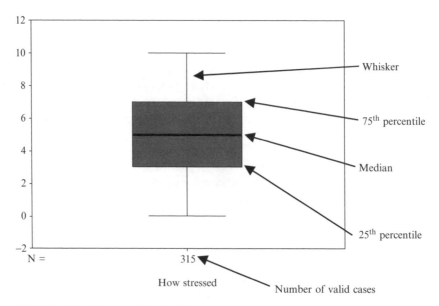

Figure 7.9   Boxplot of reported levels of stress

Boxplots and outliers

Boxplots are particularly useful for inspecting outlying cases. Outliers are defined as all those cases with a value more than 1.5 box-lengths greater than the 75th percentile or less than the 25th percentile. If you have any, they will be identified by an O. Extreme outliers (more than 3 box-lengths away from the 25th and 75th percentiles) are marked by *. The case numbers of outliers are identified on the plot, but these can be difficult to decipher where several are clustered together.

Figure 7.10 is a boxplot of weekly cigarette, cigar and tobacco consumption of smokers in our sample. It tells us that the most extreme outlier is case number 71, which lies more than 3 box-lengths away from the 75th percentile. Knowing the case number is helpful should we decide to pull out the extreme cases for a separate analysis.

Sometimes, extreme outliers turn out to be the result of errors in recording respondents' answers, in which case this can be rectified by looking back at the original questionnaire. When outliers turn out to be genuine, we might decide to set them aside to analyse separately. In the Smoking Survey, for example, we might remove the outliers shown in figure 7.10 who are smoking more than 200 cigarettes per week, for these are so far out of line with the rest of the sample that they probably deserve to be looked at separately. We can then focus on the great majority of the sample who are not 'peculiar', for we are mainly interested in generalizing about patterns rather than explaining a few exceptional cases. Taking the extreme outliers out for separate analysis also has the advantage of reducing the skew in the distribution, making it more 'normal'.

In addition to the obvious fact that it has several outliers, this boxplot looks quite different from the one in figure 7.9 because of the skew. The line through the box,

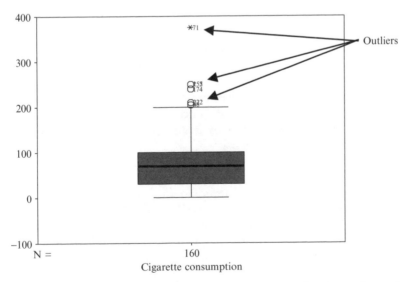

Figure 7.10   Boxplot of cigarette, cigar and tobacco consumption showing outliers and extreme outliers

indicating the median value, is closer to the bottom than the top and this indicates that the data are positively skewed. This is confirmed by the long whisker extending above the box which shows how far the values of the cases above the 75th percentile extend.

Multiple boxplots

A further feature of the 'Explore' procedure is that it allows you to create multiple boxplots which divide a single interval or ratio variable into the various categories of a nominal or ordinal variable. This means you can inspect the distribution of the first variable broken down by the categories of the second.

Suppose, for example, that we want to check whether the consumption of tobacco by smokers varies between different age groups. We might have a hunch, for example, that the younger age groups contain the most extreme smoking behaviour (both very heavy smoking and very light smoking), and that the skew in our variable 'comsmoke' might therefore be caused almost entirely by the younger smokers in the sample. We could check this out by requesting multiple boxplots.

If you are working with the **cleandat.sav** data set, use multiple boxplots to see if this hunch has any validity. In the 'Explore' dialog box, paste your interval variable ('comsmoke') into the 'Dependent list' box and your categorical variable ('var00034' – age groups) into the 'Factor list' box. From the output, you will see that there are three extremely heavy smokers in the youngest age group – take them out, and the distribution of tobacco consumption among the under-thirties looks roughly normal. In the middle-aged groups, however, there is a pronounced skew towards heavier levels of consumption.

WHEN THINGS ARE NOT NORMAL

Having investigated your data, you may well find that the values of a given variable are not normally distributed. This is not a problem unless you intend to use a statistical test that assumes that data *are* normally distributed. We shall see in subsequent chapters that many of the tests used in data analysis *do* make this assumption so what then should you do? You have three options:

♦ *Use your discretion*   Data are rarely distributed perfectly normally, but most tests will work provided there is an approximation to normality and you have a reasonably large sample. However, figures 7.8 and 7.10 show that the distribution of cigarette consumption is clearly a long way from normal, so we shall certainly violate the conditions laid down in many of the statistical procedures we shall be using in the next three chapters if we simply pretend that it is normally distributed.

♦ *Find another statistic which does not demand normality*   Not all statistical tests and measures make assumptions about the distribution of cases. Those that do not are known as *non-parametric* statistics (because they assume nothing about the parameters of the population from which the sample has been drawn), and you may be able to use these instead. However, many of the statistics you are likely to want to use are *parametric* and assume a normal distribution, so sometimes you have no choice but to try to make your distribution more closely approximate normality.

◆ *Manipulate the variable*   If you wish to use parametric statistics on a variable that is badly skewed it may be possible to transform it in order to make it more normal.

Manipulating data to make distributions more normal

One way of getting a normal distribution out of non-normally distributed data may be to *split* the cases. If the distribution of cases on a variable is bimodal, for example, you could divide them into two and analyse each cluster separately. Similarly, if you have a trail of outliers skewing the distribution, you can take out the extreme cases and treat them separately, leaving the remainder as normally distributed.

Another way to get around the problem of non-normal distributions is to *transform* the data to make the distribution more normal. This is not as devious as it sounds! You do not distort your data; you simply transform them by applying the same mathematical procedure to every case in the data set. The procedures that are most frequently used include squaring, cubing, logging and taking the square root.

Let us consider both of these strategies in turn.

> If at this stage you want to try transforming any of your variables to make them more normal, you will first need to read through the appendix to this chapter to learn how to use the 'Recode' and 'Compute' commands. Alternatively, just follow the logic of what we are doing now, and read the appendix later to find out the technical details of how it is done.

Splitting cases

Our analysis of the distribution of cigarette consumption showed that the distribution is badly skewed because there are 'too few' respondents who smoke under 20 cigarettes a week and 'too many' respondents who smoke in excess of 200 cigarettes a week (figures 7.8 and 7.10).

We could decide to analyse people who smoke fewer than 20 cigarettes a week separately from those who smoke more, for the former are probably irregular or casual smokers (e.g. they only smoke at parties, or when friends offer them a cigarette), while the latter look like regular smokers. Similarly, those who smoke more than 200 cigarettes a week are, statistically, extreme cases (i.e. outliers) and probably warrant separate analysis.

As figure 7.11 demonstrates (compare with Figure 7.8), when we remove the casual smokers and the extremely heavy smokers, the distribution of tobacco consumption among smokers begins to look more 'normal' (this trimmed variable is named 'consmcut' in the cleandat.sav data file).

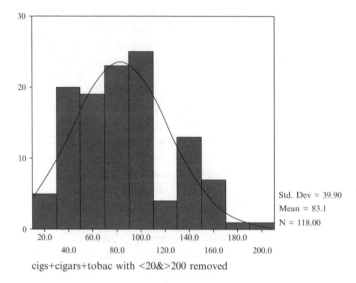

Std. Dev = 39.90
Mean = 83.1
N = 118.00

cigs+cigars+tobac with <20&>200 removed

Figure 7.11   A histogram showing the distribution of cigarettes (or cigarette equivalents) smoked in the last week, having removed those smoking under 20 or over 200 a week

Making data more normal using mathematical powers

Sometimes removing cases is not a realistic option. Where a large number of cases deviate from the expected normal distribution, you could end up having to remove the majority of the cases just to get a normal distribution! Mathematical transformations using powers such as cubing, squaring, square rooting and logging can sometimes overcome this problem by 'stretching' or 'shrinking' the scale.

♦   If the data are negatively skewed with a trail of cases below the mean, cubing or squaring the data will 'stretch' the scale and push the higher values further out.
♦   If the distribution reveals a number of cases trailing off towards the higher values, taking the square root, cube root or the natural log will 'shrink' the scale and will 'reel in' the trailing cases and outliers.

Squares, cubes and logs

The *square* of a number is the number multiplied by itself (for example $10^2 = 10 * 10 = 100$). The *square root* is its opposite (e.g. $\sqrt{100} = 10$).

The *cube* of a number is the number multiplied by itself twice (for example $10^3 = 10 * 10 = 100 * 10 = 1000$)

The *log* of a number is its index when the number is expressed to a base of 10 (e.g. the log of $10 = 1$ because $10^1 = 10$; similarly, the log of $100 = 2$ because $10^2 = 100$).

You might wonder whether it is legitimate to mess around with data in this way, but there is no need to worry. Although the *absolute distance* between the values is changed when we cube a set of numbers or log them, the *scaled distance* between them remains exactly the same, and the variables can be restored to their 'pre-transformed' state by using the opposite mathematical power (for example, if you have logged the values of a variable, you can use the antilog to restore the values, just as squaring can restore values that have been transformed with the square root).

Four mathematical transformations are commonly used to transform data:

♦ *Squaring* and *cubing* data reduces the skew when there is a straggle of low numbers trailing away to the left (squaring has a less powerful effect than cubing).
♦ Taking the *square root* or the *log* reduces the skew when a variable has a number of high values stretching a long way from the mean (logging is more powerful and is used when data are very badly skewed).

CONCLUSION

In this chapter, we have been working with single variables. We described and sum- marized the distribution of cases on single variables ('univariate analysis'), and we explored and modified variables to make them more suitable for later analysis ('ex- ploratory analysis').

All of this has involved the use of some simple descriptive statistics which are the bread-and-butter of data analysis – raw frequency counts, percentiles, measures of central tendency and measures of dispersion. We have not yet begun to test our theories by looking at how variables may be associated with each other – we turn to this next – but simple description of patterns in the data (How many people smoke? How many people express this or that opinion?) lies at the core of much social research.

It is also important to inspect your variables so that you can correct errors (by 'cleaning' the data), and get variables into a more usable form (by 'transforming' them), and in the appendix to this chapter we explain exactly how cleaning and transformation is done using SPSS.

CLEANING AND TRANSFORMING DATA IN SPSS

We begin this appendix by looking at how to check data for errors and what to do when we find them. If you are working from the Smoking Survey data set, you will need to have the dirtydat.sav file open.

Documenting changes to the data

Cleaning and transforming the data will obviously affect the raw data that you have entered. However, it is an important principle in survey research that you *never* change the raw data file without fully documenting all the changes you have made and why you made them. This is because if anyone wants to replicate your results they will be able to do so and you won't therefore run the risk of being accused of fiddling the data! It is also a good idea to keep a copy of the original uncleaned data set and save later versions, where the data has been cleaned or transformed, to a different file name.

CLEANING DATA

Coding errors can seriously affect your results. For example, instead of entering '150' for cigarettes smoked per week, '1500' was entered for one of the cases on the Smoking Survey: left uncorrected, this would distort the mean, standard deviation and skew of our estimates of tobacco consumption for the whole sample. Data that have been entered incorrectly can usually be spotted quite easily because they tend to show up as extreme values.

Twyman's Law

'The more unusual or interesting the data, the more likely it is to have been the result of error of one kind or another.'

Catherine Marsh, *Exploring Data* (Cambridge: Polity, 1988), p. 35

Screening categorical data for errors

When dealing with variables measured at the nominal level and ordinal level, frequency counts will often show up errors. Earlier in the chapter, for example, the table in figure 7.2 showed that two cases had been coded '2' for 'gender' (yet we know that the only valid responses are '0' for female and '1' for male), and that one case was coded as missing (yet we know that every respondent's gender was recorded). To correct these errors we need to find where they are in the data set. With dirtydat.sav open, bring up the Data Editor window, locate the column containing the data for the variable 'var00002' (gender), and search the column for the cases where either a '2' or a blank is recorded.

At respondent number 128 you will find that a '2' has been entered. Returning to the original questionnaires, we checked this and found that respondent number 128 is male, so highlight this cell, type in the correct code in the cell editor, and press the 'Enter' key.

The other two errors can be located and corrected in the same way (you will find that they occur at respondent number 224, where there is a value '2', and at respondent number 269, where there is a blank; in both cases, the questionnaires reveal that these respondents were males). Remember to resave the corrected data file when you have finished cleaning the data. It is sensible to resave it as a different version rather than overwriting the existing version.

Screening continuous interval/ratio data for errors

One way of correcting errors in continuous and interval level variables is to examine the summary statistics. A minimum that looks implausibly low or a maximum that appears implausibly high may well be a coding error. In the Smoking Survey, for example, question 5 asked smokers how often they had tried to stop. If you request summary statistics on this variable, you will see that the minimum is zero and the maximum is 144. However, a value of zero is logically impossible (since only those smokers who had tried to stop should have answered this question), and a maximum of 144 seems implausibly high.

Another way of identifying problems like these is to use boxplots to identify suspicious outliers. Indeed, this is a preferable method for it identifies the case numbers, which saves you having to locate them by searching through the data file.

Dealing with untraceable errors

In some instances you may not be able to check back to the original questionnaire to find the correct value to be entered in place of an erroneous code. In such instances, if you are sure the value entered is in error, it should be recoded as missing. To do this, delete the erroneous value to leave a blank which SPSS reads as 'system-missing'. Treating error values as missing is, however, only a last resort; you should first make every effort to trace what the correct value should be.

Sources of error

The dirtydat.sav file appears exactly as it was created when our students first entered the data from their interviews. Some students may have been careless; one or two were perhaps confused about what they were supposed to be doing. The result was a very 'dirty' data file. There are three common sources of coding error, and this file contains examples of all three.

1   Skipping a column

Look at case number 62. Checking the questionnaire for this respondent, we found this was a student with no occupation. For those with no occupation, var00031 (full-time or part-time) should have been left blank (signifying 'system-missing'), but in this case a code of '5' has been entered. It is clear that this code '5' should actually have been entered at var00032 (where 'student' is coded 5), and the code of 98 at var00032 should really appear under var00033. One simple mistake (failing to leave var00031 blank) has thus led to a whole sequence of errors, right the way through to the end of the row. These can now be corrected.

2   Hitting the wrong key(s)

Look at case number 147. The code entered for var00003 is '11', but the only legitimate codes are 0 or 1. Checking back to the questionnaire confirms the suspicion that the key was hit twice, and what should have been a '1' ('yes') became '11' (an impossible code).

3   Confusion over coding procedures

We saw in chapter 5 that data may be 'missing' for various reasons. One is that the question was not relevant to a particular respondent and was therefore not asked – in which case, our coding instructions were that the relevant cell on the spreadsheet should simply be left blank. An example comes early in the questionnaire, for the very first question asks whether people have had a smoke in the last week, and if they have not, then interviewers skip to question 3. For non-smokers, therefore, variable numbers 00004 to 00006 should be blank.

Some coders, however, got this instruction wrong and entered zeros on each of these items for non-smokers. This needs rectifying, for zero values will be read by SPSS as valid answers.

> Working with the **dirtydat.sav** file, see if you can locate some more of the data entry errors that have occurred. There are quite a few to find! Check variables measured at both categorical/ordinal and interval/ratio levels. By comparing the **dirtydat.sav** and **cleandat.sav** files, you can see whether and how the errors you find were detected and corrected in the final version of the data set.

TRANSFORMING DATA

In the course of analysing your results, you often need to construct a new variable (called a *derived variable*) or to change the values of an existing variable. To get rid of outliers, for example, you may wish to split an existing variable into two or more new ones, and in attempting to make a non-normal distribution more normal you may want to transform an interval variable by taking the square root or the log of all the values. In both cases, you will find yourself involved in creating newly derived variables.

There are other reasons, too, for creating new versions of existing variables, or for developing new variables by combining some features of existing ones. For example:

- *Combining variables to make a new summary variable*   You may want to calculate a summary variable from a series of separate answers. In the Smoking Survey we asked eight different attitude questions with a view to developing a single measure of people's tolerance towards smoking, and to do this we will need to combine the answers to these eight different items into a single new variable.

- *Recoding the values of a variable.* You may want to crunch the values of a particular variable to make it more manageable. For example, we might want to define those smoking fewer than 5 cigarettes a day as 'light smokers' and those smoking 20 or more as 'heavy smokers' in order to compare the two extreme groups.

If you are creating a new variable by applying some sort of arithmetic or logical procedure to your data, then you will use the 'Compute' command. If you want to change the values of a particular variable, then you will use the 'Recode' command. Both commands are found in the *Transform* menu.

The 'Compute' procedure

In the Smoking Survey, the variable measuring the age at which sample members finished full-time education is positively skewed. To reduce the skew, we might decide to create a new variable with logged values. To do this:

- Click on 'Transform' on the menu bar in the Data Editor window and then on 'Compute...' in the drop-down menu. In the dialog box, define a name for the new variable you are about to create (you type this into the 'Target Variable' box), and if you want to label it, you can do so by clicking on the 'Type&Label...' button.

- You now have to define the function. In this example, we want logarithms, so scroll down the list of functions until you see 'LG10(numexpr)'. Highlight it and transfer it to the 'Numeric Expression' box.

- Next, you select the variable you will be transforming from the list of variables in the left box. In this example, highlight 'var00033' (labelled 'Age completed FT education') and transfer it to the 'Numeric Expression' box. Click 'OK'.

The 'Compute' procedure is also commonly used to derive a summary variable from the values of other variables. We used it, for example, to produce the new variable 'comsmoke' which combines three different variables measuring people's cigarette (var00004), cigar (var00005) and tobacco (var00006) consumption over the last week. To combine these three into a single measure, we had first to make them equivalent. At the moment, a value of '1' for tobacco consumption (var00006) means 1 gram whereas a value of '1' for the variables recording cigarette and cigar consumption (var00004 and var00005) refers to a single cigarette and cigar, respectively. But one gram of tobacco is not equivalent to one cigarette, nor is one cigarette equivalent to one cigar. It would therefore make no sense simply to add the values for each of the variables together to create a summary variable. When computing the derived variable, we need to *weight* the different forms of smoking consumption to make them equivalent before adding them together.

Using weights to create equivalence scales

Weighting people's cigarette, cigar and tobacco consumption so as to express each as an equivalent of the others is an example of creating what are called *equivalence scales*. Equivalence scales are commonly used in studies of household income, for a single person household with an income of £20,000 per annum is likely to be considerably better off than a household consisting of two adults and three teenagers living on £20,000. The two household incomes are therefore adjusted to take account of variations in size and composition. One commonly used scale gives a couple-based household an equivalence value of '1'. Single adults are then given an equivalence value of '0.61' while children, depending on their age, get a value of between '0.09' and '0.38' each. Applying these weights, the single person household then receives an equivalized income of £32,787 $(20,000 \div 0.61)$ while the incomes of each of the five people in the larger household are recorded as £9,345 $(20,000 \div [1 + 0.38 + 0.38 + 0.38])$. Although their actual household incomes are the same, the equivalized income of the family of five is therefore less than a third of that of the person living on their own.

Let us say that an average cigar consists of about 2.5 grams of tobacco while an average cigarette contains about half a gram of tobacco. This means smoking one cigar is the equivalent of consuming five cigarettes, and you would need to smoke two cigarettes to smoke the equivalent of one gram of loose tobacco. Our new summary variable 'comsmoke' can therefore be computed as follows (in SPSS, multiplication is designated by the symbol *):

$$\text{Comsmoke} = (\text{cigars} * 5) + (\text{tobacco} * 2) + \text{cigarettes}$$

So that, if somebody smoked 15 cigarettes, 4 cigars and 3 grams of loose tobacco a week, on our scale she or he would be coded as smoking the equivalent of $15 + (4 * 5) + (3 * 2) = 41$ cigarettes a week.

To compute this new variable, click on 'Transform' on the menu bar in the Data Editor window, and then on 'Compute ...'. Define a name for the new variable and type it into the 'Target Variable' box. Next:

◆   Click on the brackets (parentheses) button '()' in the calculator pad and they will appear in the 'Numeric Expression' box (we need brackets to ensure that this part of the expression is calculated first).

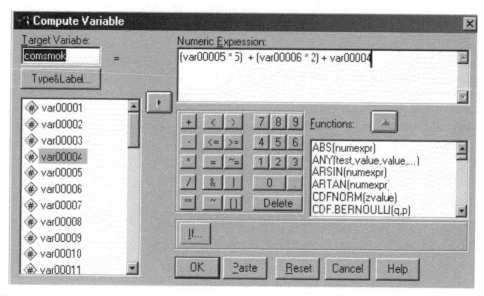

Figure 7.12   Computing a new variable using the 'Compute' command

♦   We want to multiply cigar consumption fivefold to get cigarette equivalents, so paste the 'cigar consumption' variable into the 'Numeric Expression' box inside the brackets, followed by the multiplication sign '∗' from the calculator pad, and then type in '5'. The first part of the expression should now look like this: (var00005 ∗ 5).

♦   To this equivalized cigar consumption we must add equivalized tobacco consumption. Ensuring that the cursor is placed after the last bracket, click on the addition sign '+' in the calculator pad and paste it into the 'Numeric Expression' box. You can now paste a second set of brackets, and inside them we paste the variable measuring tobacco consumption. Follow this with a multiplication sign and type '2' (because we want to weight this variable by 2).

♦   Finally, paste another addition sign after the brackets followed by the variable measuring cigarette consumption. Since we do not need to weight this variable there is no need to multiply it or place brackets around it. Your final expression now reads: (var00005 ∗ 5) + (var00006 ∗ 2) + var00004 and it should appear in the dialog box as in figure 7.12. Click on 'OK'.

Keep track of what you are doing!

When you start creating 'derived' variables, it is important that you make a note of how you did it so that other researchers can reproduce your results by following the same procedures. Keeping track of every change to the data file is a fundamental rule of data base management.

RECODING VARIABLES

When we explored our newly computed variable 'comsmoke' earlier in this chapter, we found the distribution of cases was not normal because there was a disproportionate number of light smokers as well as a few extremely heavy smokers (see figures 7.8 and 7.10). We suggested that we could make the distribution more normal by removing cases where cigarette (or cigarette equivalent) consumption is less than 20 a week or greater than 200 a week. We will now use the 'Recode' command to achieve precisely this.

There are two options when recoding a variable:

◆   you can reclassify the codes of an existing variable;
◆   you can change the codes and define the result as a new variable.

The first option is useful if you are 'tidying up' a variable (e.g. by recoding errors to 'missing'), for you will not want to keep the original version. Here, however, we shall use the second option because we want to retain the original variable with its original codes intact while *also* producing a different version of it under a new variable name.

To do this, we select 'recode' from the Transform menu and then the option 'Into Different Variables'. From the list of variables in the dialog box, select 'comsmoke' and transfer it into the 'Input Variable' list by clicking on the arrow. Next:

◆   Enter a new variable name into the 'Output Variable' box, and click on the 'Change' button (you can also define a new variable label at this stage if you wish).
◆   Define the values of the new variable by clicking on the 'Old and New Values...' button to open another dialog box. We want to recode the range from the lowest value through to 19 as 'missing', because we want those who smoke fewer than 20 cigarettes a week to be excluded, so click on the appropriate radio button on the left side of the dialog box and enter the value 19 in the box. Then select the new value that you want to put in place of these old values (in this case we want to code them as 'missing', so click on 'System-missing' and then on the 'Add' button).
◆   We also want to recode those smoking more than 200 cigarettes a week as 'missing', so repeat this procedure, this time defining the range as 201 'through highest'.
◆   Since we want all other values to remain the same in the new variable as they are in the old one, click on 'All other values' and then on 'Copy old value(s)'. When you are satisfied that everything is in order, click on 'Continue' to return to the original dialog box, then click on 'OK'.

Remember your recoded variables will need to be saved (by saving a new version of the data file) if you want to use them in later sessions.

Exercise: Creating a new summary attitude variable using 'Recode' and 'Compute'

In the Smoking Survey respondents were given eight attitude questions to measure their strength of feeling about smoking. Some were anti-smoking, others were supportive of it, but all eight statements were given the same codes (missing cases were left blank):

1 = Strongly agree
2 = Tend to agree
3 = Neither agree nor disagree
4 = Tend to disagree
5 = Strongly disagree

Given eight statements, each with a possible 'score' of between 1 and 5, we want to create a new variable which will have a range of scores between 8 (to indicate very strong antipathy to smoking) and 40 (to indicate very strong tolerance of it). However, not all of our statements run in the same direction – strong agreement on one may indicate support for smoking (e.g. var00026: 'There are already enough restrictions on where people can smoke'), while strong agreement on another may indicate opposition to it (e.g. var00021: 'Government isn't doing enough to discourage smoking'). We shall therefore have to recode some of them so that a code of 1 always indicates a positive response and a code of 5 always indicates a negative one. To do this, use the 'Recode' command.

Using the **dirtydat.sav** data file, try recoding the codes on the four pro-smoking items (var00020, var00023, var00024 and var00026) to make them consistent with the four anti-smoking ones (the other four attitude variables will therefore be left unchanged). You will need to give each a new name (when we did this, we called them var20rev, var23rev, var24 rev and var26rev, to indicate in each case that the system of coding had been *re*versed). Because you are inverting the numerical scale for these five selected variables, you will need to recode 1 as 5, 2 as 4, 4 as 2 and 5 as 1. Cases coded 3 (no opinion either way) will, of course, remain as 3, so when you enter 3 in the 'old value' box, you can simply click on 'Copy old value(s)' in the 'new value' box. The same is true for cases coded as missing.

When you have got the coding for all eight attitude items running in the same direction, you want to create a new summary variable which adds up people's scores across each of the eight items. To do this, use the 'Compute' command.

> Select 'Compute' from the Transform menu, define a name for the new variable, and then define the 'Numeric Expression' for this new variable (this is very simple, for the new variable is the sum of the scores recorded on the four recoded attitude variables plus the four non-recoded attitude variables). When you have finished, click on 'OK', and save the file so that your new variable will be available in future sessions.

When we completed this procedure, we saved the new summary variable under the name 'attit8', and this (as well as the individual recoded items) is included in the cleandat.sav data file.

Conditional transformations using the 'If' command

You can do a lot more than we have done with both the 'Recode' and 'Compute' procedures. One of the most useful ways of using these commands is in conjunction with the 'If' command, for this enables us to create conditional expressions. The 'If' command can be selected in either the 'Recode' or 'Compute' dialog boxes.

Let us compute a new variable which specifies whether or not a respondent has ever smoked (we shall need to use this in chapter 8). In the Smoking Survey, we know:

♦ whether respondents smoked in the last week (var00003);
♦ whether those who have not smoked in the last week ever smoke nowadays (var00007); and
♦ whether those who have neither smoked in the last week, nor who ever smoke nowadays, were ever regular smokers (var00008).

From these three pieces of information, we can determine whether a respondent ever smoked. Logically this can be written as a series of conditional statements:

♦ If answer to var00003 is 'yes' then respondent must have smoked.
♦ If answer to var00007 is 'yes' then respondent must have smoked.
♦ If answer to var00008 is 'yes' then respondent must have smoked.

All other respondents must never have smoked. These logical statements can be achieved within the SPSS 'Compute' and 'Recode' procedures as follows:

♦ Open the 'Compute' dialog box through the Transform menu. In the 'Target Variable' box type in the name of the new variable you want to compute. In this case, we have called the new variable 'eversmok'.
♦ By default, we will set 'eversmok' to '0', which we can later code to 'non-smoker'. Do this by typing '0' in the 'Numeric Expression' box. Click 'OK'.

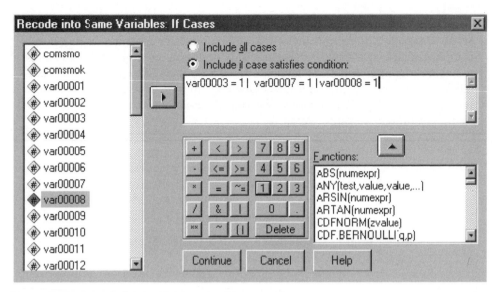

Figure 7.13 Recoding a variable using the 'If' command

♦ We now need to specify smokers using the conditional statements. To do this, click on 'Recode' and then 'Into Same Variables' from the Transform menu bar. Select the variable you have just created ('eversmok') and move it across to the 'Numeric Variables' box.

♦ Click on 'If...' at the bottom of the dialog box and another dialog box will open (figure 7.13). Highlight 'var00003' and move it across to the right-hand part of the dialog box by clicking on the arrow. Now click on the '=' sign and then type in '1'. Then click on '|' in the dialog keypad. This sign means 'or'.

♦ Next, highlight 'var00007' and move this across to the right-hand side of the dialog box. Click on the '=' sign, type in '1' and, once again follow this with the '|' sign. Highlight 'var00008', move it across to the right-hand side of the dialog box. Click on 'Continue' and you will be returned to the original dialog box.

♦ We must tell SPSS that 'eversmok' should equal '1' when the condition is satisfied. Do this by clicking on 'Old and New Value'. A new dialog box will open. Under 'Value', in the 'Old Value' section of the dialog box, type in '0'. Under 'Value' in the 'New Value' section of the dialog box type in '1'. Then click on 'Add' and, finally, 'Continue' to return to the original dialog box. What we have done here is told SPSS that when the condition is satisfied (i.e. when var00003, var00007 or var00008 equal 1) all the cases where 'eversmok' equals '0' must be recoded to '1'.

♦ Click on 'OK' to run the procedure. The variable 'eversmok' will now equal '0' if the respondent has never smoked and '1' if the respondent has smoked. You should label these values as was shown in chapter 6 through the Variable View pane of the Data Editor window.

When you have a large number of transformations to run or a complex transformation that you want to do, you are likely to find that entering the commands
in Syntax (the SPSS command 'language') through the Syntax Editor window is
quicker and easier than using the drop-down menus. However, learning the
language takes time. If you wish to find out about Syntax you will find a guide
to using it on our website (section 7).

ANALYSING THE STRENGTH OF ASSOCIATION BETWEEN VARIABLES

AIM

This chapter reviews some of the statistics and procedures used to assess the strength of relationships between variables measured at nominal, ordinal and interval/ratio levels. By the end of the chapter you will be familiar with:

- Creating and interpreting two-way contingency tables, using the SPSS 'Cross-tabs' command
- Measuring the strength of an association between categorical variables using the Chi Square statistic to derive the value of *phi* and Cramer's *V*
- Assessing the strength of association between two categorical variables using asymmetric tests such as tau
- Controlling for third variables to check for spurious association and to uncover hidden associations between variables
- Assessing the strength of association between variables measured at ordinal level using Spearman's *rho*
- Assessing the strength and pattern of association between interval-level variables by visual inspection of scatterplots and by using Pearson's correlation coefficient, *r*

INTRODUCTION

So far we have been dealing with variables one at a time. Now the time has come to look at the relationships between them so that we can start to test some of our hypotheses.

We use different procedures and statistics to analyse variables expressed at different levels of measurement. When we are dealing with interval or ratio level variables we can use much more powerful statistics than we can with nominal or ordinal level variables. For the latter, our basic tool is the *contingency table* created through a process called *crosstabulation*, and it is with this that we begin.

ANALYSIS OF ASSOCIATIONS BETWEEN CATEGORICAL VARIABLES

In social survey research, many of the variables we analyse are measured at the nominal or ordinal levels. This is because many important concepts in the social sciences draw distinctions between different categories of people (e.g. gender categories, social class categories, marital status categories, and so on). Cross-tabulation is the principal tool for analysing relationships between variables measured at these lower levels, and in SPSS, it is accessed through the 'Crosstabs' command.

'Crosstabs' creates contingency tables. A contingency table is one which cross-classifies the different values of an independent variable with those of a dependent variable. The simplest contingency table is one which cross-tabulates two dichotomous variables (sometimes referred to as a '2 × 2' table), for this consists of just four cells.

A contingency table presents the results of a two-way frequency count by showing the numbers (and often the percentages) for all possible combinations of responses in a single table. Conventionally, the values of the dependent variable form the rows in such a table, and the values of the independent variable form the columns, although these can be switched (e.g. to fit a table on to a page). Figure 8.1 gives a schematic example of a simple 2 × 2 contingency table with gender as the independent variable and whether or not people smoke as dependent.

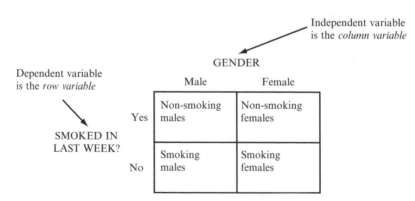

Figure 8.1   Schematic representation of a 2 x 2 contingency table

Using the 'Crosstabs' procedure to test hypothesis 2 (Peer group socialization)

If you are working with the **cleandat.sav** data set from the Smoking Survey, replicate the following procedures as we go through them. If you are working with your own data set, select two categorical variables that your theory leads you to believe should be causally related, and then replicate these procedures on your own data.

In the appendix to chapter 1, we identified a set of hypotheses which we wanted to test. One of these, hypothesis 2, suggested that people's peer groups are a major influence on their smoking behaviour:

The more friends they have who smoke, the more likely it is that people will themselves smoke.

In this hypothesis, 'smoking behaviour' is the *dependent variable* (it is causally dependent on 'peer group smoking') and 'peer group smoking behaviour' is the *independent variable* (it causes the change in the dependent variable and is not itself influenced by the other variable).

The variable that measures peer group smoking behaviour is var00016 (the proportion of family and friends that smoke). For our dependent variable we shall use var00003 (whether or not any cigarette, cigar or pipe tobacco had been smoked in the last 7 days). Both of these variables are categorical. The dependent variable has just two response categories ('yes' or 'no') which are not ranked against each other, so this is a dichotomous nominal level variable. The independent variable has four response categories ('all or most', 'about half', 'a few' and 'almost none or none') which are in rank order, making it an ordinal level variable.

Putting these two variables together will generate an eight-cell contingency table consisting of two rows (corresponding to the two values of the dependent variable) and four columns (for the four values of the independent variable).

Running 'Crosstabs'

To run the 'Crosstabs' procedure:

♦ Click on 'Analyze' in the menu bar, highlight 'Descriptive Statistics' and then 'Crosstabs...'.
♦ The dialog box that opens lists all the variables in the data set in the left window (see figure 8.2). Paste the dependent variable (var00003) into the box headed 'Row(s)' and the independent variable (var00016) into the box headed 'Column(s)'.
♦ By default the 'Crosstabs' procedure displays frequencies, but to request percentages as well, click on 'Cells...' and in the dialog box that opens select the tick box

Transfer variable from the variable list
to the 'Row(s)' box by clicking here

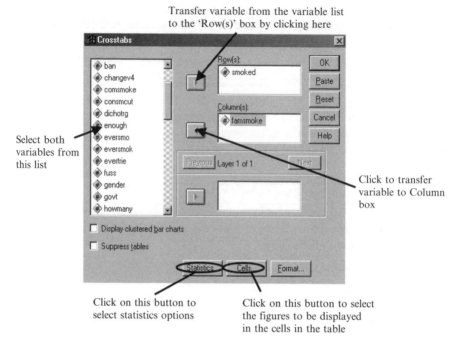

Select both
variables from
this list

Click to transfer
variable to Column
box

Click on this button to
select statistics options

Click on this button to select
the figures to be displayed
in the cells in the table

Figure 8.2   The 'Crosstabs' dialog box

next to 'Column' under 'Percentages'. Click on 'Continue' to return to the original
dialog box then click on 'OK' (we shall ignore the 'Statistics' button for now).

The output that will appear in the Viewer window should look something like that in
Figure 8.3.

Conventions when displaying 'Crosstabs'

By convention, you should ensure that your output follows these rules so that
others can interpret your work easily:

- The independent variable is arranged across the top of the table, unless lack of
  space due to the number of categories makes this impossible.
- Percentages are computed within the categories of the independent variable
  (see Figure 8.3). In other words, the percentages always sum to 100 per cent
  when you add together the column percentages.
- The number of cases on which the percentages are based always accompanies
  the total percentage for each category of the independent variable.
- Always keep the table as simple as possible and avoid cluttering a table with
  unnecessary information such as percentages by rows *and* columns.

Case Processing Summary

	Cases					
	Valid		Missing		Total	
	N	Percent	N	Percent	N	Percent
Smoked in last week? * Family/friends smoke?	327	97.9%	7	2.1%	334	100.0%

Cell frequency

Column per cent

Row marginal

Dependent variable

Independent variable

Smoked in last week? * Family/friends smoke? Crosstabulation

			Family/friends smoke?				
			All or most	about half	a few	almost none or none	Total
Smoked in last week?	no	Count	14	23	66	66	169
		% within Family/friends smoke?	20.0%	29.5%	65.3%	84.6%	51.7%
	yes	Count	56	55	35	12	158
		% within Family/friends smoke?	80.0%	70.5%	34.7%	15.4%	48.3%
Total		Count	70	78	101	78	327
		% within Family/friends smoke?	100.0%	100.0%	100.0%	100.0%	100.0%

Column marginal

Figure 8.3   Example of two-way frequency distribution generated using the 'Crosstabs' procedure

Understanding the layout of a contingency table

The output consists of two tables. The first summarizes the output, telling us how many valid and missing cases there are. We can see that 7 cases are missing (these will be people for whom we lack information on *one or both* of the two variables in the analysis), leaving us with 327 valid cases.

The second table is the cross-tabulation of the two variables. Each cell of the table contains two sets of numbers:

◆ The *frequency counts* are the first figure in each cell. For example, in the cell located in row 1, column 1 in figure 8.3 the number 14 tells us there were 14 non-smokers whose friends and family were mostly smokers. In the cell located in row 2, column 1 we see that there were 56 smokers whose friends and family were mostly smokers; and so on.

◆ The second figures are the *column percentages* and these are read down the table. We see, for example, that 80 per cent of those who reported that most or all of their friends and family smoked also smoked themselves (row 2, column 1), but this was true of just 20 per cent of non-smokers (row 1, column 1).

The row totals and column totals represent the frequency counts and percentages for each of the two variables. The sums of frequencies for each row and column appear in the totals and are known as *marginals* (or *marginal frequencies*):

♦ The *row marginals* sum the frequencies for each category of the dependent variable. They tell us that a total of 169 respondents (51.7 per cent) do not smoke and 158 (48.3 per cent) do.
♦ The *column marginals* give the frequency count for each category of the independent variable (70 people said all or most of their friends smoke, 78 said about half did, and so on).

The bottom right-hand corner of the table gives the *total number* of cases (327).

Interpreting the results of the cross-tabulation

Do the results summarized in the table in figure 8.3 offer support to our hypothesis that smoking behaviour is associated with peer group influences?

The cell percentages tell us quite a lot. We can see from the column percentages, for example, that 80 per cent of those with a lot of friends who smoked also smoked themselves, yet only 15 per cent of those with few or no smokers among their friends were themselves smokers. This looks like quite a striking difference.

There is therefore a clear association in this sample between these two variables, and this might help explain why smokers often find it so difficult to give up the habit. If smokers move mainly in smoking circles, those who want to quit will find their resolution sorely tested simply by virtue of the fact that so many of their friends and family smoke.

These initial results offer quite strong support for our hypothesis about peer group socialization, but two crucial riders need to be entered at this point.

♦ First, these results do not prove the hypothesis is correct, for as we saw in chapter 1, theories can never conclusively be shown to be true.
♦ Secondly, the fact that we have found an association between these two variables does not mean we have demonstrated the causal link suggested by our hypothesis. It may be that peer group pressure influences people to smoke, but it could also be that smokers choose to spend time with others who share their habit.

Our results thus still leave questions to be answered. All we can say at this stage is that we have found the association that we predicted between smoking and peer group behaviour, and that it appears to be quite strong.

Measuring the strength of association between categorical variables: the *phi* coefficient and Cramer's *V*

To say that the association we have found 'appears quite strong' is rather vague. Clearly it is useful to have a way of measuring the strength of association between variables.

Table 8.1   A 2 × 2 cross-tabulation of respondents' smoking behaviour by friends and family smoking behaviour

		Proportion of friends and family who smoke:		
		Many	Few	Total
	No	a	b	
Respondents		37	132	169
smoked	**Yes**	c	d	
in last		111	47	158
week:	**Total**	148	179	327

The simplest measures of strength of association between nominal variables are the *phi coefficient* (used for 2 × 2 tables) and *Cramer's V* (used for tables with more than four cells). They produce a coefficient of between −1.0 and +1.0 where 0 indicates a complete absence of association and +1 or −1 indicate a perfect association.

To keep things simple, let us work with a 2 × 2 table by recoding var00016 (the proportion of friends or family who smoke) to crunch the four categories of answers into two. We can combine 'all or most' with 'about half', and 'a few' with 'almost none' to give us a simplified, dichotomous variable. Running this against var00003 will now generate a 2 × 2 table (table 8.1) for which we can calculate the value of *phi* (whose symbol is Φ).

Look first at the so-called 'diagonals' in table 8.1 (i.e. compare cells 'a' and 'd' and cells 'b' and 'c'). The highest frequencies cluster on one diagonal (b–c) and the lowest on the other (a–d). This is because most of those who do not smoke have mainly non-smoking friends and family, and most of those who do smoke have mainly smoking friends and family. It is clear from this pattern on the diagonals that there is an association between the variables. Both the *phi* and Cramer's V coefficients measure the strength of this association by assessing the degree to which cases are concentrated on the diagonals.

Calculating the value of Chi Square

To calculate the value of *phi* we need first to work out a statistic called *Chi Square* (pronounced Kai-square, and written as χ^2). Chi Square summarizes the extent to which the frequency counts in each cell of a contingency table diverge from what we would *expect* to find in each cell of the table if the two variables were *not* associated. To work this out, the first step is to calculate these 'expected frequencies' so that we can compare them with those we have actually found (the 'observed frequencies'). The bigger the difference, the stronger will be the association between the variables and the bigger will be the value of Chi Square.

SPSS will calculate expected cell frequencies for you (it is one of the options you can select when you click on the 'Cells...' button in the 'Crosstabs' dialog box – figure 8.2), but we can easily work it out for ourselves, for in any cell the expected frequency will depend on the row and column marginals. In cell 'a' in table 8.2, for example, we can calculate the expected frequency once we know that there are 169 non-smokers (the row total), 148 people with many friends who smoke (the column total), and 327 valid cases in the sample (the overall total). The way we do it is expressed in the formula;

$$\text{Expected frequency}(e) = \frac{(\text{row total} * \text{column total})}{\text{Total observations}}$$

Thus, the expected frequency in cell 'a' $(e_a) = (169*148)/327 = 76.5$. Comparing this with the observed frequency in cell 'a' (o_a) of 37, we can see that our result is 39.5 less than we would expect to get given no association between these two variables.

The third column in table 8.2 gives the expected frequencies for all four cells in our contingency table, and the fourth column calculates how much each one differs from the observed frequencies. It can be seen from column 4 that when we calculate the difference between the observed and expected frequencies for each cell in the table, some of the differences we get are positive and some are negative, which means we cannot simply add them together to get an overall figure. We have encountered this sort of problem before when we calculated the standard deviation back in chapter 4. On that occasion, we squared all the values to make them all positive, and we shall adopt the same solution here. The results are given in the fifth column of table 8.2.

The final column of the table divides these squared differences by the value of the expected frequency in each cell to express it as a proportion. For cell 'a', for example, we divide 1560.3 (the squared difference between the observed and expected frequencies) by 76.5 (the expected frequency) to get 20.4. If we do the same thing for the other three cells, and then add the results together, we end up with a single summary statistic which expresses the extent to which all the observed frequencies in the table differ from what we would expect if there were no association between the two variables. In table 8.2 we see that this summed statistic works out at 77.1. This statistic is Chi Square (χ^2).

Using Chi Square to calculate phi

Chi Square is one of the most common statistics used in the analysis of social science data, for it summarizes the statistical association between two categorical variables. We shall encounter it again in chapter 9, when we shall use it to calculate a test of statistical

Table 8.2   Comparing expected (e) and observed (o) frequencies to calculate the value of Chi Square

Cell	Observed frequency	Expected frequency	$(o - e)$	$(o - e)^2$	$(o - e)^2 \div e$
a	37	76.5	−39.5	1560.3	20.4
b	132	92.5	39.5	1560.3	16.9
c	111	71.5	39.5	1560.3	21.8
d	47	86.5	−39.5	1560.3	18.0
					$\chi^2 = 77.1$

significance, but here we want to use it to gauge the strength of association between two variables.

As it stands, a Chi Square value of 77.1 does not tell us very much. We want to translate it into a readily understandable number that will express strength of association on a standard scale. To do this, we first need to take account of the number of cases in our sample (other things being equal, the more cases you have, the larger will be the value of Chi Square, so we need to control for this). We do this by dividing the value of Chi Square by the total number of cases (77.1 ÷ 327). We then need to take the square root so as to undo the effect of having squared all the (observed − expected) cell counts earlier. The result is the *phi* coefficient, which is always a figure between 0 (indicating no association between the variables) and 1 (indicating a perfect association − meaning in our example that if you know if somebody's friends smoke, you can make a 100 per cent accurate prediction of whether they do too). In this example, therefore:

$$\text{phi}(\Phi) = \sqrt{\frac{77.1}{327}} = 0.49$$

A rule of thumb for all statistics that measure association between fixed limits of −1.00 to +1.00 is that a value between 0 and ±0.25 indicates a non-existent to weak association; a value between ±0.26 and ±0.50 suggests a weak to moderate association; a value between ±0.51 and ±0.75 suggests a moderate to strong association, and a value between ±0.76 and ±1.00 suggests a strong to perfect association. In our case, the figure of 0.49 suggests that there is a moderate association between the two variables.

Odds ratios

Another way of measuring the strength of association between two categorical variables is by using odds ratios. An odds ratio compares the probability of being in one situation with the probability of being in another. For example, in the Smoking Survey, we can calculate the odds of a non-smoker having many friends and family members who smoke, and the odds of a non-smoker having few friends and family who smoke. Expressing these two sets of odds in a single statistic gives us an odds ratio. Referring to table 8.1, for example:

♦ We calculate the odds that someone whose friends smoke will not smoke themselves by dividing cell 'a' (many friends smoke but the respondent does not) by cell 'c' (many friends smoke, and so does the respondent). This comes to 37/111 = 0.33, or 3:1 against (i.e. there is only 1 chance in 3 that such a person will be a non-smoker).

♦ Next, we calculate the odds that someone whose friends do not smoke will not smoke themselves. This entails dividing cell 'b' (few friends smoke, nor does the respondent) by cell 'd' (few friends smoke, but the respondent does), which comes to 132/47 = 2.81, or odds of nearly 3:1 *on* (i.e. there is only 1 chance in 3 that this person will not be a non-smoker).

♦   Finally, we express the first set of odds as a proportion of the second. Thus:

$$(a/c) \div (b/d) = 37/111 \div 132/47 = 0.119$$

An odds ratio of 0.119 tells us that the odds of somebody smoking when their friends tend not to smoke are about 8.5 times lower than the odds of somebody smoking when most of their friends do. It therefore indicates a fairly strong association (if there were no association between these two variables, there would be an odds ratio of 1).

Odds ratios can stand on their own, but they are more often used in two more advanced and more powerful methods for analysing categorical variables (loglinear modelling and logistic regression). We discuss both of these in the additional material available on the website (in appendices H and I in section 5). When you run a 'Cross-tabs' procedure, you can get odds ratios by clicking on 'Risk' under the statistical options.

Asymmetrical measures of strength of association for nominal variables

Odds ratios, like the *phi* coefficient and Cramer's V, are *symmetrical measures* of the strength of association between variables, for they are indifferent as to which of the variables is independent and which is dependent. When testing hypotheses, however, we are often testing a claim that one variable causes change in the other, and this means that the relationship between them is 'asymmetrical' – X is said to cause change in Y, but not vice versa. To measure the extent to which knowledge of an independent variable improves the best prediction we can make of the value of a dependent variable, we need to use an *asymmetrical* statistic such as *lambda* or *Goodman and Kruskal's tau*.

Asymmetric measures express the degree to which total errors in predicting the dependent variable are reduced when we take account of the values of the independent variable. Both lambda and tau can be selected in SPSS (select both by clicking on 'Lambda' in the statistics dialog box when running 'Crosstabs') and both give figures between 0 and 1. A value of 0 means that the independent variable is of no use in predicting the dependent variable, while a value of 1 tells you that it predicts the dependent variable perfectly.

Referring back to table 8.1, the best prediction we can make for any one respondent is that they are a non-smoker, for there are 169 people who said they did not smoke in the last week as compared with 158 who said that they did. This is a pretty awful prediction, though, for we will be wrong nearly half the time.

We can improve on this rate of error if we are told whether the respondent has many or few friends who smoke. We will then predict that

♦   the respondent is a smoker (if he or she has many smoking friends) and we will be right three-quarters of the time (111/148 = 75 per cent of predictions will be correct);
♦   the respondent is a non-smoker (if he or she has few smoking friends), when we will also be right about three times out of four (132/179 = 74 per cent of predictions correct).

Directional Measures

			Value	Asymp. std. Error[a]	Approx. T[b]	Approx. Sig.
Nominal by Nominal	Lambda	Symmetric	.247	.042	5.283	.000
		Smoked in last week? Dependent	.468	.056	6.459	.000
		Family/friends smoke? Dependent	.093	.040	2.218	.027
	Goodman and Kruskal tau	Smoked in last week? Dependent	.260	.045		.000[c]
		Family/friends smoke? Dependent	.083	.015		.000[c]

a. Not assuming the null hypothesis.

b. using the asymptotic standard error assuming the null hypothesis.

c. Based on chi-square approximation.

Figure 8.4 Lambda and Goodman and Kruskal's tau statistics for the cross-tabulation of smoking behaviour by family and friends smoking behaviour

Overall, therefore, we shall make far fewer errors by knowing this additional information. Lambda and Goodman and Kruskal's tau express this proportionate reduction of error as a simple statistic.

The output in figure 8.4 was computed for the full (eight-cell) table produced in figure 8.3. It shows that, with respondents' smoking behaviour as the dependent variable, we get a lambda value of 0.468 and a tau value of 0.260. This means that knowing the smoking behaviour of friends and family, we reduce the error in predicting whether the respondent smokes by 47 per cent (according to the lambda statistic), or by 26 per cent (according to the tau statistic).

Although the principle underlying the two measures is the same, they differ in the way they are calculated and there is some debate about which is the better one to use. You may be safer using tau, for it tends to give the lower measure of association and it is always good practice to err on the side of caution. Also, lambda can be unreliable, occasionally throwing up a value of 0 even when there is a relatively strong association between the variables.

Note that SPSS produces statistics for lambda and tau with each variable dependent and with the association as symmetrical. It is only your theory that tells you which variable is independent and which dependent, and therefore which of these results you should use.

Controlling for third variables: a test and further exploration of the parental influence hypothesis

When testing for associations between variables, you may often need to go beyond bivariate analysis (the analysis of just two variables). In chapter 3 we saw that:

◆   If you find a reasonably strong association between two variables, X and Y, you may need to check that it is not *spurious* (e.g. that the apparent relation between them has not been produced by a common third variable, Z). We can test for this by seeing whether the association between X and Y disappears once we *control* for the third variable, Z, by adding it to the analysis.

♦ If you fail to find an expected association between two variables, X and Y, which your theory led you to believe would be associated, it may be premature to conclude that your theory was wrong, for it is possible that the association between them is being disguised by the influence of a third variable. For example, the association may only occur in a particular subgroup of the population, which means it will not be visible until we break the analysis down further, or a third variable may be exerting a positive influence on X but a negative one on Y, thereby making it appear that they are not covarying when in fact they are.

In both of these cases, we need to check for possible *interaction effects* brought about by the influence of a third, *intervening* or *mediating* variable.

The influence of intervening variables: the case of Durkheim's study of suicide

One criticism of Durkheim's study in *Suicide* is his willingness to conclude from an absence of association between two variables that they are not related when further analysis might have shown that they are. For example, looking at 15 Austro-Hungarian provinces, he found no association between the suicide rate and the proportion of German speakers in each province. However, Selvin shows that while there was no association in the westerly provinces, there was a strong one to the east which was hidden when all the data were aggregated.

H. Selvin, 'Durkheim's *Suicide*: further notes on a methodological classic', in R. Nisbet (ed.), *Émile Durkheim* (Englewood Cliffs: Prentice Hall, 1965)

An illustration of how it can be important to add third variables to your analysis arose in our Smoking Survey when we came to test hypothesis 1:

Smokers are more likely than non-smokers to have had parents who smoked.

We can test this by running a cross-tabulation of var00003 (whether the respondent smoked in the last week) and var00015 (whether the respondent's parents smoked while he or she was growing up). The results (Figure 8.5) show that people brought up by non-smoking parents are more likely to be non-smokers (57%), and that those brought up in households where both parents smoked are more likely to smoke (54%). However, the pattern does not look strong, for the percentage differences are small, and the tau test confirms that the association is very weak (0.014). It seems that the peer group has much more influence on our smoking behaviour than our parents do.

Although this finding is in line with that from other studies, we decided to explore the data further by controlling for gender differences. Perhaps girls' smoking behaviour is influenced by their mothers and boys might only be influenced to smoke if their fathers smoked? To check on this, we ran a three-way crosstabulation of parents' smoking behaviour (var00015) by respondents' smoking behaviour (var00003) by

Smoked in last week? * Did parents smoke? Crosstabulation

			Did parents smoke?				
			Neither did	Only mother	Only father	Both did	Total
Smoked in last week?	no	Count	48	16	61	47	172
		% within Did parents smoke?	57.1%	43.2%	57.0%	46.1%	52.1%
	yes	Count	36	21	46	55	158
		% within Did parents smoke?	42.9%	56.8%	43.0%	53.9%	47.9%
Total		Count	84	37	107	102	330
		% within Did parents smoke?	100.0%	100.0%	100.0%	100.0%	100.0%

Directional Measures

			Value	Asymp. std. Error[a]	Approx. T[b]	Approx. Sig.
Nominal by Nominal	Lambda	Symmetric	.058	.048	1.178	.239
		Smoked in last week? Dependent	.082	.071	1.105	.269
		Did parents smoke? Dependent	.040	.044	.897	.370
	Goodman and Kruskal tau	Smoked in last week? Dependent	.014	.013		.210[c]
		Did parents smoke? Dependent	.005	.005		.193[c]

a. Not assuming the null hypothesis.

b. using the asymptotic standard error assuming the null hypothesis.

c. Based on chi-square approximation.

Figure 8.5   Cross-tabulation of parental smoking history against respondents' smoking behaviour

gender (var00015). The results are given in the tables in figure 8.6 (to request a three-way cross-tabulation in SPSS, paste the control variable into the third, empty window in the 'Crosstabs' dialog box).

When we control for a third variable, we produce two parallel cross-tabulations, known as *partial tables*. Examining the partial table for female respondents, we see there is no pattern of association between the two variables (tau = 0.005). In fact, a slightly higher proportion of female respondents smoked if neither parent smoked (46%) than if both parents smoked (43%)! When we look at the partial table for males, the tau statistic is still very weak (0.041), but there seems to be some association with mothers having smoked. Of the 77 males whose mothers smoked (the 19 where only the mother smoked plus 58 where both mother and father smoked), 49 were themselves smokers, but of the remaining 91 whose mothers did not smoke, only 41 were smokers.

To investigate the possibility that male smoking is associated specifically with the mother having smoked, we created a new independent variable (derived from var00015) which distinguishes those whose mother smoked from everybody else (this derived variable can be found in the cleandat.sav data file where it is named 'mumsmoke'). We then reran our three-way cross-tabulation using this new variable, and found that 64 per cent of males whose mothers smoked were themselves

Smoked in last week? * Did parents smoke? gender Crosstabulation

gender				Did parents smoke?				Total
				Neither did	Only mother	Only father	Both did	
female	Smoked in last week?	no	Count	25	10	34	25	94
			% within Did parents smoke?	54.3%	55.6%	63.0%	56.8%	58.0%
		yes	Count	21	8	20	19	68
			% within Did parents smoke?	45.7%	44.4%	37.0%	43.2%	42.0%
	Total		Count	46	18	54	44	162
			% within Did parents smoke?	100.0%	100.0%	100.0%	100.0%	100.0%
male	Smoked in last week?	no	Count	23	6	27	22	78
			% within Did parents smoke?	60.5%	31.6%	50.9%	37.9%	46.4%
		yes	Count	15	13	26	36	90
			% within Did parents smoke?	39.5%	68.4%	49.1%	62.1%	53.6%
	Total		Count	38	19	53	58	168
			% within Did parents smoke?	100.0%	100.0%	100.0%	100.0%	100.0%

Directional Measures

gender				Value	Asymp. std. Error[a]	Approx. T[b]	Approx. Sig.
female	Nominal by Nominal	Lambda	Symmetric	.006	.036	.056	.876
			Smoked in last week? Dependent	.000	.000	[c]	[c]
			Did parents smoke? Dependent	.009	.059	.156	.876
		Goodman and Kruskal tau	Smoked in last week? Dependent	.005	.011		.835[d]
			Did parents smoke? Dependent	.002	.005		.779[d]
male	Nominal by Nominal	Lambda	Symmetric	.074	.072	1.008	.313
			Smoked in last week? Dependent	.115	.115	.946	.344
			Did parents smoke? Dependent	.045	.062	.715	.474
		Goodman and Kruskal tau	Smoked in last week? Dependent	.041	.030		.079[d]
			Did parents smoke? Dependent	.013	.011		.085[d]

a. Not assuming the null hypothesis.

b. using the asymptotic standard error assuming the null hypothesis.

c. Cannot be computed because the asymptotic standard error equals zero.

d. Based on chi-square approximation.

Figure 8.6 Cross-tabulation of parental smoking history against respondents' smoking behaviour, controlling for gender

smokers, while this was true of only 45 per cent of males whose mothers had not smoked.

Breaking the data down by gender thus hints at the possibility of an association between mothers smoking and male smoking behaviour which had initially been obscured in our early contingency tables. It would be interesting to test for this in subsequent surveys.

Trawling the data: a note of caution

We should remember that we did not originally hypothesize that mothers' smoking habits would influence their sons, nor that fathers' smoking habits would have no impact on either sons or daughters. By following our noses in an attempt to dig out a possible hidden relationship from our data, we have crossed the boundary between *analytical research* and *exploratory research*, for what we have done is to go looking for patterns rather than testing a prediction of what we expect to find. There are two problems with this:

- Findings must make theoretical sense. Mere correlation means little unless we have good theoretical grounds for believing that certain patterns should arise in our data.
- If we dredge around in any data set looking for patterns, we shall almost certainly find some, but the key question is whether these findings can be repeated on a fresh data set.

We certainly would not be justified in publishing this finding unless (a) we could explain it theoretically (perhaps Freudian theory has something to offer here?), and (b) we could replicate it by testing it as a new hypothesis on a fresh data set. In fact, we did try replicating it when we repeated the Smoking Survey with a later cohort of students, but we failed to get an association second time around. If you have been replicating the Smoking Survey on your own sample of respondents, see whether you find any association between mothers' and sons' smoking behaviour. Send us your results, and we shall post them on the website that accompanies this book (for details of how to send us material, see p.301).

Beyond three-way cross-tabulations

The procedure we have been following, where we start by examining a two-way cross-tabulation and then enter a third control variable to see what effect it has, is known as *elaboration* and it is frequently used in the social sciences to explore findings. Of course, elaboration need not end here, for we could in principle try controlling for a fourth or even a fifth variable. In practice, however, there are two problems with taking the procedure of elaboration beyond three-way cross-tabulation:

- The first is the sheer number of partial tables that are produced with four or more variables. If we tried to elaborate further on this example by controlling, say, for age group, we would end up with eight partial tables, and this is just too many for anyone to be able to make much sense of.
- The second is that as we break the data down into more and more partial tables, so the cell counts decrease. If we tried to control for age group as our fourth variable,

eight partial tables, each containing four cells, would give us a total of 32 cells, with an average frequency in each of a little over 10. This is really too small for us to place much faith in the findings.

When we need to take the analysis of categorical data beyond three-way cross-tabulation, we therefore use a different method for analysing contingency tables, known as *loglinear modelling*. We explain loglinear models in appendix I on our website.

Measuring strength of association between two ordinal-level variables

When we move from analysing nominal to ordinal level variables, we can use more powerful measures of association which take advantage of the fact that cases are now rank ordered. There are several different statistics that do this including *Spearman's rho, Kendall's tau-b and tau-c, Goodman and Kruskal's gamma,* and *Somer's d.* All are non-parametric statistics and produce a result between −1 (for a perfect negative correlation: as the independent variable increases, the dependent variable decreases) and +1 (a perfect positive correlation: both rise or fall together).

Spearman's rho is more commonly used than tau (mainly because tau gets into difficulties with ties in rankings). Gamma treats the variables symmetrically (i.e. it makes no distinction between the independent and dependent variables), while Somer's d allows an asymmetric test for the effect of the independent variable on the dependent variable. All are available on SPSS when you run a 'Crosstabs' command.

Calculating Spearman's rank correlation coefficient (rho)

We shall focus here on Spearman's rho, which we shall use to test hypothesis 8 in the Smoking Survey:

The higher somebody's social class and level of education, the less likely they are to smoke, and the less tolerant they will be of smoking.

We shall focus here on differences in class attitudes to smoking, leaving the test of whether the classes differ in their actual smoking behaviour to chapter 10. The hypothesis suggests that attitudes towards smoking are the dependent variable, and that class position is the independent variable. Our dependent variable will therefore be measured by the combined attitude variable ('attit8') that we created in the appendix to chapter 7 (this consists of a scale from 8, indicating extreme intolerance, to 40, indicating extreme tolerance). Our independent variable will be var00042, a derived variable which classifies people's occupations according to the old Registrar-General's six-category social class schema. Although there is some debate about the level of measurement of this schema (see appendix B on the website), we shall treat it here as an ordinal scale.

A worked example

Let us first run through the logic of the test with an imaginary sample of ten individuals. Table 8.3 shows their ranking on both the attitude scale (low scores are ranked highest) and the social class scale (class I ranks highest). If the higher social classes are less tolerant of smoking, then we should expect that those who rank highly on one variable should also rank highly on the other (note that people sharing the same social class position are given a tied ranking).

To calculate Spearman's rho, we first work out the difference between the ranks (given in the sixth column in table 8.3). These values are then squared to make all the differences positive (column 7), and summed (in this example it comes to 42). What follows next is rather convoluted, for the resulting statistic is manipulated to ensure that its value will fall somewhere between +1 and −1. To get this outcome, we first multiply the sum of the squared differences by 6 ($42 * 6 = 252$); then we take the square of the number of cases in our sample, minus 1, and multiply this value by the number of cases ($(100 − 1)^*10 = 990$); and finally we divide 252 by 990 and subtract this value from 1:

$$\frac{252}{990} = 1 - 0.255 = 0.745$$

The Spearman's rho value of +0.745 tells us that there is a strong positive relationship between the rankings of our two variables. As social class rises, so individuals are more likely to express negative attitudes towards smoking.

Table 8.3 Example of calculation for Spearman's rho

Case number	Social class	Social class rank	Attitude score	Attitude rank	Difference between ranks	Difference squared
1	I	1.5	20	4	−2.5	6.25
2	I	1.5	14	3	−1.5	2.25
3	II	3.5	9	1	2.5	6.25
4	II	3.5	11	2	1.5	2.25
5	IIIN	5.5	23	5	0.5	0.25
6	IIIN	5.5	29	7	−1.5	2.25
7	IIIM	7	38	9	−2.0	4.0
8	IV	8.5	34	8	0.5	0.25
9	IV	8.5	39	10	−1.5	2.25
10	V	10	24	6	−4.0	16.00
					Total =	42.00

The Spearman's rho test in SPSS

> If you are using **cleandat.sav,** you can replicate the steps we take. If you are using data you have generated yourself, find two comparable variables to the ones we are using here, and follow what we do using your own material. Remember that both of the variables that you select should be ordinally ranked.

You run the test from the 'Crosstabs' menu item – select the 'Statistics…' button and then select 'Correlations'. We do not want to generate an unwieldy 4x32 contingency table, so you should also click in the box next to 'Suppress tables' before clicking 'OK'.

The first table in figure 8.7 tells us that just 172 (51.5%) of our respondents have been included in this analysis while 162 (48.5%) are 'missing'. The reason why nearly half of the cases are missing is that many of our respondents had no occupation and were not therefore allocated to any social class.

The second part of the output gives us the results from the statistical test. Since we have run the test on two ordinal variables we should read from the second row, which gives the Spearman correlation for ordinal by ordinal variables (note that this test can also be run on interval-level data; because it is non-parametric, it is useful for analysing interval-level variables that fail the normal distribution assumptions often made by parametric tests). The value of 0.054 informs us that there is a very weak positive association between our two variables. As we move up the class categories, people tend to be more intolerant towards smoking, which is what our hypothesis predicted, but

Case Processing Summary

	Cases					
	Valid		Missing		Total	
	N	Percent	N	Percent	N	Percent
Attitude score (8 items) *Reg-Gen Social Class	172	51.5%	162	48.5%	334	100.0%

Symmetric Measures

		Value	Asymp. std. Error[a]	Approx. T[b]	Approx. Sig.
Interval by Interval	Pearson's R	.068	.080	.893	.373[c]
Ordinal by Ordinal	Spearman Correlation	.054	.078	.709	.479[c]
N of Valid Cases		172			

a. Not assuming the null hypothesis.

b. using the asymptotic standard error assuming the null hypothesis.

c. Based on normal approximation.

Figure 8.7   Spearman's rho test of association between class and attitude towards smoking

the relationship is so weak as to be virtually non-existent. We cannot, therefore, claim support for this hypothesis from our data.

What to do when hypotheses are refuted

We saw earlier that hypotheses that fail should not be discarded too swiftly, but when there really is no evidence to support them, as in this case, we must have the resolution to discard them. People often fiddle around, transforming variables, using different variables or using different statistical tests, but unless you think there was some kind of flaw in the way you originally set up the test, it is not acceptable to make post hoc changes to the conditions of the test in an attempt to scrape together support for a weak hypothesis. Remember what Popper said: we should be looking to falsify our theories, not confirm them.

A hypothesis that has been refuted should not be seen as an 'unwanted' finding or as something to be ignored. In fact, a finding like this can often be helpful in enabling us to refine our ideas and formulate new ones. Knowledge that something is *not* the case is still valuable.

ANALYSING THE STRENGTH OF ASSOCIATION BETWEEN TWO INTERVAL VARIABLES: CORRELATION

The most commonly used measure of the strength of association between two variables which are both measured on an interval or ratio scale is *Pearson's Product Moment Correlation Coefficient*. This statistic is symbolized by the letter r and is often referred to as *Pearson's r*. Like other coefficients discussed in this chapter, it is measured on a scale from +1 through to −1. A value of r close to +1 represents a strong positive correlation, a value of r close to −1 represents a strong negative relationship, and an r value close to 0 indicates a weak or non-existent association.

Graphing the relationship between two variables

Suppose we have collected the IQ score and the points score in school exams for every individual in a sample of students, and we want to know whether the two sets of scores are related. Because both are measured as interval scales, we can plot each student's scores on a graph (known as a *scatterplot*). For example, if person A has an IQ score (plotted on the X axis) of 98 and an examination score (plotted on the Y axis) of 25, we put a cross on the graph where X = 98 and Y = 25. All the other students' scores are plotted in the same way to produce a scatter of crosses, and we end up with something like the pattern in figure 8.8.

There is not much consistency in this pattern. Although respondents A and B have the same IQ score of 98, their examination points are quite different (25 and 16 respectively). Similarly, although respondent C is relatively 'bright', with an IQ of 115, her or his exams point score is much lower than the 'less bright' respondent A.

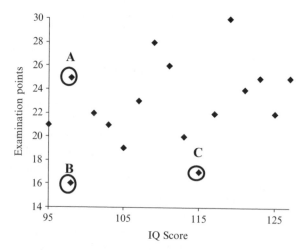

Figure 8.8   Scatterplot showing a weak linear relationship between an independent and dependent variable

Nevertheless, there does seem to be some kind of association between the two variables, for there is a weak pattern in the scatter of the dots. There is a tendency for students' exam points to rise as their IQ score increases – at an IQ of around 125, the average exam points score of students appears to be about 24, whereas for those with an IQ score around 105, the average exam score seems to be about 20 – but there is a lot of variation around these averages, and the pattern is far from perfect.

Linearity, direction and strength of association

When assessing the pattern of association between two interval or ratio variables, it is always good practice to begin by producing a scatterplot to get a visual idea of their relationship. A scatterplot can not only tell us something about the *strength* of association between them, but it can also indicate the *direction* of the association (positive or negative), and the *form* of the association (in particular, whether the relationship is linear or not).

Strength of association

Look at figure 8.9. In scatterplot (a), the association between the two variables is very strong. We know this because all the cases lie close to a straight line drawn through them. Cases where the value of X is a long way below the mean of X (those cases falling towards the left end of the X axis) also have a value of Y a long way below the mean of Y (they fall towards the bottom of the Y axis) – and vice versa. There is therefore a high degree of *co-variation* between X and Y, which will produce a high value of *r*.

Conversely, in scatterplot (b) there is virtually no relationship between the two variables, for there is a random scatter of points and no line drawn in any direction would fit the data any better than any other. In this example, high values of X (those above the mean of X) can be found at many different values of Y, just as low values of X can. X and Y are clearly not covarying, in which case *r* will equal, or be close to, zero.

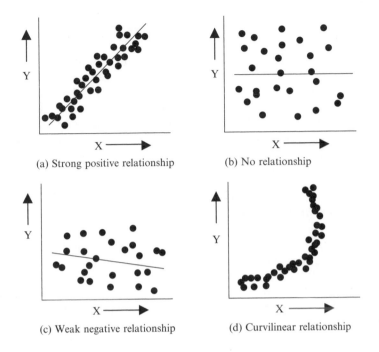

(a) Strong positive relationship

(b) No relationship

(c) Weak negative relationship

(d) Curvilinear relationship

Figure 8.9   Scatterplots showing different patterns of association

Direction of association

Scatterplots can also be used to tell us whether a relationship between two variables is positive or negative. Scatterplot (a) in figure 8.9 shows a positive relationship, indicated by the clustering of cases around a line that rises from left to right (as the value of Y increases, so does the value of X). Scatterplot (c), however, shows a negative relationship between the variables because the line decreases from left to right (as Y increases, X tends to decrease).

The fit of the line is different from the slope of the line

You might be tempted when inspecting a scatterplot to interpret a steep line as indicating a strong relationship and a shallow line as indicating a weak one, but this is incorrect. A shallow line indicates that Y only changes *slightly* as X changes, but this might simply be due to the fact that the total amount of variation in Y is already very small, in which case no amount of change in X can shift Y much since Y does not vary much.

If all the points are close to the line, the relationship is a strong one, irrespective of how steep or shallow the gradient of the line might be. What matters for correlation (a measure of the strength of association) is not the gradient of the slope, but the extent to which the cases all fall on a straight line.

Form of association

It is possible for two variables to be associated but not in a linear fashion. In scatterplot (d) on figure 8.9, there is a strong association between the two variables, but the form of their relationship is *curvilinear* (as the value of X increases, the value of Y increases exponentially). Pearson's *r* assumes a linear relationship, so it is important to check the scatterplot to see whether this assumption actually applies in any given case (in scatterplot (d), trying to fit a straight line to the data would produce a misleadingly low value for the correlation coefficient, for many of the cases fall a long distance away from the best-fitting straight line).

Making curved lines straight

Correlation requires that there be a (roughly) linear relationship between variables, so what can you do if your scatterplot fails to find one? One possibility is to transform one or both of the variables to make the relationship more linear. We saw in chapter 7 that non-normal distributions can be made more normal by transforming data (for example by logging, squaring and so on); so too non-linear associations can be 'bent' into linear ones in much the same way. For example, the relationship shown in scatterplot (d) in figure 8.9 could be made somewhat more linear by logging the variable on the Y axis.

Running a scatterplot in SPSS

Hypothesis 9 in our Smoking Survey holds that:

Ex-smokers will become increasingly intolerant of smoking, the longer they have given up.

For this hypothesis to be supported, we should expect people's tolerance scores to fall as the time since they stopped smoking lengthens. To test this, the independent variable will be the length of time (measured in months) that ex-smokers have given up smoking (var00009) – a ratio measure. The dependent variable will be the combined attitude scale ('attit8'), which we shall treat for these purposes as an interval scale (but see chapter 5 on the problems in such an assumption).

If you are working with your own data set, select two variables measured at interval or ratio level which your theory leads you to believe should be associated, and follow these procedures using them.

Let us first run a scatterplot to see whether these two variables are related. Do this by selecting 'Scatter' from the Graphs menu – we want the default setting of a simple scatterplot, so click 'Define' to open the simple scatterplot dialog box, and select the variables you want.

Your scatterplot will appear in the Viewer window but it may be difficult to make sense of it if you have a lot of cases. To make it clearer, click on 'Edit' in the menu bar, highlight 'SPSS Chart Object' and then click on 'Open'. A new window called the Chart Editor will open. We last used this window when editing our bar graph in chapter 7 and, as with the bar graph, within this window we can make a number of changes to the style and format of our scatterplot.

♦   In the Chart Editor, click on 'Chart' in the menu bar and then on 'Options'. This will open a dialog box headed 'Scatterplot Options'.
♦   In the dialog box, click on the box next to 'Show sunflowers'. This will change all the squares on your plot into 'sunflower heads' – the more 'petals' a sunflower has, the more cases there are at that point in the plot.
♦   Now click on the box below 'Fit line' to ask SPSS to superimpose the best-fitting straight line (the *line of best fit*) on to your plot. This line will be drawn so as to minimize the total vertical distance from all points on the graph (i.e. it minimizes the total dispersion on the Y axis).
♦   Click on 'OK', close the Chart Editor window, and inspect the modified scatterplot you have created. It should look something like the one in figure 8.10.

We can see that as the time since giving up smoking increases, attitude scores tend to fall (i.e. ex-smokers become more intolerant towards smoking the longer they have given up smoking). This negative relationship is demonstrated by the line of best fit sloping downwards from left to right. This result is consistent with hypothesis 9. Less satisfactory, however, is the strength of this association, for the wide scatter of points about the line suggests it is quite weak.

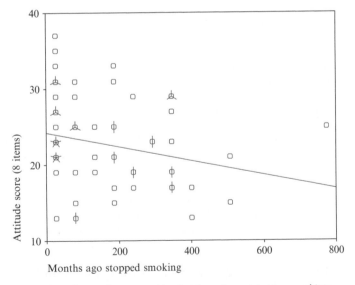

Figure 8.10   Scatterplot of attitudes to smoking by time since giving up smoking

Having visually inspected the association between the two variables to satisfy our-selves that there is a relationship between them and that it is roughly linear in shape, we can now move on to calculate how strong it is. We do this by finding the value of the Pearson correlation coefficient.

Calculating the value of Pearson's *r*

The logic behind the calculation of the value of Pearson's *r* is that we want to know to what extent the values of one variable change as the values of another variable change. In technical language, this means we want to calculate their *covariance*.

Calculating the variance in a single variable (a short refresher)

We saw in chapter 4 that the total *variation* (known as the sum of squares) in a single variable is the *total* amount (squared, to allow us to add positive and negative amounts together) by which all observations vary from the mean. We took as an example a sample of six students aged 19, 19, 19, 28, 31 and 38. Their mean age was calculated as 25.67, and for each student we then calculated how far their age was from this mean age of the sample. In each case, this difference was then squared, and the six squared deviations were added up to give a total variation (sum of squares) of 319.42 (see p. 110). The equation which expresses this procedure is:

$$\sum (x - \bar{x})^2$$

We further saw in chapter 4 that the *variance* of a variable is the *average* amount by which all observations vary from the mean. It is calculated by dividing the sum of squares by the number of cases in the sample, minus 1 (for the sample size itself takes up one degree of freedom):

$$\frac{\sum (x - \bar{x})^2}{n - 1}$$

With a total variation of 319.42 and a sample size of six, we calculated the variance in the ages of our sample of students as $(319.42 \div 5) = 63.89$ (p. 111).

Calculating the covariance of two variables

We calculate the strength of association between *two* variables by looking at how the variation in one is associated with the variation in the other – i.e. by calculating their *covariation*:

◆   If X and Y covary positively, then when X has a high value, so (on average) will Y, and when X has a low value, then again, so generally will Y.
◆   If X and Y covary negatively, then when X is high, Y will tend to be low, and vice versa.

The way we calculate covariation is (looking at each case in turn) to calculate the amount by which each value of X varies from the mean of X, and the amount by which each value of Y varies from the mean of Y, and then to multiply the differences together in order to get a single figure. If we then add up all these figures, we end up with a statistic that represents the total amount of covariation between our two variables. The bigger this figure (whether positive or negative), the greater the degree of covariation.

Calculating the covariation between age and exam results in a sample of six students

Suppose we are interested in the association between the age of the students in the sample drawn in chapter 4 and their examination results (given in column D below):

A Age	B Average age	C Difference from mean	D Exam score	E Average score	F Difference from mean	G Product C*F
19	25.67	−6.67	57	59.5	−2.5	+16.675
19	25.67	−6.67	63	59.5	+3.5	−23.345
19	25.67	−6.67	41	59.5	−18.5	+123.395
28	25.67	+2.33	78	59.5	+18.5	+43.105
31	25.67	+5.33	54	59.5	−5.5	−29.315
38	25.67	+12.33	64	59.5	+4.5	+55.485
						+186.0

The covariation of age with exam performance is calculated by seeing for each student how their distance from the mean age of the group (column C) compares with their distance from the mean exam score of the group (column F). (Note that we do not square these differences, as we do in calculating the variation in one variable, for we do not want to cancel out negative differences. If, for example, people with ages *below* the mean tend to score *above* the mean on exams, then this represents a negative association between age and exam performance, and we would lose this information if we were to square the differences.)

If age is related to exam performance, high figures in column C should be matched by high figures in column F, and the plus or minus sign will tell us whether the association is positive or negative. By multiplying these differences from the mean age and the mean exam score together (column G), and then summing the results, we can get an overall statistic that summarizes the extent to which the two covary. In this example, the covariation statistic comes to +186 (the positive sign shows that the two variables vary positively with each other – as age increases, exam scores tend to increase).

This procedure for calculating the covariation of two variables can be expressed by the equation:

$$\sum(x - \bar{x})(y - \bar{y})$$

Covariance is the average amount of covariation. In this example, the average amount of covariation (allowing 1 degree of freedom) will be $(+186 \div [6 - 1]) = +37.2$. The equation for calculating covariance is therefore:

$$\frac{\sum(x - \bar{x})(y - \bar{y})}{n - 1}$$

Standarizing the covariance to get Pearson's r

Covariance gives us a measure of the average amount by which two variables vary with each other. The higher it is, the stronger the association. If it is positive, the association is positive; if negative, the association is negative.

On its own, however, this statistic is not very informative. In the example of the six students, we have found a covariance between age and exam results of +37.2, but is this large or small? Clearly we need to express this covariance on a standardized scale which is readily understandable, and Pearson's correlation coefficient does this by creating what are called *z scores*.

Standardizing the covariance to find Pearson's correlation coefficient

In chapter 4 we calculated the standard deviation in the age distribution of our sample of six students as 7.99. The standard deviation of their exam scores can also readily be calculated as 12.28. We can therefore calculate standardized (z) scores (scores expressed in standard deviations from the mean) for age (column B) and exam performance (column D), and from these we can calculate the product of the standardized age and exam scores for each student (column E):

A	B	C	D	E
Age − mean age	Column A ÷ 7.99	Exam score − mean score	Column C ÷ 12.28	Column B * column D
−6.67	−0.70	−2.5	−0.20	+0.14
−6.67	−0.70	+3.5	+0.29	−0.20
−6.67	−0.70	−18.5	−1.51	+1.06
−2.33	+0.29	+18.5	+1.51	+0.44
+5.33	+0.67	−5.5	−0.45	−0.31
+12.33	+1.54	+4.5	+0.37	+0.57

If we now sum the product of the z scores we arrive at a figure of +1.7. Divide this by $(N - 1)$ to find the average standardized covariance: $1.7 \div 5 = +0.34$. This is the Pearson correlation coefficient.

We explain in detail how to calculate z-scores in appendix C in section 4 of the website but, in essence, to standardize the values of a variable in the form of z scores, we calculate for each case in the sample the degree of variation from the mean and then express this as a proportion of the standard deviation in the sample as a whole. When dealing with covariance, we have two variables, of course, so we have to calculate each person's z score on each of the two variables being compared. These are then multiplied together, the results are all added up, and the total is averaged to produce a standardized covariance statistic. The result is Pearson's correlation coefficient, a number between −1 and +1.

We can express this procedure in the form of the following equation:

$$\frac{\left(\sum z_x z_y\right)}{n - 1}$$

Which can be written out more fully as:

$$r_{xy} = \frac{\sum (x - \bar{x})(y - \bar{y})}{\sqrt{\left[\sum (x - \bar{x})^2 \sum (y - \bar{y})^2\right]}}$$

Generating Pearson's r using SPSS

Let us return to testing hypothesis 9 from the Smoking Survey.

To calculate the Pearson's correlation coefficient for the association between tolerance of smoking and the time that people have given up smoking, open the 'Bivariate...' dialog box from the 'Correlate' item under the Analyze menu. SPSS calculates the Pearson correlation coefficient as the default setting. If you want to request descriptive statistics on both variables, select 'Options' and click on the radio button next to 'Means and standard deviations'. Leave the 'Missing Values' option at its default setting. Click on 'Continue', then on 'OK' to obtain a correlation matrix in the Viewer window.

Analysing the output of a bivariate correlation

The output comes in two parts (figure 8.11). The first provides information on the mean and standard deviation of the two variables, and the second is a correlation matrix.

With just two variables, we get a 2×2 matrix, and two of the four cells equal 1 (because a variable correlates with itself perfectly). In this output, for example, cell A correlates 'attit8' with itself, and cell D correlates var00009 with itself. The interesting figures are those on the other diagonal – where the *correlation coefficient* between the independent and dependent variables is reported. In this example the correlation coefficient, or r, $= -0.257$.

Interpreting the correlation coefficient

The correlation matrix confirms our visual inspection of the scatterplot – there is an association. On a scale from 0 (absence of correlation) to 1 (total correlation), the variables correlate with each other at −0.257. The correlation coefficient (Pearson's *r*) expresses the proportion of variation in the Y variable explained by the linear relation-

Descriptive Statistics

	Mean	Std. Deviation	N
Attitude score (8 items)	23.6888	6.5678	331
Months ago stopped smoking	163.6984	160.6510	63

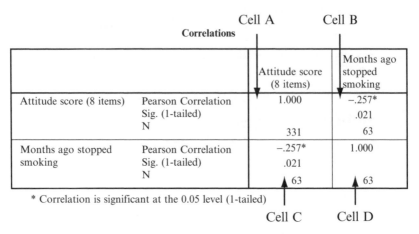

Cell A   Cell B

Correlations

		Attitude score (8 items)	Months ago stopped smoking
Attitude score (8 items)	Pearson Correlation	1.000	−.257*
	Sig. (1-tailed)		.021
	N	331	63
Months ago stopped smoking	Pearson Correlation	−.257*	1.000
	Sig. (1-tailed)	.021	
	N	63	63

* Correlation is significant at the 0.05 level (1-tailed)

Cell C   Cell D

Figure 8.11 A bivariate correlation of months given up smoking by attitude towards smoking (pairwise deletion)

ship between X and Y (i.e. how well the line fits the data). A coefficient of −0.257 indicates that our ability to predict the value of Y (attitudes to smoking) is improved by 26 per cent if we know the value of X (months since stopping smoking). In other words,

---

Two notes of caution in interpreting what a correlation coefficient means

(1)   Pearson's r measures the strength of association between two variables by calculating their standardized covariance. This is not the same as the 'proportion of variation' in Y explained by X (this proportion is given rather by r^2, the square of the correlation coefficient, which is known as the *coefficient of determination*). Only by squaring the correlation coefficient can we find the *ratio* of explained variation in X to total variation in X (i.e. the *proportion* of variance explained). In our example the $r^2 = (-0.257 * -0.257) = 0.066$, indicating that the length of time for which somebody has stopped smoking accounts for only 7 per cent of the variance in former smokers' attitudes about smoking.

(2)   It is also important to remember that correlation does not of itself imply causation. It only indicates the extent to which the variables associate with each other in a linear way. Only our theory allows us to say whether there is a cause-and-effect relationship (in this case, our hypothesis led us to predict that the time elapsed since quitting smoking *causes* a shift in attitudes).

we will make 26 per cent fewer errors predicting Y if we know X as compared with the predictions we will make if we do not know it.

The correlation matrix also contains a test of significance, based on a t test (in the table in figure 8.11, its value is 0.021, which tells us that a result as strong as this would only occur by chance 2 times in 100). We shall see how to interpret inferential statistics like this one in chapter 9, so ignore this for the time being.

Note that Pearson's *r* can be affected by a few extreme outliers, so it is always a good idea to check for these with a boxplot for each variable. Even without producing a boxplot we can see from our scatterplot (figure 8.10) that there is one extreme case of somebody who gave up smoking nearly 800 months – 67 years – ago! Try taking this person out and see if it makes much difference to the correlation coefficient you get.

Correlation matrices for multiple pairs of variables

We can produce correlation matrices involving many pairs of variables. One reason for doing this is as a first step in more complex statistical procedures such as factor analysis and structural linear equations modelling (these are discussed in appendices F and G in section 5 of the website). Another is that correlation matrices can be useful for checking whether different variables are interrelated (i.e. when exploring a data set).

When we developed our eight attitude questions in chapter 5, we raised the question of whether all eight items were equally good measures of people's tolerance to smoking. One way of checking this is to inspect the correlation coefficients between them. If they are measuring the same thing, they should all correlate strongly with each other.

Figure 8.12 shows a bivariate correlation matrix correlating these attitude variables against each other, thereby creating an 8x8 table. We are only interested in half the cells, since the others provide redundant information:

◆ One set of redundant cells consists of those where variables are correlated with themselves. These are the cells that run on what is known as the *principal diagonal* from the top left to the bottom right of the matrix.
◆ A second set of redundant cells comes from the fact that each pair of variables is correlated twice (once above the principal diagonal, and then again below it). Obviously, the correlation coefficient between, say, attitude 2 and attitude 3 is the same as that between attitude 3 and attitude 2, so we only need examine one instance of the correlation.

Some of the correlations look reasonably strong – many are greater than 0.3, and some are near or exceed 0.6 (for example, look at the correlation coefficient between variable 1, *Smoking should be banned in places like restaurants*, and variable 4, *Employers should ban all smoking in workplaces*). Some, however, look rather weak. There is, for example, a coefficient of just −0.20 between variable 2 (*Our society has*

Correlations

		Attitude 1: ban in restaurants	Attitude 2: too much intolerance	Attitude 3: govt not doing enough to discourage	Attitude 4: ban in workplaces	Attitude 5: too much fuss being made	Attitude 6: shouldn't persuade to stop	Attitude 7: should be made illegal	Attitude 8: already enough restrictions
Attitude 1: ban in restaurants	Pearson Correlation	1.000	-.286**	.365**	.595**	-.362**	-.296**	.603**	-.553**
	Sig. (2-tailed)		.000	.000	.000	.000	.000	.000	.000
	N	332	332	332	331	332	331	331	331
Attitude 2: too much intolerance	Pearson Correlation	-.286**	1.000	-.201**	-.270**	.497**	.282**	-.357**	.536**
	Sig. (2-tailed)	.000		.000	.000	.000	.000	.000	.000
	N	332	332	332	331	332	331	331	331
Attitude 3: govt not doing enough to discourage	Pearson Correlation	.365**	-.201**	1.000	.293**	-.388**	-.305**	.362**	-.329**
	Sig. (2-tailed)	.000	.000		.000	.000	.000	.000	.000
	N	332	332	332	331	332	331	331	331
Attitude 4: ban in workplaces	Pearson Correlation	.595**	-.270**	.293**	1.000	-.304**	-.256**	.551**	-.491**
	Sig. (2-tailed)	.000	.000	.000		.000	.000	.000	.000
	N	331	331	331	331	331	331	331	331
Attitude 5: too much fuss being made	Pearson Correlation	-.362**	.497**	-.388**	-.304**	1.000	.420**	-.383**	.536**
	Sig. (2-tailed)	.000	.000	.000	.000		.000	.000	.000
	N	332	332	332	331	332	331	331	331
Attitude 6: shouldn't persuade to stop	Pearson Correlation	-.296**	.282**	-.305**	-.256**	.420**	1.000	-.296**	.431**
	Sig. (2-tailed)	.000	.000	.000	.000	.000		.000	.000
	N	331	331	331	331	331	331	331	331
Attitude 7: should be made illegal	Pearson Correlation	.603**	-.357**	.362**	.551**	-.383**	-.296**	1.000	-.609**
	Sig. (2-tailed)	.000	.000	.000	.000	.000	.000		.000
	N	331	331	331	331	331	331	331	331
Attitude 8: already enough restrictions	Pearson Correlation	-.553**	.536**	-.329**	-.491**	.536**	.431**	-.609**	1.000
	Sig. (2-tailed)	.000	.000	.000	.000	.000	.000	.000	
	N	331	331	331	331	331	331	331	331

** Correlation is significant at the 0.01 level (2-tailed)

Figure 8.12 Correlation matrix of eight attitude variables from the Smoking Survey

How strong is strong?

'What is a large correlation? ... below 0.19 is very low; 0.20 to 0.39 is low; 0.40 to 0.69 is modest; 0.70 to 0.89 is high; and 0.90 to 1 is very high. However, these are rules of thumb and should not be regarded as definitive indications, since there are hardly any guidelines for interpretation over which there is substantial consensus'

Alan Bryman and Duncan Cramer, *Quantitative Data Analysis for Social Scientists* (London: Routledge, 1990), p. 168

become too intolerant towards people who smoke) and variable 3 (*Government isn't doing enough to discourage smoking*).

Where items seem poorly correlated with the others, we could try dropping them and recomputing the summary variable without them in order to produce a more robust and internally coherent overall measure of tolerance to smoking. In the **cleandat.sav** data set, we have included both a six-item and seven-item attitude scale created by deleting the weakest items in the correlation matrix. If you are working with this data set, try using these alternative indexes to retest some of the hypotheses in which the combined attitude score is the dependent variable, and see if it makes any difference to the results (the two new variables are named 'attit6' and 'attit7' respectively). If you are working with your own data set, inspect your correlation matrix and decide whether any items could profitably be deleted from your summary attitude variable.

CONCLUSION

In this chapter we have seen how to assess the strength of association between variables measured at different levels. The higher the level of measurement, the more rigorously we can measure the strength of association. A simple statistic like *phi*, used to assess the association between two dichotomous nominal variables, can do little more than compare 'expected' and 'observed' patterns in the data, but once we move to interval-level measures, we can plot relationships between variables on a graph and can measure their covariance using a statistic like the Pearson correlation coefficient.

In the course of this chapter, we have also begun to test some of the hypotheses from the Smoking Survey. We found no evidence to support our belief that tolerance of smoking will vary by social class (hypothesis 8). Our prediction that parental smoking behaviour influences that of their children when they become adult (hypothesis 1) was also not supported – although further investigation did suggest a possible link between the smoking patterns of mothers and sons, which would need to be tested in further research. More positively, we found good evidence to support hypothesis 2 (that peer groups influence smoking behaviour), and hypothesis 9 (that ex-smokers become less tolerant of smoking, the longer they have given up) also received moderate support (the correlation of 0.26 is fairly low, but is still of some interest).

All of this analysis, of course, has been carried out on quite a small sample of just 334 individuals. The question we have not yet addressed is whether we are justified in assuming that the patterns found in this sample would also be found in the whole population from which it was drawn. To answer this crucial question, we need to look at a group of statistics known collectively as 'inferential statistics' – and this is where we go next.

INFERRING POPULATION PARAMETERS FROM SAMPLE STATISTICS

AIM

This chapter introduces you to 'inferential statistics' (so called because they are used to infer estimates about population parameters from sample data). We look at both univariate and bivariate statistics. By the end of the chapter you should understand:

- What the 'sampling distribution of the mean' is, and why it forms a 'normal' distribution
- How the 'standard error of the mean' is calculated, and how it can be used to find confidence intervals for population estimates
- How the Chi Square statistic can be used to estimate the probability that associations between variables in a sample point to real associations in the population from which the sample was drawn
- The way a Mann-Whitney U Test is calculated to test the significance of associations between variables measured at ordinal level
- The use of Student's t test to assess the significance of associations between variables at interval level, and how other ANOVA designs can be used to test the significance of more complex patterns of association
- The assumptions made, and the conditions required, by different tests of statistical significance
- The difference between 'Type I' and 'Type II' errors

INTRODUCTION

Until now we have been analysing *sample* statistics. But we are not really interested in samples – the only reason we draw a sample is so that we can make estimates about a *population*. It is all very well to describe and find associations between variables in our sample, but what we really want to do is to use these findings to make confident and reliable estimates about patterns in the whole population from which the sample was drawn. To do this, we use 'inferential statistics'.

Inferential statistics can be used to make estimates about single population parameters (e.g. to estimate within a given range how many smokers there are in a population), or to gauge whether an association between variables is likely to exist in the population as a whole (e.g. the probability that the association we found in our sample between peer group smoking and people's own smoking behaviour really does exist in the whole population).

- To make inferences about single population parameters from interval/ratio level sample statistics, we use a statistic called the *Standard Error of the Mean*;
- To make inferences about associations found between sample variables, we use one of a number of statistical *significance tests* (different tests are used at different levels of measurement).

ESTIMATING A SINGLE POPULATION PARAMETER USING THE STANDARD ERROR

Probability sampling revisited

Let us return to the class exercise on sampling that we carried out in chapter 4. There we drew a single probability sample of six students from a room of 32 students, and we calculated some simple sample statistics:

The sample mean age $(\bar{x}) = 25.67$ years
The sample standard deviation $(s) = 7.99$ years

How accurate were these sample statistics as estimates of the mean and standard deviation for all 32 students? When we analysed the ages of all 32 students we found:

The population mean $(\mu) = 28.16$ years
The population standard deviation $(\sigma) = 13.06$

Our sample mean age was therefore about $2\frac{1}{2}$ years below the actual population mean age, and the standard deviation was out by more than 6 years. We saw in chapter 4 that these inaccuracies would probably have been reduced had we taken a bigger sample, for the smaller the sample, the less accurate our population estimates are likely to be.

In this exercise we were able to check the accuracy of our sample estimates because we knew the ages of all 32 people in our population. In real research, however, we cannot do this (if we had information on everybody, we would not need to sample in the first place). We therefore have no choice in real research but to base our population estimates on our sample statistics – even though they may be inaccurate. Given this reliance on sample data, what is needed is some way of gauging how accurate our estimates are likely to be and how much confidence we can put in them. This is what the Standard Error of the Mean is used for.

The sampling distribution of the mean

The Standard Error of the Mean, $SE(\bar{x})$, is the standard deviation of a very special kind of sample that in reality we never actually draw – a sample of sample means. We would get a sample of sample means if we were to keep drawing samples from a population and calculating the mean in each of the samples we draw (for example, we might draw lots of samples and calculate the mean age of the people in each one). In reality, of course, we never do this – we draw one sample and we make our population estimates from this. But let us see what happens when we do take repeated samples from the same population – we can do it easily enough by continuing to draw samples of 6 from our population of 32 students, and for each sample, calculating the average age.

> Go back to the population of 32 students identified in chapter 4. Rather than drawing only one sample of 6, try drawing many repeated samples. For each sample you draw, calculate the mean age. To make things simpler, round the results to the nearest whole number and plot them as a histogram. When we did this, we drew 45 different samples and ended up with the graph reproduced in figure 9.1. If you do it, you will end up with something similar.

Figure 9.1 plots the mean ages (rounded to the nearest whole number) of 45 different samples drawn from our population of 32 students. Each sample was very small (N = 6), as was the original population, and we gave up drawing samples after we had 45 of them (for this exercise to work properly, we would need to draw an infinite number of

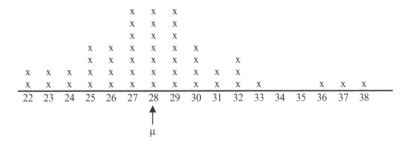

Figure 9.1   Plot of 45 sample mean ages showing clustering around mean age of whole population

fairly large samples from a much larger population). Nevertheless, we can see a clear pattern emerging:

- Most of the sample estimates cluster in quite a narrow range, and there is a tailing off in the number of samples falling a substantial distance away from the main cluster. As we plot more and more sample means, so we see a familiar bell-shaped 'normal' curve beginning to form.
- The *actual* mean age of this population of 32 students ($\mu = 28$) falls in the middle of this sampling distribution. Most of the sample means come fairly close to it, and only a few fall a long way from it (26 of the 45 samples have a mean age within 2 years of the population mean). If we work out the average value of all these sample mean ages – the mean of all these means, or what statisticians call the *Grand Mean* – we find that it equals the mean age of the population from which all the samples were drawn.

The Grand Mean equals the population mean

We drew 45 different samples in the class exercise. If we add up all of the mean values of all of these samples $(22 + 22 + 23 + 23 + 24 + 24 + 25 \ldots$ etc.) and divide by the total number of samples (45), the answer comes to $1268/45 = 28.178$. This figure is the mean of all of the 45 sample means, and is known as the 'Grand Mean'.

The average age of all the 32 students making up our population was 28.16. This is almost exactly the same as the value of the Grand Mean of all the 45 sample means (28.178). If we continued drawing samples (and if we calculated the exact mean ages in each case rather than rounding them), we would find that the Grand Mean is *exactly* the same as the population mean.

Three important principles emerge from all this:

- Provided our sample sizes are not too small and we draw a sufficient number of samples, the sampling distribution of means will tend to form a normal distribution. The significance of this is that it is more likely that any single sample will be close to the true population mean than that it will be a long way from it.
- The bigger the 'sampling fraction', the lower is the spread of sampling means away from the true mean. In other words, the bigger our sample relative to the size of the population, the less likely it is that the mean of any one sample will lie a long way from the true mean of the whole group. You can check this for yourself by putting, say, three of your samples together and calculating the mean age of the total of 18 cases. It will almost certainly be closer to the true mean age of the whole group than any of your smaller samples was. The significance of this is that bigger samples are likely to generate more accurate estimates.
- The greater the variance within a population, the greater is the chance that the mean of any one sample will lie a long way from the true mean. In our group of 32

students, where ages ranged from 19 to 62, the relatively wide scatter of ages meant that some sample means inevitably fell quite a distance from the true population mean (figure 9.1 shows three of the 45 samples had mean ages in the mid to high 30s – up to ten years away from the true mean age of the whole population – and this occurred because some samples inevitably picked up two or three of the older students who then 'pulled up' the average age of the sample). The significance of this is that sample estimates will be the more inexact, the greater the spread of values in the population as a whole.

Calculating the Standard Error from a sampling distribution of means

Looking at the distribution of sample means in figure 9.1, we can work out how far on average each sample mean falls from the Grand Mean by calculating the standard deviation. We saw how to work out a standard deviation by hand in chapter 4, but we also saw how to make the computations easier by means of the following formula:

$$\text{Standard deviation}(s) = \sqrt{\frac{\sum x^2 - \frac{(\sum x)^2}{n}}{n - 1}}$$

To apply this formula to find the standard deviation for our 45 sample means, we do the following:

- Find the value of $\sum x$ (to get this, we must add together all the 45 sample mean ages). The result comes to 1,268. It follows that the value of $(\sum x)^2$ therefore $= 1268^2 = 1,607,824$.
- Find the value of $\sum x^2$, which entails squaring each value of x and then adding them all together. We take the square of the first sample mean of 22 (484), add it to the square of the second sample mean, which is also 22 (484 + 484), add this to the square of the third sample mean of 23 (484 + 484 + 529), and so on through all 45 samples. The result $= 35,886$.

Now that we know the value of $(\sum x)^2$ and $\sum x^2$ we can compute the formula:

$$\left(\sum x\right)^2 \div n = 1,607,824 \div 45 = 35,729.$$

... which subtracted from $\sum x^2 = 35,886 - 35,729 = 157$.
... which divided by $(n - 1) = 157/44 = 3.568$.
Finally we take the square root: $\sqrt{3.568} = 1.89$.

So the standard deviation of this distribution of sample means $= 1.89$. This statistic is the Standard Error of the Mean. What it tells us is that, on average, the mean age of each of the samples we drew in our class exercise was 1.89 years away from the Grand Mean (the mean of all the 45 sample means).

Calculating the Standard Error from a single sample

In real life, we never produce a distribution of sample means. We draw but one sample from a population , not hundreds or thousands of them. How then can we calculate the Standard Error if we only have one sample?

The formula for calculating the Standard Error

The formula is simple enough. We take the standard deviation of the one sample that we have, and we divide it by the square root of the number of cases in the sample. This, magically, gives us the Standard Error. Expressed as an equation:

Standard Error of the Mean = standard deviation ÷ square root of n

or:

$$SE(\bar{x}) = \frac{s}{\sqrt{n}}$$

But what is the logic behind this simple bit of maths?

The logic behind the formula

Let us return to our population of 32 students. How many possible different samples of six students could we draw (with replacement) from a population of this size? The answer is the following (for the exclamation marks, see the box on 'Factorial numbers'):

$$32! \div (24!*6!) = 589,024,800$$

Factorial numbers

The exclamation mark symbol (!) in equations means 'factorial'. This means that the number must be multiplied by each successive number below it. For example, 6! equals 6*5*4*3*2*1 which comes to 720. 24! is 6,204,484 followed by 17 zeros, and 32! is 2,631,308 followed by 29 zeros.

Suppose we drew all 589 million possible samples, and that we calculated the mean age for each of them and plotted the results on a graph. You already know that the result will be a normal distribution (because the sampling distribution of means tends towards normality), but the variance within this sampling distribution of means will be much smaller than the variance within the original population from which all the samples were drawn.

This is because very few of the samples will include many people at the extremes of the age distribution, so the means will tend to cluster tightly around the true mean age in the population. For example, only one out of these millions of samples will consist of the oldest student in the room selected six times (remember that we are sampling with replacement). In fact, with sample sizes of six each time, the variance within the sampling distribution of means will be six times smaller than the variance within the whole population.

It follows from this that we could calculate the variance of the sampling distribution of means by dividing the variance within the whole population by six (the size of each sample). To find the standard deviation of this sampling distribution of means, we would then take the square root of this variance (because, as we know, variance = standard deviation squared). Thus we arrive at the calculation for the Standard Error (i.e. the standard deviation of the sampling distribution of means) as the standard deviation of the population (σ) divided by the square root of the size of each sample (n).

So far, so good. But there is still a problem, for in a real life research project, we will not know the standard deviation in the whole population. All we have to go on is the standard deviation of the one sample we have taken from that population.

However, *provided the sample was drawn randomly and was reasonably large*, its standard deviation should be much the same as that of the whole population. This is because the amount of variability in the whole population should be reflected in the amount of variability picked up in our sample.

To calculate the Standard Error, we therefore take the standard deviation of our particular sample, and assume that this is the same as the standard deviation in the whole population from which the sample is drawn. Divide this sample standard deviation (s) by the square root of the sample size, and you end up with the equation for calculating the Standard Error:

$$SE(\bar{x}) = \frac{s}{\sqrt{n}}$$

Applying this formula to the single sample of six students with which we have been working, we estimate the Standard Error of the Mean as:

$$\frac{7.99}{\sqrt{6}}$$

which comes out at 3.26. This is considerably larger than the actual Standard Error, which we calculated earlier as 1.89. The reason for the difference is that our sample standard deviation is a poor reflection of the standard deviation in the population (see chapter 4). With a larger sample, we would expect the standard deviation more accurately to represent that of the population, in which case the Standard Error would be more accurate too.

Making estimates based on the Standard Error

Why bother doing all this? The answer is that the Standard Error allows us to calculate confidence limits when we use sample statistics to infer the value of population parameters.

In the case of our sample of six students, we know that the mean age is 25.67 and the standard error is 3.26. This tells us that the average sample estimate will be 3.26 years away from the actual mean age of the population (because the Standard Error is the standard deviation of a hypothetical distribution of thousands of sample mean ages, and the mean of all these samples – the *Grand Mean* – equals the mean age of the whole population from which they are drawn).

Knowing that, on average, any one sample is likely to be 3.26 years above or below the mean age of the population tells us that, if our sample is an average one, the population mean age will usually fall somewhere in the range 25.67 ± 3.26 – i.e. anywhere between 22.41 and 28.93.

But how likely is it that our sample is an 'average' one? We can calculate this probability because we know that the sampling distribution of the mean is normally distributed – and any normal distribution curve has certain invariant properties:

♦   about 68% of cases cluster in a range of ±1 standard deviation from the mean;
♦   roughly 95% of cases will fall within ±2 standard deviations;
♦   approximately 99% of cases will fall within ±3 standard deviations.

Because the sampling distribution of the mean is normally distributed, and the Grand Mean is equal to the true population mean, μ, it must follow that

♦   about two-thirds of all the samples that we might draw will have a mean age within ±1 standard error of the true mean in the population as a whole;
♦   around 19 out of 20 samples will have a mean age within ±2 standard errors of the true population mean;
♦   some 99 out of 100 samples will have a mean age within ±3 standard errors of the true mean.

But if 68% of all samples will lie within + or −1 standard error of the true population mean, then there must be a 68% chance that our sample is one of them. This means there are 2 chances in 3 that the mean age recorded in our sample is within 1 standard error of the true mean age of the population from which the sample was drawn. Similarly, there is a 95% probability that our sample mean is no more than 2 standard errors away from the true population mean, and there is a 99% chance that our sample mean is no more than 3 standard errors from the true population mean.

Returning to our original sample of six students, where the mean age is 25.67 years, and the standard error is 3.26, we can therefore say that:

♦   there is a 68% probability (i.e. 2 chances in 3) that the mean age of the population from which this sample was drawn is somewhere between 22.41 and 28.93 (i.e. the sample mean of 25.67 + or − the standard error of 3.26);
♦   there is a 95% probability (i.e. 19 chances out of 20) that the mean age of the population lies between 19.15 and 32.19;
♦   there is a 99% probability (i.e. 99 chances out of 100) that the mean age lies between 15.89 and 35.45.

Of course, in this hypothetical example we know the mean age of the whole population of students from which this sample was drawn. It is 28.16. In this case, therefore, we can see that even the first of these estimates is accurate. Normally, though, we look for a higher level of confidence than 68 per cent (a one in three chance of being wrong is too risky), and select either 95 or 99 per cent.

Calculating the Standard Error using SPSS

When running 'Frequencies' in SPSS, it is a simple matter to request that the Standard Error be calculated. Indeed, we did it back in chapter 7 when we generated summary statistics for the number of cigarettes smoked per week by respondents in the Smoking Survey. The table in figure 7.5 above (p. 179) shows that the mean number smoked was 77.25, and that the Standard Error was 4.787. You are now able to interpret what this means:

♦ There is a 68% probability that average cigarette consumption in the whole population from which the sample was taken is in the range 77.3 ± 4.8 (i.e. between 72.5 and 82.1).
♦ We can be a lot more confident if we stretch the estimate to cover 2 standard errors, for there is a 95% probability that average consumption is in the range 77.3 ± 9.6 (= 67.7 to 86.9).
♦ We can be 99% confident that the average lies within 3 standard errors −77.3 ± 14.4 (= 62.9 to 91.7).

Try running some summary statistics on other continuous interval- or ratio-level variables in the data set you are using. Work out population estimates at different confidence levels based on the Standard Error.

ASSESSING THE SIGNIFICANCE OF AN ASSOCIATION BETWEEN TWO CATEGORICAL VARIABLES USING PEARSON'S CHI SQUARE TEST

The Standard Error is useful when we want to estimate a single population parameter from a sample statistic, but surveys are not limited to describing the characteristics of populations. We also use them to test hypotheses about relationships between social phenomena, and to do this we look for evidence of association between variables.

In chapter 8 we learned about a range of statistics used to measure the *strength* of association between two or more variables. But if we find an association between two variables in a sample, how confident can we be that it points to a real relationship in the population as a whole? We need some way of assessing the probability that an association detected in our sample exists in the whole population.

This is what a test of statistical *significance* is used for. One of the most common is the Pearson Chi Square test, which is used to gauge the probability that a statistical association between two categorical variables in a sample reflects a real relationship in the whole population.

Testing the null hypothesis

The table in figure 8.3 (p. 205) showed a moderately strong association in the Smoking Survey data between people's smoking behaviour and that of their family and friends. How confident can we be that this is an association which exists in the population? It is possible that our sample of just 334 people is not really representative of the whole population of Brighton, in which case the discovery of an association in our sample between peer group smoking and people's own smoking behaviour might tell us nothing about the way the other quarter of a million people in the city are behaving. What we need is some way of judging the likelihood that the pattern in our sample reflects the pattern in the wider population. This is where the Chi Square significance test can help.

We saw in chapter 8 that the Chi Square statistic summarizes the extent to which observed frequencies in a contingency table diverge from what would be expected given the row and column totals. In chapter 8, we used Chi Square to work out the *phi* coefficient (a standardized measure of strength of association between two variables), but we can also use it to calculate the probability that any pattern of association discovered in a sample reflects an association in a population.

The Popperian logic in Pearson's Chi Square test

The basic principle of Pearson's Chi Square test is that we set out to *falsify* (rather than confirm) a hypothesis. This is in line with Popper's argument, outlined in chapter 1, that we can never be certain that a proposition is true, but can only demonstrate empirically that certain hypotheses are false. The hypothesis that we hope to falsify by using Chi Square is the *null hypothesis* (sometimes expressed symbolically as H_0), which states that that there is *no* association between parameters in the *population*, and that any association observed between variables in the *sample* could have arisen due to random error.

Looking at the data in figure 8.3, the null hypothesis which we have to test states that there is no association in the wider population between people's smoking behaviour and the smoking behaviour of their friends and family, and that the association found in our particular sample is therefore a fluke. If our statistical test shows that the association we have found in our sample is highly unlikely to have occurred by chance, then the null hypothesis will be rejected. This would then offer support to (but not conclusive proof of) our *research* hypothesis, which states that there is an association between these two population parameters.

The way we test the null hypothesis is by looking at the size of the association between the variables, and deciding whether an association this big (or small) is likely to have occurred in a sample if it did not actually exist in the population as a whole.

♦   We first calculate the 'model of no association' predicted by the null hypothesis. This involves calculating the *expected* frequencies for each cell of the table in figure 8.3.

- This model is then compared with the actual cell frequencies (the *observed* frequencies).
- The larger the summed differences between the observed and the expected frequencies, the less likely it is that they occurred as a fluke, and the more inclined we become to reject the null hypothesis and conclude that the association between our variables probably does indicate a real association between these parameters in the population.

Using Chi Square to test the null hypothesis

We saw how to work out the value of Chi Square (χ^2) in chapter 8:

- The first step is to calculate the expected frequency, *e*, for each cell (we do this by multiplying the row total by the column total and then dividing by the total number of cases – the expected frequencies for the table in figure 8.3 are given in the third column in table 9.1).
- Next, we calculate the extent to which the expected frequency in each cell differs from the observed frequency, *o* (table 9.1, column 4) and we square these differences to make them all positive (column 5).
- Because cells with large numbers will tend to have larger absolute differences between *e* and *o*, we express the result in each cell as a proportion of its expected frequency (i.e. we find out proportionately by how much *o* varies from *e* – column 6), and we then sum them to arrive at the Chi Square statistic. In table 9.1, we see this is 84.96.

We noted in chapter 8 that the more cells there are in a table, the higher the Chi Square statistic is likely to be. To allow for this, we must calculate the 'degrees of freedom' in the table in figure 8.3 (i.e. the number of cells which are free to vary given that we know the row and column totals). The simple formula for calculating the *degrees of freedom (df)* in a table is:

$$df = (\text{no. of rows} - 1) \times (\text{no. of columns} - 1)$$

Table 9.1   Calculation of Chi Square statistic (based on table in figure 8.3)

Cell	Observed	Expected	$(o-e)$	$(o-e)^2$	$(o-e)^2 \div e$
a	14	36.18	−22.18	491.95	13.60
b	23	40.31	−17.31	299.64	07.43
c	66	52.20	+13.80	190.44	03.65
d	66	40.31	+25.69	660.00	16.37
e	56	33.82	+22.18	491.95	14.55
f	55	37.69	+17.31	299.64	07.95
g	35	48.80	−13.80	190.44	03.90
h	12	37.69	−25.69	660.00	17.51
				Chi Square $= 84.96$	

Table 9.2   Distribution of Chi Square (up to 3 degrees of freedom)

df	Probability												
	.99	.98	.95	.90	.80	.70	.50	.30	.20	.10	.05	.02	.01	.001
1	.0001	.0006	.0039	.0158	.0642	.148	.455	1.074	1.642	2.706	3.841	5.412	6.635	10.827
2	.0201	.0404	.103	.211	.4460	.713	1.386	2.408	3.219	4.605	5.991	7.824	9.210	13.815
3	.115	.185	.352	.584	1.005	1.424	2.366	3.665	4.642	6.251	7.815	9.8371	1.341	16.268

Source: Hubert Blalock, *Social Statistics*, 2nd edn (Singapore: McGraw-Hill, 1979)

In a 4×2 table like this one, there are therefore $(4 - 1) \times (2 - 1) = 3$ degrees of freedom (once we know the values of any three of the cells, the values in all the others are necessarily predetermined given the row and column totals).

We now have all the information we need to calculate the probability that the pattern in figure 8.3 would have occurred in our sample if there were no association in the population between people's smoking behaviour and that of their peer groups. Knowing the value of Chi Square (84.96) and the degrees of freedom (3), we can look up the probability on a *Distribution of Chi Square* table.

Table 9.2 tells us the probabilities of finding different magnitudes of Chi Square (given 1, 2 or 3 degrees of freedom) assuming no association between two variables. We can see that there is a good chance of finding low values of Chi Square even when two variables are not related (e.g. at 1 degree of freedom, there is a 90 per cent chance of finding a value of Chi Square of 0.0158 or less). This is because we can expect a small difference between expected and observed frequencies to occur in any sample, simply as a matter of chance. But as the values of Chi Square increase, so the likelihood that they will occur by chance falls. There is, for example, only 1 chance in 1,000 ($p = 0.001$) of finding a Chi Square as large as 10.827 in a table with 1 degree of freedom if the two variables are not in fact associated with each other.

In our case, we have a Chi Square value of 84.96 with 3 degrees of freedom. Reading along the relevant row in table 9.2, we see that this far exceeds even the value (16.268) that might be expected to occur just one time in a thousand. In other words, there is less than one chance in a thousand that the association found in our sample

---

When should we reject the null hypothesis?

Conventionally, with anything less than 95 per cent likelihood ($p < 0.05$) we can reject the null hypothesis, but with large data sets it is often safer to look for 99 per cent ($p < 0.01$). You should decide what level of significance you will accept *before* you calculate Chi Square. On a sample the size of our Smoking Survey ($N = 327$, with 7 missing cases in this table), 95 per cent is probably OK, and 99 per cent is certainly acceptable. The larger your data set, the more conservative you should be in stipulating an acceptable level, for with large data sets quite small differences can turn out to be statistically significant.

between smoking and peer group behaviour would have occurred if the association did not also exist in the wider population from which the sample was drawn. The null hypothesis can therefore be rejected fairly confidently – we are pretty sure (though not *absolutely* certain) that our result holds true for the population about which we are making our claims. We therefore say we have a *statistically significant* finding.

Calculating statistical significance using SPSS

SPSS will calculate both the Chi Square statistic and the probability of its distribution – select it under 'Statistics' in the 'Crosstabs' dialog box. Figure 9.2 gives the output for the cross-tabulation in the table in figure 8.3 (p. 205 above). It confirms the value of Chi Square (which we calculated by hand) as 84.954, and it tells us that the probability of such a high value occurring by chance is 0.000 (the probability is only given to 3 decimal points, but it is not literally zero; we would record this probability as $p < 0.001$ – less than 1 in 1,000).

> How are the probabilities in table 9.2 calculated? If you are happy to take these probability calculations on trust, carry on reading. But if you are curious about how these calculations were derived, you may want to read appendix D 'The binomial distribution' on the website (www.surveymethods.co.uk) before you go on.

Assumptions and limitations of the Chi Square test of significance

Assumptions

Although Chi Square is a non-parametric statistic, there are a number of assumptions that need to be met if it is to be used to test for statistical significance:

♦ *The data are categorical*   The variables to be used in the analysis should be either nominal or ordinal categories.

Chi-Square Tests

	Value	df	Asymp. Sig (2-sided)
Pearson Chi-Square	84.954[a]	3	.000
Likelihood Ratio	90.965	3	.000
Linear-by-Linear Association	81.010	1	.000
N of Valid Cases	327		

a. 0 cells (.0%) have expected count less than 5.
The minimum expected count is 33.82

Figure 9.2   Pearson Chi Square test result using SPSS

◆ *The sample has been randomly generated*   The logic of the test is that everybody in the target population had an equal chance of being selected. If (as in our Smoking Survey) you used a non-probability technique such as a quota sample, this assumption may have been violated, in which case you should treat the test results with caution.

◆ *The expected cell frequency (e) should not fall below 5 in more than 20 per cent of cells*   The Chi Square statistic may be distorted if used on small samples, or on tables with empty cells or where more than 20 per cent of cells have expected frequencies lower than 5. This problem can be avoided by using *Fisher's exact test* instead.

Tests for small samples and 2 x 2 contingency tables

If you are producing a 2×2 cross-tabulation with a small sample size (around 20 or less), and/or expected values in a given cell are small (less than 5), then *Fisher's exact test* should be used instead of Chi Square. SPSS automatically produces Fisher's test if you request a Chi Square on a 2×2 table where any expected frequency is less than 5.

If your sample size is greater than 20 or so, then with two dichotomous variables *Yates' correction* (which appears in the SPSS output as the 'continuity correction') should be applied to the Chi Square statistic. This correction reduces positive differences between observed and expected frequencies by 0.5 while increasing negative differences by the same amount (this takes account of the fact that the values in the binomial distribution are whole numbers – because they are sample proportions – and that a more accurate approximation to normality can therefore be achieved by taking the mid-points between numbers; for an explanation of the binomial distribution, see appendix B on the website). The effect is marginal, and the correction is unnecessary on any table larger than a 2×2. SPSS automatically gives you this correction when you request Chi Square for a 2×2 table.

Type I and Type II errors

Statistically significant results are easier to achieve with a large sample than a small one. Associations that may be of very little *substantive* significance may nevertheless appear to be *statistically* significant when using Chi Square on large samples.

A *Type I error* is said to occur when we believe that an association between two variables is significant when really it is not. One way to minimize Type I errors is to set a higher level of significance with large samples (for example, only rejecting the null hypothesis when $p < 0.01$ rather than $p < 0.05$). In surveys where the sample size is very large, statistical tests may be of limited value and you should examine the size of the difference and make a sensible judgement yourself. Indeed, even on smaller samples, we should resist the temptation to be driven by the results of significance tests – always inspect the cell percentages visually and decide whether the difference looks large enough to get excited about.

With small samples the opposite problem may arise. Differences between observed and expected values may have to be huge before Chi Square gives a significant result. This can lead to a *Type II error*, where we reject an association as not significant when in reality it is. Again, you need to use your common sense.

Spurious association

A Chi Square test that is statistically significant only tells you that you can safely reject the null hypothesis – i.e. that there is probably an *association* between the parameters in the whole population. The test cannot, however, tell you whether this association is *causal*. This means that it cannot demonstrate that your hypothesis is correct. Remember that statistical association does not demonstrate causation. As we saw in chapter 3, just because two variables covary, it does not necessarily follow that one is causing the change in the other.

MEASURING SIGNIFICANCE OF ASSOCIATION WITH ORDINAL DATA: THE MANN-WHITNEY U TEST

In cases where the dependent variable is measured at ordinal level or higher, and where the independent variable is dichotomous, we can use a more powerful test than Chi Square – the Mann-Whitney U test.

Assumptions

Like Chi Square, the U test calculates the likelihood that an observed association between an independent and a dependent variable could have arisen by chance. It therefore tests the null hypothesis that there is no association between them in the population. It is a more powerful test than Chi Square because it makes use of the fact that the dependent variable is ordered on a scale from low to high.

The U test is one of a range of *independent samples* tests. It assumes that the two groups being compared are independent of each other and are not matched in any way. For example, we should not use an independent samples test to compare male and female attitudes about smoking if our sample consists of husband and wife pairs because the two samples would be linked. Fortunately, if the overall sample has been randomly selected, any subsamples selected from within the main sample will automatically be independent of each other (because the selection of one individual to be included in the sample will have had no effect on the probability of another also being included).

Like Chi Square, the U test assumes that the sample has been drawn randomly, but it makes no assumptions about the population from which the sample has been drawn (i.e. it is a non-parametric test).

Calculating the value of U

The Mann-Whitney U test examines whether two groups differ significantly with respect to their overall rank location on a dependent variable. It does this by testing the null hypothesis that their median locations on the ranking of the dependent variable do not differ significantly.

'Sorry, sir — this is a non-smoking ocean.'

We can illustrate this with reference to hypothesis 6 from the Smoking Survey (the 'self-interest' hypothesis):

Smokers will express greater tolerance of smoking than will non-smokers. Non-smokers will be more supportive of smoking restrictions than smokers.

To test this hypothesis we take var00003 (whether the respondent has smoked in the last week) as our independent variable, and the derived variable 'attit8' (the combined attitude score) as our dependent variable. The Mann-Whitney U test is the appropriate statistic to test the significance of the association between these two variables, for the independent variable is dichotomous, and the dependent variable is measured on an ordinal scale (scores range from 8 to 40, with low scores indicating intolerance towards smoking).

Imagine we have a sample of just 11 respondents (labelled A to K), five of whom (A through E) have smoked in the last week. Inspecting their scores on our combined index of smoking attitudes ('attit8') we might find a distribution something like this:

Smokers		Non-smokers	
A	12	F	11
B	8	G	14
C	9	H	20
D	16	I	16
E	10	J	9
		K	21

These 11 people can be ranked in ascending order of their scores. For example, person B ranks first with a lowest score of 8; respondents C and J tie for second place with scores of 9 (which means that each occupies position 2.5 on the ranking, midway between second and third); and so on as follows:

Overall rank order

B	1
C & J	2.5
E	4
F	5
A	6
G	7
D & I	8.5
H	10
K	11

The first part of the Mann-Whitney U test involves adding the total rank scores of the smaller of the two groups (in this example, the smokers). This gives us the W statistic:

$$W = 6 + 1 + 2.5 + 8.5 + 4 = 22$$

This figure is then averaged to give a mean rank for smokers: $22/5 = 4.4$. The question is whether this mean ranking is sufficiently different from the overall rankings in the total sample to allow us to conclude that smoking is significantly associated with attitudes. To see if this is the case, we compare the W statistic with the total ranking scores when the value of W is removed. The resulting statistic is known as U. Thus, U equals (total ranked scores of the whole sample) minus W (total ranked scores of smokers only).

In this example, the total ranked scores of the whole sample equals

$$1 + 2.5 + 2.5 + 4 + 5 + 6 + 7 + 8.5 + 8.5 + 10 + 11 = 66$$

It follows that $U = 66 - W$, which is $66 - 22 = 44$. The probability of a difference of this magnitude occurring by chance can then be looked up on a table (derived from the binomial distribution) giving the values of U, in much the same way as we did for the Chi Square test.

Running a U test using SPSS

If you are working with the Smoking Survey data set, run a U test using var00003 and 'attit8' from the **cleandat.sav** data set. If you are working with your own data, select two appropriate variables (the independent variable should be dichotomous and the dependent variable should be ordinal) and follow the same procedure

To run a U test using SPSS, click on 'Analyze' in the menu bar and select 'Nonparametric tests' and then '2 independent samples...'. Your dependent variable should be pasted into the 'Test variable list' box, and your dichotomous independent variable will be your 'Grouping variable' (you need to tell SPSS what the values of the groups are – for example, var00003 coded non-smokers '0' and smokers '1') When you click on OK, the Mann-Whitney test is preselected by default.

Our hypothesis predicts that smokers will score significantly higher on the attitude variable than non-smokers. We therefore need to test the null hypothesis, that attitudes between the two groups do not differ.

We can see from the table in figure 9.3 that the average non-smoker ranked 118th out of 330 on the attitude scale, while the average smoker ranked 216th. Clearly there is a difference between the two groups. To see whether it is statistically significant, the

Ranks

	Smoked in last week?	N	Mean Rank	Sum of Ranks
Attitude score (8 items)	no	170	117.63	19996.50
	yes	160	216.37	34618.50
	Total	330		

Test Statistics[a]

	Attitude score (8 items)
Mann-Whitney U	5461.500
Wilcoxon W	19996.500
Z	−9.406
Asymp. Sig. (2-tailed)	.000

a. Grouping Variable: Smoked in last week?

Figure 9.3   Results of a Mann-Whitney U test assessing the significance of the variation in attitudes to smoking between smokers and non-smokers

test works out how many times non-smokers come before smokers in the rank ordering. This is expressed in the total figure, U (given as 5461.5). The probability that U would be as great as it is if smokers and non-smokers in the total population from which this sample has been drawn did not in fact differ in their attitudes is then calculated (this is done by working out how many samples of smokers and non-smokers would reveal a difference of this magnitude if we drew all the different samples that were possible).

Finally, we are given a two-tailed probability statistic. Anything higher than 0.05 will mean we cannot reject the null hypothesis (i.e. the difference in scores between smokers and non-smokers is not big enough to be considered significant). In this case, however, the difference appears highly significant (p is less than 0.001). In fewer than 1 in 10,000 random samples would we expect to find a difference in attitudes of this magnitude if smokers and non-smokers in the population from which the subsamples are drawn did not have different attitudes.

We can therefore reject the null hypothesis – that the two groups do not differ on the dependent variable – in favour of our research hypothesis, that people's attitudes regarding the regulation of smoking will vary according to self-interest (i.e. smokers will oppose regulation, non-smokers will support it). We conclude, therefore, that hypothesis 6 is supported by our data.

MEASURING STATISTICAL SIGNIFICANCE USING INTERVAL/RATIO LEVEL DATA: STUDENT'S t TEST

When a dependent variable is measured at ordinal level, we use a test of statistical significance which compares group rankings, thereby making use of the fact that the data are ordered. When a dependent variable is measured at interval level, however, we can test the statistical significance of differences even more rigorously, for we can now compare the mean scores for different groups.

The simplest test which involves comparison of means is *Student's t test*. The name derives from the pseudonym adopted by William Gosset, the man who developed it around the turn of the twentieth century.

The logic of a t test

Student's t test is used to test the significance of a difference between the mean values recorded for two groups on an interval-level dependent variable. Assuming the two groups are independent of each other, we use the *independent samples t test* (if they are not, then we use a *paired samples t test*).

To assess whether the mean scores for two groups are significantly different, we have to take account of the variability of the scores *within* each group as well as the difference in means *between* them. To see why, look at the examples in figure 9.4 which plots two different hypothetical distributions of scores of two different groups (say, smokers and non-smokers). The difference between the group means is the same in both examples, but the spread about the means is clearly very different.

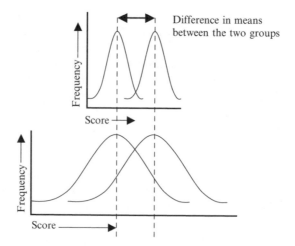

Figure 9.4 Variation within and between groups

In the first example there is little variability about the mean score for each group and there is little overlap between the distributions of the two groups, but in the second, there is much more variability about the means and there is considerable overlap of the scores. Clearly, the scores for the two groups in the first example are more distinct than in the second (i.e. the independent variable is producing a much clearer difference in the values of the dependent variable in the first example than it is in the second). The t test takes this into account by looking at the degree of variability *within* the groups as well as the differences *between* the group means.

Assumptions

Unlike the Chi Square and Mann-Whitney U tests, the t test is a *parametric* statistic which means that it makes certain assumptions about the population from which the sample has been drawn (and hence about the sample itself). Two, in particular, are important:

◆ It assumes that the population is normally distributed on the dependent variable. If this requirement of normality cannot be met (even after transforming the values of the variable by logging, cubing, or whatever – see chapter 7), then you should probably use a non-parametric test (e.g. the Mann-Whitney U test) instead.
◆ It also requires that the variance within each of the groups being compared should not be too dissimilar.

Like all other inferential statistics, the t test also assumes that the sample has been randomly generated from a population.

A worked example of a t test

Hypothesis 5 in the Smoking Survey predicts:

The more stressed people claim to be, the more they are likely to smoke.

When we developed this hypothesis, we thought that people who feel stressed would be more likely to smoke (stress is the independent variable), but we also speculated that smokers would claim to feel more stressed because this would help to rationalize their smoking (stress is the dependent variable). In this example, we shall test the second of these interpretations.

We measured stress by asking people to tell us how stressed they felt, on a scale from 0 to 10 (var00029). For hypothesis 5 to be supported (i.e. for the null hypothesis to be rejected), we should find significantly higher reported mean stress levels among smokers than among non-smokers (var00003).

To see how a t test is calculated, imagine that we wish to compare the reported stress levels of just five smokers and five non-smokers. Their stress scores are as follows:

x_1 (smokers): 7 6 8 10 3

x_2 (non-smokers): 5 4 5 2 8

We need to test the null hypothesis that there is no statistically significant difference in the means of these stress scores (i.e. that $u_1 = u_2$).

Step 1: Calculate the difference in means between the groups

Given that the test involves comparing the mean stress levels of smokers and non-smokers, we begin by calculating what these are:

$$\text{Mean of } x_1 = (7 + 6 + 8 + 10 + 3)/5 = 6.8$$

$$\text{Mean of } x_2 = (5 + 4 + 5 + 2 + 8)/5 = 4.8$$

The difference of means between the two groups therefore $= 6.8 - 4.8 = 2.0$. The t test will work out the likelihood of drawing two samples of 5 individuals each and finding a difference of 2.0 in their mean stress scores.

Step 2: Calculate the variance in scores within each group

Next, we calculate the variance within each group (i.e. the sum of the squared deviations from the mean). For the smokers, this works out as in table 9.3.

Table 9.3 Variance in scores of the smokers

Case number	Deviation from the mean	Squared deviation
1	$7 - 6.8 = 0.2$	0.04
2	$6 - 6.8 = -0.8$	0.64
3	$8 - 6.8 = 1.2$	1.44
4	$10 - 6.8 = 3.2$	10.24
5	$3 - 6.8 = -3.8$	14.44
	Sum of squares $=$	26.80

From this:

$$\text{Variance} = 26.80/(n - 1) = 26.80/4 = 6.7$$

$$\text{Standard deviation} = \text{square root of variance} = 2.5884$$

Similarly for the non-smokers, the variance can be calculated as $= 4.7$ and the standard deviation $= 2.1679$.

Step 3: Determine the degree of difference in group means, given the variation in scores within the groups (the value of t)

William Gosset ('Student') proved mathematically that if you took an infinite number of samples, the variance of the resulting distribution would be the same as the average variance in any one sample plus the average variance in any other sample. This means that we can work out the variance (and hence the standard deviation) of a hypothetical sampling distribution of means from our two independent samples – which in turn means we can work out the Standard Error.

We have already calculated the variance within each of our groups (step 2). Given Gosset's proof, we can therefore work out what the variance would be in a distribution of mean scores of an infinite number of samples of five people per sample. For each of our two groups, we divide the variance by the number of cases (to get an average of the variation of each case from the mean):

$$\text{Smokers:}\quad 6.7/5 = 1.34$$

$$\text{Nonsmokers:}\quad 4.7/5 = 0.94$$

We add these together to find the variance in the sampling distribution of means (because Gosset proved that this is the same as the sum of averaged variances in any two samples). Thus $1.34 + 0.94 = 2.28$. If we then take the square root of this ($\sqrt{2.28} = 1.51$), we will find the standard deviation of the sampling distribution of means – i.e. the Standard Error.

To complete the t test, we simply need to express the difference of means between our two groups (which is 2) as a proportion of the Standard Error:

$$\text{t value} = \frac{2}{1.51} = 1.32$$

This figure of 1.32 tells us that the difference in mean stress scores between smokers and non-smokers, relative to the scatter of scores within each group, equals 1.32. Put another way, the stress scores of smokers and non-smokers are 32 per cent more different than we would expect given the overall variation in patterns of reported stress. But is this enough to convince us that there really is a difference in the population from which these samples were drawn?

Step 4: Calculate the probability that this degree of difference in sample mean scores could arise if the mean scores of these groups in the population were the same

To answer this we refer to a table of t values to see how many times we could expect to get a difference this big between two samples (one of five smokers and one of five non-

Table 9.4   Distribution of t (extract)

df	Level of significance for one-tailed test					
	.10	.05	.025	.01	.005	.0005
6	1.440	1.943	2.447	3.143	3.707	5.959
7	1.415	1.895	2.365	2.998	3.499	5.405
8	1.397	1.860	2.306	2.896	3.355	5.041
9	1.383	1.833	2.262	2.821	3.250	4.781
10	1.372	1.812	2.228	2.764	3.169	4.587

Source: Extract of table D from Hubert Blalock, *Social Statistics*, 2nd edn (Singapore, McGraw-Hill, 1979), p. 603

smokers) drawn at random from a population where there is no association between smoking and levels of stress. The degrees of freedom will be $N-2$ (for each group mean costs us 1 degree of freedom). In our example, this is $10-2=8$ degrees of freedom.

Table 9.4 reproduces an extract from a table of t values. We can see that at the crucial 5 per cent probability threshold, the value of t is 1.86. We have fallen short of this (a value of 1.32 will be obtained by chance in more than one sample in ten) so the null hypothesis cannot be rejected. There is no statistically significant difference between the scores in our imaginary example of two samples of smokers and non-smokers.

Running a t test using SPSS

> Either replicate the following procedure using the Smoking Survey data, or run a test on your own data set by selecting a dichotomous variable as your independent variable, and a continuous interval- or ratio-level variable for your dependent variable.

To run a simple t test, select 'Compare Means' and then 'Independent-Samples T Test...' from clicking the Analyze menu. Your dependent variable should be pasted into the 'Test Variable(s)' box, and the dichotomous independent variable is pasted into the 'Grouping Variable' box. You also need to click on the button labelled 'Define groups' so you can specify the values for the two groups defined by the independent variable (in the Smoking Survey, non-smokers – the first group – were coded '0' and smokers – the second group – were coded '1').

Figure 9.5 shows output from a t test for the significance of the difference in stress levels reported by smokers and non-smokers in our survey. From the first part of the output we see that non-smokers have a lower mean stress score (4.57 against 5.61 for smokers), which is what the hypothesis predicted, but we need to check the second part of the output to see whether this difference is big enough to be significant.

Group Statistics

	Smoked in last week?	N	Mean	Std.Deviation	Std.Error Mean
How stressed (scale 0 to 10)	no	162	4.5710	2.5446	.1999
	yes	152	5.6118	2.4952	.2024

Independent Samples Test

		Levene's Test for Equality of Variances		t-test for Equality of Means					95% Confidence Interval of the Difference	
		F	Sig.	t	df	Sig. (2-tailed)	Mean Difference	Std. Error Difference	Lower	Upper
How stressed (scale 0 to 10)	Equal variances assumed	.153	.696	−3.657	312	.000	−1.0409	.2847	−1.6009	−.4808
	Equal variances not assumed			−3.659	311.388	.000	−1.0409	.2845	−1.6006	−.4811

Figure 9.5   T test comparing mean reported stress levels of smokers and non-smokers

A t test requires that the variance within the two groups being compared should not be too dissimilar. Levene's test (in the second part of the output) checks this:

♦   If the result is not significant (p > 0.05) then the t test requirement (that the variances of the two groups are similar) has not been violated. We can therefore read the statistics from the row that corresponds to 'Equal variances assumed'.
♦   If the result is significant (p < 0.05) then the variances of the two groups are different, in which case we read the statistics from the row that corresponds to 'Equal variances not assumed'.

The probability in this case is 0.696, which tells us that the difference in variance between the stress scores of smokers and non-smokers is not significant. We can therefore rely on the statistics from the first row ('Equal variances assumed').

The t value (−3.657) tells us that the difference in scores between smokers and non-smokers is more than 3 times greater than we might have predicted from the scatter of scores within the two groups. The significance level of 0.000 tells us that a mean difference in stress scores of 1.04 with 312 degrees of freedom would occur by chance in fewer than 1 in 1,000 samples.

The results from the analysis therefore indicate that we can reject the null hypothesis that the means of the two groups are not significantly different. Hypothesis 5, that smokers and non-smokers differ significantly in the levels of stress that they report, is therefore supported.

ANALYSIS OF VARIANCE (ANOVA) MODELS

The t test is the simplest version of a cluster of tests which are collectively known as *analysis of variance*, or ANOVA. A t test is a *one-way* analysis of variance:

♦ there is only one independent variable (e.g. whether people have smoked in the last week or not), *and*
♦ the independent variable is dichotomous (it has only two values – in this case, either people have smoked in the last week, or they have not).

Things, however, are often more complicated than this. Let us consider briefly some examples of more complex models that can be tested.

One-way ANOVA using an independent variable with more than two values

Sometimes, our independent variable may have *more than two values*. Suppose, for example, that we want to test a slightly different version of hypothesis 9 in the Smoking Survey. The original hypothesis is that ex-smokers tend to become less tolerant of smoking, the longer they maintain their abstinence, and in chapter 8 we found some evidence to support this. But do ex-smokers ever become as intolerant as those who never smoked at all?

One way of testing this would be to design an ANOVA model comparing the mean attitude scores of smokers, ex-smokers and non-smokers (we assume for the purposes of this and subsequent analyses that the summary attitude score created in the analysis of the Smoking Survey, 'attit8', can be treated as an interval scale). We still have a single independent variable (so this is still a *one-way* ANOVA), but it now has three values.

Figure 9.6 gives most of the SPSS output from a one-way ANOVA comparing the mean attitude scores of those who have never smoked (Group 0), those who still smoke (Group 1), and those who used to smoke (Group 2). We can see from the 'Descriptives' summary that their mean scores vary from a low of 18.7 for the non-smokers, through 22.8 for the ex-smokers, to a high of 26.9 for the current smokers. With higher scores indicating greater tolerance towards smoking, these results seem to lend support to our hypothesis that smokers are most tolerant, non-smokers are least tolerant, and ex-

Descriptives

Attitude score (8 items)

	N	Mean	Std. Deviation	Std. Error	95% Confidence Interval for Mean Lower Bound	Upper Bound	Minimum	Maximum
non-smoker	100	18.7400	5.6936	.5694	17.6103	19.8697	8.00	30.00
current-smoker	169	26.9467	5.2839	.4065	26.1443	27.7492	13.00	40.00
ex-smoker	62	22.7903	5.7862	.7348	21.3209	24.2597	13.00	36.00
Total	331	23.6888	6.5678	.3610	22.9787	24.3990	8.00	40.00

ANOVA

Attitude score (8 items)

	Sum of Squares	df	Mean Square	F	Sig.
Between Groups	4292.914	2	2146.457	70.814	.000
Within Groups	9942.035	328	30.311		
Total	14234.949	330			

Figure 9.6   Average tolerance levels of non-smokers, smokers and ex-smokers (a one-way ANOVA model)

smokers fall midway between the two. But are the differences between these three groups *significant*?

Figure 9.6 suggests that they are. A glance at the 95 per cent confidence intervals for each group's mean score in the 'Descriptives' table shows that these do not come close to overlapping with each other, so we can be pretty sure that the differences between them have not arisen by chance. This is confirmed by looking at the F ratio in the ANOVA output where we see that the average amount of variation in scores *between* the three groups is some 70 times higher than that *within* them, and that a difference of this magnitude is likely to occur by chance less than 1 time in 10,000 ($p < 0.001$). We can therefore conclude with some confidence that the three groups really do differ in their level of toleration of smoking (see p. 268 for explanation of the F test).

Why not use a series of t tests?

With an independent variable with three values, we could in principle run three separate t tests to compare:

- smokers' mean attitude scores with the mean scores of non-smokers;
- smokers' mean attitude scores with the mean scores of ex-smokers;
- non-smokers' mean attitude scores with the mean scores of ex-smokers.

But suppose we were using a five-category independent variable rather than one with just three categories. The number of possible combinations of pairs now rises to ten, but carrying out ten separate t tests would be unwieldy. Furthermore, if we run lots of simultaneous t tests, we increase the likelihood of finding a large difference between two sets of sample means even when no difference exists in the population. If, for example, we take 0.05 as our significance level, then we know that 1 time in 20 we can expect to find a 'significant' difference in mean scores even though there is no difference in the population from which the sample has been drawn (i.e. a Type I error). We can live with a probability like that if we are testing only one statistic, but if we decide to run ten t tests, the chances of throwing up one spurious 'significant' difference increase from 20:1 to just 1.5:1. ANOVA avoids problems like these because it expresses the difference in mean scores in a single statistic – which is why it is preferred to sequences of t tests.

Two-way ANOVA designs

Sometimes, we may have *more than one independent variable* to deal with. For example, we know that respondents' own smoking behaviour (X_1) and the smoking behaviour of their family and friends (X_2) are both significantly associated with their attitudes about smoking. The problem is that we also know that smokers tend to associate with other smokers, and non-smokers with other non-smokers. So how

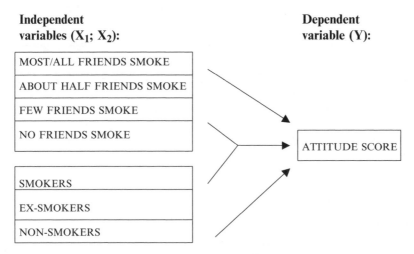

Figure 9.7   A two-way ANOVA design, with interaction effect

much of the variation in people's tolerance of smoking can be explained by whether they themselves smoke, and how much is explained by whether or not they socialize with other smokers?

To answer this, we need to test a causal model involving two independent variables, a *two-way ANOVA* in which we determine, not only whether each of the independent variables is significantly associated with people's attitude scores, but also whether each independent variable continues to have an effect once we *control* for the influence of the other. The model depicted in figure 9.7 will also test whether there is a further, interaction effect in which attitude scores are the product of a particular combination of smoking behaviour and pressure or influence from family and friends.

Figure 9.8 gives the results of this test (the total number of respondents has fallen slightly, for six respondents for whom data were missing on either of our two independent variables have been excluded). Inspecting the significance levels tells us that people's own smoking profile ('smokhist') continues to have a highly significant association with their attitudes, but that the influence of their family and friends (var00016) seems questionable (a significance level of 0.066, just outside the 0.05 cut-off). The hypothesis that there is an interaction effect (smokhist*var00016) also fails to achieve the required level of statistical significance (p = 0.100). Summing this up, we could conclude that, while having family and friends who smoke might have some influence on people's attitudes about smoking, the more important influence is their own smoking behaviour, now and in the past.

CONCLUSION

Inferential statistics enable us to gauge how far findings from a sample survey can be generalized to the population from which the sample was drawn. We can estimate population parameters within known levels of confidence by calculating the Standard

Tests of Between-Subjects Effects

Dependent Variable: Attitude score (8 items)

Source	Type III Sum of Squares	df	Mean Square	F	Sig.
Corrected Model	4925.690[a]	11	447.790	15.920	.000
Intercept	96160.300	1	96160.300	3418.692	.000
SMOKHIST	1830.932	2	915.466	32.547	.000
VAR00016	204.355	3	68.118	2.422	.066
SMOKHIST * VAR00016	302.662	6	50.444	1.793	.100
Error	8804.003	313	28.128		
Total	197347.000	325			
Corrected Total	13729.692	324			

a. R Squared = .359 (Adjusted R Squared = .336)

Figure 9.8   Testing for the effects of smoking behaviour and of family/friends on tolerance of smoking (a two-way ANOVA model with interaction effect)

Error of the Mean, and we can determine the likelihood that associations between variables would be found in whole populations by using various tests of statistical significance.

Some of the material in this chapter is quite difficult to follow when you first encounter it. The logic of deriving the value of the Standard Error from the 'sampling distribution of the mean' can be difficult to grasp (and the additional twists involved in estimating the probability of Chi Square from the binomial distribution – discussed on the website – makes this even more challenging). The calculation of the Mann-Whitney U test and Student's t test are not simple either, and the prospect of working out a complex ANOVA without the help of SPSS is so daunting that we have not even attempted it in this chapter!

But the point, of course, is that you *do* have SPSS to do all these things for you. You will never have to work out the value of Chi Square using pen and paper, still less a t test or an ANOVA. But it is still important to try to understand what these statistics involve, for only in this way will you begin to use them with confidence. You must also pay close attention to the conditions and assumptions which they entail, for in the end it is you, and not SPSS, who has to decide what is appropriate and what is not.

MODELLING ASSOCIATIONS BETWEEN VARIABLES

AIM

Social scientists develop statistical models to test hypotheses and to explore data for associations between variables. One of the most common modelling techniques is least squares regression – the focus of this chapter. By the end, you should:

- Understand how to construct and interpret a simple, bivariate regression model
- Know how to check 'residuals' for evidence of linearity, homoscedasticity and collinearity
- Be able to build a multiple regression model, including the use of 'dummy variables' as required

Least squares regression is suitable only for modelling data measured at interval or ratio level. The website that accompanies this book contains details on logistic regression (for use with a dichotomous dependent variable) and loglinear modelling (for use with categorical data), as well as path modelling.

INTRODUCTION

Social life is complex. Whenever we try to explain why and how something happens, we find that many different factors are at work, and that many of them seem to influence each other as well as impacting on the phenomenon we want to analyse.

The essence of a good explanation, however, is simplicity. Theories which list dozens of contingent conditions – ifs, buts and maybes – are not much use. What we are looking for is explanatory theories which simplify the way the world works without hopelessly distorting it. We want to cut to the essence of things.

This is what models try to do. A model isolates a small number of factors deemed to be important in explaining something, it specifies their relative importance, and it takes account of how they act on each other. Models do not try to include everything, but they must include enough so that they do not diverge too much from the reality they are trying to represent. A good model is parsimonious yet powerful.

We began to encounter social science modelling at the end of chapter 9 where we developed some ANOVA designs. Some of these got quite complex. The model in figure 9.7 (tested in figure 9.8), for example, juggled the effects on people's attitudes of their peer group, their own self-interest, and the interaction between the two, in an attempt to sort out which of these effects was 'significant' and which was not. In this chapter we introduce another common modelling technique in social science – least squares regression. This can be used to test hypotheses, or to explore relations between variables as a prelude to developing new hypotheses.

Least squares regression is intended for use only with interval/ratio level data, although we shall see how categorical independent variables can be included in models by turning them into what are called 'dummy variables'.

♦   If you are modelling influences on a dichotomous dependent variable, you should not use least squares regression, but should use a technique called 'logistic regression'.
♦   If you are modelling associations between categorical variables, you should not use least squares regression, but should develop and test what are known as 'loglinear models'.

We explain both of these techniques in appendices H and I which you can download from our website.

BIVARIATE REGRESSION

The regression equation

When we looked at correlation in chapter 8, we produced a scatterplot and we saw how it is possible to draw a straight line which 'best fits' all the points on the graph (figure 8.10). This line is drawn so as to minimize the sum of the vertical distances of all the data points to the straight line (see figure 10.1). It is sometimes called the *least squares line* because it is the line which produces the smallest total of squared distances from each case plotted on the graph (the distances are squared so we can add the positive figures above the line to the negative ones below it). If we drew any other line, squared the distances of the data points from that line and summed the values, this sum would always be greater than the sums of squares for the best-fitting line.

A regression model uses this 'line of best fit' to predict the values of a dependent variable from given values of an independent variable. Indeed, the line is also know as the *regression line*.

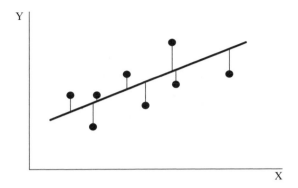

Figure 10.1 Minimizing the vertical distances to fit the regression line

Like any straight line on a graph, the regression line can be expressed as an equation:

$$Y = a + bX$$

where:

♦ a is the intercept. This is the value of Y at the point where the regression line crosses the Y axis. It is referred to as the *regression constant*.
♦ b is the slope. It indicates the number of units by which Y changes for each change in a unit of X. It is known as the *regression coefficient*.

If $b = 1$, then the line is at 45 degrees. If $b > 1$ then the slope is steeper, and if $b < 1$, then it is less than 45 degrees. If $b = 0$, it means changes in X have no effect on values of Y. If b is positive, it means Y increases as X increases (the line rises from left to right), and if it is negative, it means Y decreases as X increases (the line falls from left to right).

Don't forget about 'error'!

The actual value of Y for any individual in our sample will obviously be influenced by more than just the constant a and the value of X, for our model does not contain everything that has an effect. All the influences not included in the model are referred to collectively as *error*, for together they make the actual value of Y different from what it 'should' be according to our model (i.e. they explain the error in the model).

Taking account of error (*e*), the equation to predict any value of Y is:

$$Y = a + bX + e$$

However, when we construct a regression model, we ignore the error term, *e*. What we are interested in is how far X predicts the value of Y, and all the other influences on Y are irrelevant for the model we are testing. We therefore treat *e* as zero and we look for the best-fitting line to predict the value of Y at any given value of X. Once we have built our model, we look at what is left unexplained (the *residual* variance in Y) to see how well it fits the data.

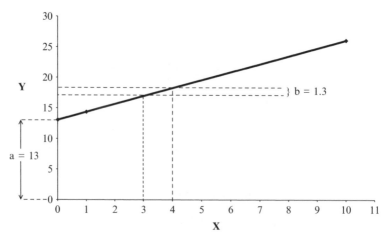

Figure 10.2   A geometric interpretation of the regression equation

Figure 10.2 illustrates how we can calculate the value of Y using the regression equation $Y = a + bX$. Suppose we want to know the value of Y when X has a value of 10:

- The first thing we need to know is the value of the intercept a. This is the point at which the regression line crosses the Y axis when X is at 0. In figure 10.2, a = 13.
- Next we need to calculate b. This indicates the slope of the line and is calculated by the magnitude of change in Y for every unit change in X. In figure 10.2 we see that for every unit change in X, Y changes by 1.3.

We can now predict Y when X = 10:

$$Y = 13 + (1.3 \times 10) = 26$$

Developing a regression model using SPSS

If you are working with the Smoking Survey data set, replicate the following procedures using the variables from the **cleandat.sav** data file. If you are working with your own data set, select two continuous variables measured at interval or ratio level. Be clear which is 'independent' and which 'dependent'. You should select for your dependent variable one which is roughly normally distributed and without too many extreme outliers.

Let us use our Smoking Survey data to test the first part of hypothesis 8 (the 'social class effect' hypothesis):

The higher somebody's social class and level of education, the less likely they are to smoke, and the less tolerant they will be of smoking.

We tested the second part of this hypothesis in chapter 8 where we used Spearman's rho to test the association between social class (measured as an ordinal scale using the Registrar-General schema) and tolerance about smoking. We shall now test the first part of the hypothesis by testing whether consumption of tobacco falls the higher we go up the social class ladder (you can test for the effect of education on tobacco consumption yourself later on).

Selecting suitable variables

For this exercise we shall measure social class using the Cambridge scale (var00030). Unlike the Registrar-General class categories, this is a continuous, interval measure, which makes it suitable for our independent variable (see appendix B on the website for a detailed explanation of the Cambridge social class scale). For our dependent variable we would like to use the variable 'Comsmoke' which we computed as a combined measure of cigarette, cigar and tobacco consumption, but when we explored this variable earlier using a boxplot (figure 7.10) we found a number of outliers that skewed the distribution.

Outliers on a dependent variable can be a problem, because they exert a disproportionate effect on the slope of the best-fitting line (they are said to have high *leverage*). The regression line is forced to pivot towards these points. An example of this can be seen in the scatterplot in figure 10.3. Regression line A has been fitted to the data with the outliers excluded, while line B has been fitted with the outliers included. Not only does the slope of the line change dramatically when the outliers are included, but the fit of line B to the data is clearly poorer than that of line A.

In chapter 7 we recoded 'comsmoke' into a new variable called 'consmcut' which excludes all outliers where weekly cigarette (or equivalent) consumption was above 200 or below 20. We shall therefore use this truncated variable as the dependent variable in our model.

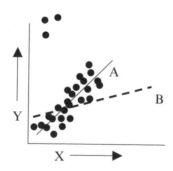

Figure 10.3   A scatterplot showing the effect that outliers have on the regression line

Obtaining the regression output

To calculate a simple regression of Y (the dependent variable, 'consmcut') on X (our independent variable, the Cambridge occupational scale score):

◆   Under 'Analyze' highlight 'Regression' and then click on 'Linear'.
◆   A dialog box opens headed 'Linear Regression'. Scroll down the list of variables, find your independent and dependent variables, and transfer them into the appropriate boxes.
◆   There is no need to select 'Statistics...' because by default SPSS produces regression coefficients and 'model fit' statistics (including Pearson's *r* and R^2 – see below). You can also ignore the 'WLS' button (standing for 'weighted least squares'), the 'Options' button and the 'Save...' button, but click on 'Plots...' and select the 'Histogram' and the 'Normal probability plot' (to obtain plots of standardized residuals).
◆   We shall also want to obtain a casewise plot of standardized residuals ('ZRESID') by standardized predicted scores ('ZPRED'), so paste 'ZRESID' into the box next to 'Y' and 'ZPRED' into the box next to 'X'. Click on continue in order to return to the 'Linear Regression' dialog box, and then on 'OK'.

Interpreting the output

Figure 10.4 contains the first three parts of the output obtained from this job. The first part of the output tells us which independent variables have been entered into the regression. We entered only one, and this appears in the column 'Variables Entered'. Ignore the 'Variables Removed' and 'Method' columns for the time being – we shall see what these are referring to when we look at multiple regression.

   The second part of the output, headed 'Model Summary', presents four statistics summarizing our model:

◆   'R' is the correlation coefficient. With only two variables, as in this case, this is exactly the same as the Pearson's *r* statistic at 0.376.
◆   'R Square' is, as the name implies, the squared correlation coefficient, or the 'determination coefficient'. It tells you the extent to which X predicts Y, that is, the proportion of variation in the dependent variable explained by the independent variable. In this case, 14 per cent of the variance in smoking consumption is explained by occupational class.
◆   'Adjusted R Square' corrects for the fact that the R^2 for any sample tends slightly to exaggerate the goodness of fit actually found in the population from which it is taken. In this case, the R Square is reduced from 0.141 to 0.126.
◆   The Standard Error is the standard deviation of the residuals of the estimate. In plain English, it is the amount by which any prediction of the value of Y (based on the value of X) is likely to be wrong. In this case, try predicting the smoking consumption of any respondent from their position on the Cambridge scale and there is a 1 in 3 chance that you will be out by as much as 37 cigarettes either way

Variables Entered/Removed[b]

Model	Variables Entered	Variables Removed	Method
1	Occupation Cambridge scale [a]		Enter

a. All requested variables entered.
b. Dependent Variable: cigs+cigars+tobac
   with <20&>200 removed

Model Summary[b]

Model	R	R Square	Adjusted R Square	Std. Error of the Estimate
1	.376[a]	.141	.126	37.2598

a. Predictors: (Constant), Occupation: Cambridge scale
b. Dependent Variable: cigs+cigars+tobac with
   <20&>200 removed

ANOVA[b]

Model		Sum of Square	df	Mean Square	F	Sig.
1	Regression	13001.607	1	13001.607	9.365	.003[a]
	Residual	79132.529	57	1388.290		
	Total	92134.136	58			

a. Predictors: (Constant), Occupation: Cambridge scale
b. Dependent-Variable: cigs+cigars+tobac with <20&>200 removed

Figure 10.4 Regression statistics from the Smoking Survey predicting tobacco consumption from Cambridge scale score

(for 1 standard error either side of the mean covers 67 per cent, or 2 in 3, of the possible samples which might be drawn).

The third part of the output, headed 'ANOVA', contains the statistics that calculate whether the impact of X on Y is significant. This is calculated by dividing the variation in Y (the dependent variable) which is explained by the model by the variation in Y that is left unexplained (i.e. it is an analysis of the proportion of variance that we have explained). What the model leaves unexplained is known as the *residual*.

♦ The first column gives the 'Sum of Squares'. This is the distance between each observation of Y and the mean of Y, squared to remove minus signs, and all added together (i.e. the total variation in Y). The Sum of Squares of the Regression (in the first row) is the amount of variance explained by the model (i.e. the variation in Y that can be attributed to the association with X), while the Sum of Squares of the Residual (in the second row) is the amount of variance still left unexplained (which must therefore be caused by other variables not in the model, and/or by inaccurate measurement of Y). These two added together give the Total Sum of Squares. If we divide the sum of squares of the regression by the total sum of squares, we get the *R square* statistic (i.e. the proportion of the total variance in Y explained by the regression). Thus, the sum of squares of the regression (13001.6) divided by the total sum of squares (92134.1) produces the R^2 value of 0.141.

◆ The column headed 'Mean Square' is the average amount by which each observation of Y differs from the mean. It is calculated by dividing the sum of squares by the degrees of freedom.

◆ The F test is a statistical test of significance. It expresses the mean square of the regression and the mean square of the residual as a ratio. If this ratio is sufficiently high, then the probability is slight that this degree of fit of the model to the data could have occurred by chance. In this case, $p = 0.003$ so the relationship exceeds the 99 per cent significance level. We can be fairly confident that the association between class and smoking consumption does exist in the population from which this sample was drawn.

Now consider the next part of the output reproduced in figure 10.5. This provides the figures from which we can construct the equation for the regression line. There are five statistics in this table that are of interest:

◆ 'B' is the regression coefficient, or the slope of the line. The figure for the dependent variable tells you the amount by which Y changes for each unit increase in X. In this case, for every unit we move up the Cambridge scale, tobacco consumption changes by 0.161 cigarettes. The minus sign tells us that there is a negative relationship between the two variables indicating that tobacco consumption *decreases* by this amount as we move up the Cambridge scale from more 'working class' to more 'middle class' occupations.

◆ The figure for the Constant gives you the intercept. It is the predicted value of Y when the dependent variable is zero. In this case, tobacco consumption equals 76.855 cigarettes at the point where the Cambridge scale is zero (this, of course, is the result of extrapolation of the line, for the Cambridge scale does not extend down to zero).

Coefficients[a]

Model		Unstandardized Coefficients		Standardized Coefficients	t	Sig.
		B	Std. Error	Beta		
1	(Constant)	76.855	5.660		13.579	.000
	Occupation: Cambridge scale	−.161	.053	−.375	−3.060	.003

a. Dependent Variable: cigs+cigars+tobac with <20&>200 removed

Figure 10.5   The regression equation

♦ 'Std. Error' is the Standard Error of B. It is the number of standard errors by which the predicted value of Y (based on the value of X) could be wrong. A figure greater than 2 would indicate a problem, for 2 or more standard errors from the mean takes you beyond accepted probability levels of 95 per cent, so your predictions will not be statistically significant. In our case, the standard error of B is 0.053 – perfectly acceptable.

♦ 'Beta' is the standardized regression coefficient. In a simple regression this is the same as Pearson's *r*, but in multiple regression models with more than one independent variable, the betas indicate the relative strength of the different independent variables in influencing the dependent variable (we discuss multiple regression later).

♦ The t is the t test which assesses whether the relation of the independent variable to Y could have occurred by chance. The value of t is calculated by dividing B by the Standard Error of B. In our example, the t value is statistically significant ($p < 0.001$).

Predicting the value of the independent variable using the regression statistics

Based on the statistics in the table in figure 10.5, we can now develop our regression equation. We know that $Y = a + bX$. This generates the prediction that somebody's level of cigarette consumption (Y) will be:

76.855(a, the constant)

plus – 0.161(b, the regression coefficient) for every unit increase in the Cambridge scale(X)

For example, the model predicts that a smoker who is a primary school teacher (an occupation scored at 65.06 on the Cambridge scale) would have a tobacco consumption of:

$$76.855 - (65.06 \times 0.161) = 66.380 \text{ cigarettes per week}$$

On the other hand, a smoker who is a mechanic (scored at 21.15 on the Cambridge scale) would be predicted to have a consumption of:

$$76.855 - (21.15 \times 0.161) = 73.471 \text{ cigarettes per week}$$

Before we get carried away, though, remember that we have only explained 13 per cent of the variance in smoking (the adjusted R Square). This is not too bad for one independent variable but still leaves 87 per cent of the variance in the dependent variable unexplained. This suggests there are other influences on tobacco consumption besides social class, and/or that one or both of our variables has not been measured very accurately and is therefore producing some 'error' in our predictions. Both explanations seem likely.

We have also to remember that any predictions we make of people's cigarette consumption are likely to be out by as much as 37.26 either side for each Standard

Error (which works out at $37.26 \times 2 = 74.52$ either side if we want to achieve 95 per cent confidence). For example, the best prediction we can make for a smoking primary school teacher is that he or she will smoke $76.855 - (65.06 \times 0.161) = 66.380 \pm 74.52$ cigarettes per week (i.e. somewhere between none and 141). This is not a very impressive prediction!

We shall see in a moment how we might try to improve this degree of predictive accuracy by including some additional explanatory variables in our model.

Examining the residuals

A residual is the difference between an observed value of the dependent variable and the value predicted by the equation. In other words, it is the variation in Y left unexplained by X. The final part of our output provides information on the residuals.

In the table labelled 'Residual Statistics' (Figure 10.6), we are given statistics on the four variables we created during the regression calculation. 'Predicted Value' refers to the distribution of the predicted values of Y based on the values of X. 'Residual' refers to the distribution of values of Y left unexplained. 'Std. Predicted Value' and 'Std. Residual' are these two sets of values standardized as z scores to enable comparison between them. (Look up appendix C on the website if you need to remind yourself about standardizing values as Z scores.)

We can see from this output that the predicted values range from 44.68 to 105.17 cigarettes per week and that the residuals (i.e. the difference between the observed value and predicted value) range from -62.83 to 105.71. When these values are standardized and compared we can see that the range of standardized residual values $(-1.7 \text{ to } 2.8)$ is a little greater than the range of the standardized predicted values $(-2.7 \text{ to } +1.3)$. This indicates that the spread of values left unexplained is still very large. Ideally, we would hope to find a much smaller spread for residuals than for predicted values.

Checking that the regression assumptions have been met

When we construct a regression model like this one, we make two important assumptions about our data that we need to check:

Residuals Statistics[a]

	Minimum	Maximum	Mean	Std. Deviation	N
Predicted Value	44.6777	105.1704	85.7797	14.9722	59
Residual	-62.8295	105.7069	-4.34E-15	36.9372	59
Std. Predicted Value	-2.745	1.295	.000	1.000	59
Std. Residual	-1.686	2.837	.000	.991	59

a. Dependent Variable: cigs+cigars+tobac with <20&>200 removed

Figure 10.6 Residuals statistics

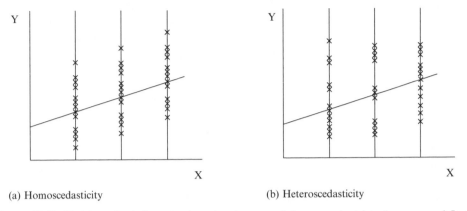

(a) Homoscedasticity   (b) Heteroscedasticity

Figure 10.7 Two hypothetical scatterplots showing normal (homoscedastic) and non-normal (heteroscedastic) distribution of Y at each value of X

♦ We assume that the dependent variable (Y) is normally distributed at each value of the independent variable (X). This is known as *homogeneity of variance* and is sometimes called *homoscedasticity*. This requirement is not simply that the dependent variable should be normally distributed, but is that it should be normally distributed *at each value of* X. Figure 10.7(a) shows a hypothetical scatterplot of homoscedastic data, where the values of Y are normally distributed at all three values of X. Compare this with scatterplot (b) in the figure, where the distribution of Y values is skewed or even bimodal at different values of X. A distribution like this is *heteroscedastic*. In our example, homoscedasticity means there should be a normal distribution of tobacco consumption at each value of the Cambridge scale (i.e. that tobacco consumption should be normally distributed at every level of the class system). Regression does not, however, require that the independent variable (X) be normally distributed.

♦ We also assume that the relationship between the two variables is linear. In other words, our model assumes the relation between X and Y is best expressed by a straight line.

Both the assumptions of homoscedasticity and linearity can be checked with the graphs of residuals which were produced when we ran the regression procedure. There are three graphs: a histogram, a normal plot and a scatterplot. All three enable us to check for violation of the assumptions on which regression depends. If the assumptions have been violated, the statistics will be misleading.

Checking for homoscedasticity

The assumption of homoscedasticity is necessary because, if X is said to cause variations in Y, then it should do so equally well for all values of Y. Suppose, for example, that occupational rank quite accurately predicted smoking consumption among those whose tobacco consumption is low, but that it had very little predictive power among heavy smokers. If we then attempt to fit a straight line to this graph, it would understate the strength of association between the variables among light smokers, and would overstate it among heavy smokers.

This would show up in the *residuals* – among light smokers, for example, there would be many observations falling a long way below the line and only a few falling above it. Put another way, the distribution of the residuals would not approximate normality. In such a case, it might then be better to divide the sample into light smokers and heavy smokers and to apply the model only to the former.

We can test for the homogeneity of variance in the residuals by inspecting the histogram of standardized residuals. If the condition of homoscedasticity is being met, most of the residuals should be close to the best-fitting straight line and there should be fewer and fewer the further away we move from the line on either side. If we standardize the residuals, this means that most should be within + or −1 standard error from the line, and there should be very few more than 2 standard errors away. In other words, the distribution of standardized residuals should approximate normality.

Figure 10.8 shows the distribution of the standardized residuals for our dependent variable – tobacco consumption. It does not seem that the normality condition is fulfilled, for there are too many residuals at around −1.00 and 1.00, and too few at about −0.5 and 0.5. However, we need to bear in mind that we only have 59 cases in our analysis (because the dependent variable only includes respondents who smoked between 20 and 200 cigarettes per week) and that it only takes a few cases to make the distribution appear non-normal.

We can also test for normality with a *normal plot* (not shown here). If you have constant variance on the dependent variable, this plot will form a 45 degree straight line.

Testing for linearity

The *linearity assumption* is necessary because we are trying to find the best-fitting straight line. A scatterplot of standardized residuals (ZRESID) against standardized predicted values (ZPRED) is one way of checking for linearity. If the linearity assumption is met, there should be no pattern in the scatterplot, for if the best-fitting line

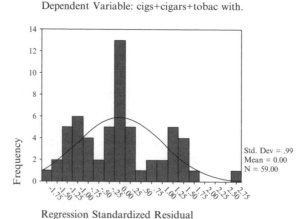

Histogram
Dependent Variable: cigs+cigars+tobac with.

Std. Dev = .99
Mean = 0.00
N = 59.00

Regression Standardized Residual

Figure 10.8   Testing for homogeneity of variance using a histogram of standardized residuals

through all the points on the original graph is indeed a straight line, then the pattern of points away from the line will be random.

When assumptions are violated

It is important when constructing regression models to check the residuals to see whether the conditions assumed by the model are in fact being met. If they are being violated, you can try modifying the data by, for example, splitting the sample or transforming the measurement scale by logging, cube-rooting, or one of the other methods outlined in chapter 7. If none of this works, then you may have to make do with lower level, non-parametric statistics (such as Spearman's rho) and abandon the attempt to use least squares regression.

BUILDING A MULTIPLE REGRESSION MODEL

The simple bivariate regression model which we have constructed is quite weak. Occupational class (measured by the Cambridge scale) does seem significantly to predict how many cigarettes smokers consume, but it only accounts for 13 per cent of the variance in their consumption. Perhaps by adding further information to our model, we can improve on this?

Once we start adding extra independent variables to a regression model, we move from bivariate to *multiple regression*. The logic and procedure of multiple regression is virtually identical to that for bivariate regression, except that you are looking at the relative impact on the dependent variable of a number of different independent variables, rather than just one.

The multiple regression equation

The equation for a multiple regression model is:

$$Y = a + b_1X_1 + b_2X_2 + b_3X_3 + \ldots b_kX_k$$

We predict the value of Y as the constant (the intercept on the Y axis of the graph) plus a multiple of the value of the first independent variable, plus a multiple of the value of the second independent variable, and so on.

In principle, we are still trying to find a line of best fit on a scatterplot, although it is increasingly difficult to represent this visually (indeed, it is impossible to represent it visually once we add more than two independent variables).

Interpreting the output

When we enter more than one independent variable in a regression model, the influence that each has on the dependent variable is calculated while holding the influence of all the other independent variables constant. In a multiple regression equation with just two independent variables, for example:

$b_1 =$ the change in Y for each unit change in X_1 while holding X_2 constant

$b_2 =$ the change in Y for each unit change in X_2 while holding X_1 constant

Let us take an example. We have seen that occupational class (measured by the Cambridge scale) has a small but significant influence on the amount of tobacco that smokers consume. Now, assume we have reason to believe that somebody's gender will further affect how much they smoke. What we want to know is the effect of class on smoking when gender is kept constant, and the effect of gender on smoking when class is kept constant.

Use of dummy variables

Regression can only be used where we have independent and dependent variables measured at interval or ratio level. However, models can include categorical variables if they are dichotomous because, in a sense, a dichotomous variable *is* measured at interval level – it is just that it only has one interval. If we plot a dichotomous independent variable like gender (X) against a continuous dependent variable like tobacco consumption (Y), we still get a scatter of dots (although they are vertically aligned around just two values of the X axis), so we can still find the line of best fit that runs through them.

If we want to include a categorical variable with more than two values in a regression model, it follows that we can do it if we first transform it into a series of dichotomous variables, each with values of 0 and 1. For example, if we wanted to use the Registrar-General's social class schema (var00042), we could do so by transforming it into a series of dichotomous *dummy variables*:

- DummyI (coded 1 if respondents are in class I and 0 if they are not);
- DummyII (coded 1 if respondents are in class II and 0 if they are not);
- DummyIII (coded 1 if respondents are in class IIIN or IIIM and 0 if they are not);
- DummyIV (coded 1 if respondents are in class IV and 0 if they are not).

With five categories of social class, we create four dummies. One class category is not included as a dummy (in this example, Class V), for its members are already identified by a unique combination of values on the four dummies (i.e. they are coded 0 on all four).

Note that dummy variables can only be used as *independent* (predictor) variables. If you want to develop a regression model for a dichotomous dependent variable, you should use *logistic regression*, otherwise you could end up with impossible results when you come to fit your least squares line.

Model Summary^b

Model	R	R Square	Adjusted R Square	Std. Error of the Estimate
1	.453^a	.205	.176	36.1699

a. Predictors: (Constant). Occupation: Cambridge scale, gender

b. Dependent Variable: cigs+cigars+tobac with <20&>200 removed

Coefficients^a

Model		Unstandardized Coefficients		Standardized Coefficients	t	Sig.
		B	Std. Error	Beta		
1	(Constant)	65.204	7.774		8.387	.000
	gender	20.185	9.529	.252	2.118	.039
	Occupation: Cambridge scale	−.161	.051	−.376	−3.159	.003

a. Dependent Variable: cigs+cigars+tobac with <20&>200 removed

Figure 10.9   Multiple regression of Cambridge scale score and gender on tobacco consumption

The model summary statistics and coefficients from a multiple regression of Cambridge scale score and gender on tobacco consumption are given in figure 10.9 (we have not included the ANOVA table).

The model summary statistics

The model summary statistics refer to the model as a whole, rather than to the association between Y and any specific independent variable:

- The R statistic is the *multiple correlation coefficient* (a capital letter is used in notation to distinguish it from the Pearson coefficient, *r*, which is used only for bivariate correlations). In a multiple regression, R refers to the extent to which *all* the independent variables together are correlated with the dependent variable.
- The 'R Square' and 'Adjusted R Square' tell us the proportion of the linear variance in Y explained by the model as a whole (i.e. by all the independent variables acting together). Note that the difference produced by the adjustment is greater now that we have added an additional variable to our model. The adjusted R^2 is the one you should use.
- The Standard Error measures the amount by which predictions of Y based on all independent variable values are likely to be wrong, and the F test (included in the ANOVA table not shown here) is a test of the significance of the model as a whole (in this case, p = 0.002).

The adjusted R square is now 0.176. Between them, the Cambridge scale score and gender are accounting for 18 per cent of the variance in tobacco consumption of smokers. This is an improvement over our earlier model in which the Cambridge score alone predicted just 13 per cent of the variance. But which of our two variables is doing most of the predictive work? To answer this, we need to inspect the coefficients output in figure 10.9.

The partial regression coefficients

SPSS calculates two sets of coefficients – unstandardized b values and standardized *Beta* values. The *unstandardized coefficients* are interpreted in exactly the same way as before – these are the values that can be entered into our regression equation in order to predict values of the dependent variable. Given that both occupation and gender appear to have statistically significant independent effects on tobacco consumption (p [occupation] = 0.003; p [gender] = 0.039), we can predict from the second table in figure 10.9 that a smoker's consumption of cigarettes will be:

65.2(the constant) − 0.16(for each point up the Cambridge scale) + 20.2(if male)

(Because gender was coded 0 for females and 1 for males, the coefficient of +20.2 means that tobacco consumption rises by that amount as we shift from the lower to the higher value on this dichotomous variable).

Allowing for the standard error of $\pm$ 36.17, we can say that there is a 95 per cent probability that:

♦ a smoker who is a male bus conductor (code −158 on the Cambridge scale) is likely to smoke the equivalent of 65.2 +(− 0.16* − 158) + 20.2 = 110.68 ($\pm$ 2 standard errors = 72.34) cigarettes per week, while
♦ a smoker who is a female university teacher (Cambridge scale = +131) is likely to smoke the equivalent of just 86.16 ($\pm$ 72.34) cigarettes each week (65.2 + [− 0.16* + 131] + 0).

What we cannot deduce from these b coefficients, however, is the *relative contribution* that occupation and gender make to smoking consumption. The two different b coefficients cannot be directly compared because the different Xs are scaled differently. Our version of the Cambridge scale (X_1) runs from −182 (production process workers) to +132 (electrical engineers), but gender runs only from 0 (female) to 1 (male). The unstandardized coefficient for X_1 (0.16) is much smaller than that for X_2 (20.2), but that obviously has something to do with the fact that there are many more points on the scale of occupations than on the scale of gender.

To compare the relative weights of these two independent variables, we obviously need to standardize these coefficients, and this is what the Beta coefficients represent in the second table in figure 10.9. Beta coefficients can be directly compared with each other, for they take account of the spread of values (i.e. the standard deviation) within each variable. Thus, occupational class (Beta = −0.376) has more impact on the consumption of smokers than their gender does (Beta = 0.252). To be precise, it is (0.376 ÷ 0.252) = 1.49 times more powerful in predicting their consumption.

Both the unstandardized and standardized coefficients in multiple regression are calculated so as to control for the effects of all the other independent variables in the model (they are what is termed *partial regression coefficients*, for they tell us how much of an effect the variable has when the linear effects of all the other variables have been removed). This means we can do a straight comparison of Betas to tell us how much each variable contributes independently to the variance in Y.

Dealing with missing cases in multiple regression

Missing data can become a major problem in multiple regression. In our regression in figure 10.9, for example, only 59 cases out of a sample size of 334 were included in the analysis. This is because we included only those cases where we had information on all of the variables in the model. While there were 118 respondents who smoked, 334 with a recorded gender and 182 allocated to a class, there were just 59 cases with data on all three variables.

Pairwise versus listwise deletion of missing cases

You might have noticed when you opened the 'Options' dialog box that you were offered the choice between excluding missing cases 'pairwise', 'listwise' or 'replace with mean'. The default option is 'listwise', and this is the one we selected. Listwise analyses only those cases where data are available on *all* variables.

Pairwise deletion on the other hand includes as many cases as are available for each *pair* of variables in the model. Had we selected this option, we would have had 59 cases where we knew the social class of smokers, but 118 where we knew their gender, and our regression model would have been calculated using the maximum number of cases available for each independent variable.

Clearly, pairwise deletion makes better use of the information we have (just because one respondent may not have a social class code, for example, does not mean we cannot include them in an analysis of the relationship between gender and smoking). The problem with it, however, is that we end up with a series of coefficients which are actually based on different subsamples, so when we compare the relative predictive strength of gender and class, we do so using different sets of cases. This suggests we should probably use listwise deletion but this can often mean we rapidly deplete the number of usable cases, and the fact that we drop a lot of respondents means that we might end up biasing our results quite dramatically.

Alternative ways of dealing with missing cases: mean substitution

There are other solutions to the problem of handling missing cases besides pairwise and listwise deletion. One possibility is to substitute *mean scores* for missing data. For example, respondents who were not allocated a position on the Cambridge scale can be given a score corresponding to the mean score of the whole sample.

This procedure can be further refined by substituting 'group means'. Here missing cases are given a score corresponding to the mean score of other people like themselves. For example, women smokers with a 'missing' Cambridge scale score might be given the mean value of other women smokers, while their male counterparts get the average value of all men who smoke.

But these solutions too have their problems. Where there are many missing cases, substituting means will accentuate the influence of 'moderate' answers while marginalizing 'extreme' ones, for it increases the proportion of cases clustering at the midpoint of the distribution.

Building a multiple regression model in SPSS

Methods for entering the variables

SPSS offers different methods for entering independent variables when building a multiple regression model:

◆ *Enter* is the default option. This allows you to specify the order in which you want independent variables to be put into the model. You can enter them all together in one step, or you can enter one new variable (or block of variables) at a time in order to test specific theoretical presuppositions or hypotheses.

◆ *Forward* selection tells the computer to inspect the strength of association between each of your independent variables and the dependent variable before constructing the model. It then enters the independent variables in order of their relative strength up to the point where the next variable is no longer statistically significant.

◆ *Backward* elimination starts with all the independent variables included in the initial equation and then eliminates them one at a time, starting with the weakest, until you end up with a model where no more variables can be removed without significantly reducing the model fit.

◆ *Stepwise* selection combines the previous two procedures by adding variables one at a time while at the same time checking to see whether any that were added earlier can now be removed.

If you are using multiple regression to test a theory, then you should probably use the *Enter* method, for this is the only method that allows *you* to specify whether and how various combinations of independent variables are to be analysed. But if you are exploring the data to see whether there are any interesting findings which might later be tested on a new data set (or on a different subset of the data you are using), then one of the other methods is probably appropriate, for they sift and sort the patterns of association in the data to find the best-fitting model.

The model produced for figure 10.9 was generated using the *Enter* method – both occupation and gender were entered simultaneously. In a sense, we *forced* SPSS to compute a model which simultaneously took account of both of our independent variables.

How many variables should we include in our model?

There is in principle no limit to the number of independent variables that can be included in a multiple regression model – if they achieve significance, then you can

The importance of variable order

We shall see later that one condition of multiple regression modelling is that the independent variables should not be highly correlated with each other. But having said that, there is always likely to be *some* degree of correlation between our independent variables, which means some of the variance in Y is always likely to be 'shared' by X_1 and X_2. This means that the order in which we enter these variables into our model can be crucial, for the first one will mop up, not only the variance in Y that it is uniquely producing itself, but also the variance in Y that it shares in common with the other independent variable(s) which have yet to be entered. The next variable entered into the model will then only be credited with its own unique contribution to the variance in Y, for any shared contribution has already been claimed by the first one.

The *Enter* method allows you to determine the order in which variables are entered – if necessary, by *forcing* one variable into the model ahead of another. There may be times where your theory tells you that the effect on Y of X_1 must be prior to the effect of X_2, in which case you will enter X_1 first – even though, left to its own devices, SPSS might decide to enter X_2 ahead of X_1 because it has a higher F value.

include them. However, models which include many variables can be difficult to interpret, and the point is to achieve the simplest model that adequately reproduces the main patterns of association in the data. Adding more and more variables will not normally give you a better and better model – very soon, the improvements in model fit (measured by R^2) become very small, while the Standard Error may start to increase as you use up degrees of freedom (every new variable adds 1 degree of freedom to the regression sum of squares and deletes 1 from the residual sum of squares, thereby altering the means of these two statistics). The basic rule in modelling is the simpler, the better.

However, we do not want to stop developing our model prematurely, for we might end up including weak predictors while neglecting stronger ones. As the following example demonstrates, we sometimes find when we add further variables to a model that some existing variables drop out of it yet we end up with a higher R^2 than before.

Finding the strongest model: exploratory uses of multiple regression

If we run a series of bivariate correlations, we find that several other variables (besides occupation and gender) appear to be associated with the number of cigarettes people smoke. These include:

*   The proportion of their family and friends who smoke (var00016). This is not, strictly speaking, an interval variable (although it is not far off). If we want to

include it in a regression model, we could stretch a point and treat it as an interval measure, or we could create three new dummy variables and enter them.

♦ Parental smoking. We have created a new variable, 'parsmok' by recoding var00015 to tell us whether 2, 1 or neither of a respondent's parents smoked. This is a ratio scale, running from 0 to 2, and is therefore suitable for use in regression.

♦ Views about whether smoking can be beneficial (var00028). This is a dichotomous (dummy) variable coded 0 if people believed there are no positive benefits from smoking and 1 if they thought there were some. In the sample as a whole, 37 per cent saw some benefits while 63 per cent saw none, but among smokers, these proportions were almost reversed (57 per cent against 44 per cent).

Our original hypotheses led us to expect that some of these variables should affect smoking consumption, while others will not:

♦ Our two 'socialization' hypotheses (hypotheses 1 and 2) suggest that the smoking behaviour of parents and of peer groups should be important influences on how heavily people smoke, so it makes sense to include both in our regression model.

♦ The 'cognitive dissonance' hypothesis (hypothesis 10) suggests that smokers will define smoking as beneficial, but we also hypothesized that a belief in its beneficial effects will further reinforce their smoking behaviour. The causation, in other words, runs both ways. By including beliefs as an independent variable in a regression model, we can test the latter proposition – that beliefs reinforce smoking behaviour.

Our original hypotheses did not tell us which of these possible influences on smoking were likely to be more important. Thus, while it makes sense to include them all in a regression model, we do not really know what we expect to find. We are at this stage therefore moving away from confirmatory analysis (theory testing) and towards exploratory analysis. It may therefore make sense to choose a method like *Forward* or *Backward* in order to build this model, so that SPSS can determine which variables should be included and the order in which they should be entered or eliminated.

Table 10.1 summarizes the model outcomes when occupation, gender, parental smoking, peer group smoking and belief in the benefits of smoking are included in a model predicting the amount of tobacco (measured in cigarette equivalents) smokers consume each week. We have run the same model three times using three different methods (*Enter, Forward* and *Backward*). Two points should be noted:

♦ No matter how we build our model, gender no longer achieves a significant effect on tobacco consumption. Clearly, our earlier model was oversimple, for once other predictor variables are taken into account, most of the variance in Y that we had attributed to gender is accounted for by other, stronger, variables.

♦ Different methods of building the model produce somewhat different outcomes.

The first method (simultaneous entry of all variables) includes all five of our predictors in the final model (because we force it to), but only one of these (occupation,

Table 10.1 Modelling tobacco consumption of smokers, using three different methods of model building

Method	No. of iterations	Model fit (adj. R^2)	Model fit (ANOVA sig)	p of variables in final model	Final Betas
1 *Enter* 5 independent variables in one block	1	0.205	0.007	Occupation 0.033 Smoking benefit 0.064 Parents 0.176 Gender 0.365 Peer group 0.698	−0.300 0.245 0.180 0.118 −0.052
2 *Forward* (probability of *F* for entry = 0.05)	2	(1) 0.126 (2) 0.188	(1) 0.005 (2) 0.002	Occupation 0.021 Smoking benefit 0.032 *Not entered:* Parents 0.082 Gender 0.192 Peers 0.527	− 0.308 0.285 0.219 0.165 −0.086
3 *Backward* (probability of *F* for removal = 0.10)	3	(1) 0.205 (2) 0.219 (3) 0.222	(1) 0.007 (2) 0.003 (3) 0.002	Occupation 0.016 Smoking benefit 0.051 Parents 0.082 *Removed:* (2) Peers 0.721 (3) Gender 0.368	−0.314 0.255 0.219 −0.048 0.116

Figures in parentheses refer to iteration number.

$p = 0.033$) achieves statistical significance. Given this result, we would conclude that our best-fitting model is the simple bivariate regression which we developed in the tables in figures 10.4 and 10.5 (the Adjusted R^2 of 0.126 in figure 10.4 is rather lower, because none of the other variables is contributing to it, but the model is much simpler and may therefore be preferred).

The second method (forward entry) ends up with two variables in the model – occupation and the belief that smoking is beneficial. Occupation was entered on the first iteration, but belief in benefits of smoking was still contributing a statistically significant additional effect to the variance in amount of tobacco consumed ($p = 0.032$), so it too was entered. None of the other three variables then achieved significance (although parental smoking came close), and the iterations therefore terminated.

Why did belief in benefits of smoking achieve significance in our second method of building the model, but not in the first? The answer is that the first model assessed the significance of each variable when the effects of *all* the other variables were included, so the 'benefits' variable got squeezed out as some of its variance was shared out among the others. In our second model, however, variables were entered one at a time, so the 'benefits' variable (entered second) could claim all the variance that it shared with the remaining three that had not been included in the model.

The third method (backward elimination) gives us yet another final model. This one includes three predictor variables, for parental smoking is added to occupation and the belief that smoking can be beneficial. With $p = 0.082$, parental smoking never got included when we built our model forwards, for variables needed $p \leq 0.05$ to be entered, but in backward elimination, SPSS sets a default of $p > 0.10$ before knocking variables out (this is a safeguard against a Type II error, where we reject associations which are in fact valid).

So which 'final model' should we accept? There is no self-evidently correct answer, although two things *are* clear:

- We should not include gender in our final model. Once we take account of other possible influences on the number of cigarettes smoked, gender loses statistical significance. Our earlier model, where we predicted tobacco consumption from a combination of occupation and gender, can be rejected.
- Occupation, as measured by the Cambridge scale, is unambiguously significant in all of the models we have built. Clearly, it needs to be included in whatever final model we decide on (which means that the first part of hypothesis 8 is supported).

We noted at the start of this section that the R^2 of just 0.13 for a model which predicts tobacco consumption solely from occupation is not very impressive. It is tempting, therefore, to include the belief that smoking is beneficial, for (as we see from method 2 in Table 10.1), this raises the final adjusted R^2 to 0.19 with the loss of only 1 degree of freedom.

Should we go further and accept the results from the backward elimination (method 3), where parental smoking was also included in the final model? This raises our R^2 further still (to 0.22), and the significance of the overall model ($p = 0.002$) is no worse than in method 2, which excluded this variable. However, the significance of the effect of parental smoking falls short of the conventional 0.05 significance criterion. There may be times when we might be willing to accept this – but on this occasion, we think it is probably wise to quit while we are ahead and accept the results from method 2 as our final model (the parental socialization hypothesis was in any case rejected back in chapter 8, so the case for including parental smoking in our model is not strong).

We can therefore claim to have explained 19 per cent of the variance in the amount that smokers smoke with just two predictor variables – their occupation, and whether or not they believe smoking can be beneficial. With Betas of -0.308 and 0.285, these two variables seem to have a roughly equal effect on the dependent variable. The probability that our model might be wrong (i.e. that these two variables do not influence how much people smoke) is just 0.002, or 1 chance in 500. However, since we did not set out to test precisely this model – it derives partly from an exploration of the data – we should probably test it again using new data before accepting it as valid.

Checking conditions have not been violated

Tests for linearity and heteroscedasticity

When developing a multiple regression model, you still need to check for:

- linearity – is there a linear relationship between our dependent variable, Y, and all of our independent variables taken together?
- homoscedasticity – are the values of Y normally distributed at each value of each of the independent variables?

We can make these checks in the same way as for bivariate regression. Using SPSS, we check for linearity by plotting the residuals against the predicted values for each of the independent variables in the model, as well as for the model as a whole. We check for normality by requesting a histogram and a normal plot for the standardized residuals for the model as a whole. We have not reproduced this output here – if you are working with the Smoking Survey data, you can do this for yourself and decide whether the conditions have 'more or less' been met in the model we have developed.

Checking for collinearity

In addition to heteroscedasticity or absence of linearity, there is an additional problem to look out for now that we are dealing with a model with more than one independent variable. Because multiple regression assumes that the various independent variables in the model are not themselves highly correlated, we must check for what is called *collinearity* (or sometimes, *multicollinearity*) between them. In other words, we need to ensure that there is no strong linear association between any of the independent variables in our model.

Why is collinearity a problem?

When two independent variables are highly correlated, it becomes difficult to disentangle the variance in Y that is caused by one from the variance in Y that is caused by the other. As one increases or decreases, so does the other, so we cannot tell which of them is causing any resultant change in the dependent variable. This is why we should not construct models which include highly intercorrelated independent variables.

If we do develop such models, our results will almost certainly be invalid. A strong correlation between two independent variables, X_1 and X_2, may produce a high R for the model as a whole, even if *neither* of them correlates strongly with Y. Such cases will tend to show up in impossibly high Beta coefficients.

One simple way of checking for collinearity is to produce a *correlation matrix* to look at the strength of association between your independent variables (we saw how to do this in chapter 8). As a rough rule of thumb, statistically significant correlations above about 0.6 should set alarm bells ringing. In the model we have developed, there is no significant correlation between our two independent variables ($r = -0.061$, $p = 0.432$), so we do not seem to have a problem.

You can also check for collinearity by requesting a set of 'collinearity diagnostics' under the 'Statistics' option in the regression dialogue box. When you run your model, this will produce two additional columns of output (headed 'Collinearity Statistics') in the coefficients table, plus an additional table of 'Collinearity Diagnostics'. An example of this output is given in figure 10.10.

This output offers two tests of collinearity. One is the *tolerance* and *variance inflation factor (VIF)* for each variable, given in the two final columns of the coefficients table:

♦ The tolerance of a variable is determined by the extent to which its values can be predicted from the values of the other independent variables in the model. Expressed on a scale from 0 to 1, the smaller the tolerance, the greater is the association between this variable and the other independent variables taken together (i.e. small tolerance levels indicate problems of collinearity). In this example, both our independent variables have the same tolerance (0.939) because in each case there is only one other independent variable in the model.
♦ The VIF is derived by dividing 1 by the tolerance – a high VIF thus indicates collinearity.

In our model, the very high tolerances and low VIFs indicate that there is no problem of collinearity.

The other method for testing for collinearity involves comparing the *eigenvalues* derived from our correlation matrix, and these are given in the table in figure 10.10 headed 'Collinearity Diagnostics'. Eigenvalues are a way of measuring the extent to which different variables share variance in common (they do this by looking to see how well a single linear function, or underlying 'dimension', in the data can minimize the

Coefficients^a

Model		Unstandardized Coefficients		Standardized Coefficients	t	Sig.	Collinearity Statistics	
		B	Std. Error	Beta			Tolerance	VIF
1	(Constant)	65.737	7.543		8.715	.000		
	Occupation: Cambridge scale	−.126	.053	−.308	−2.391	.021	.939	1.065
	Smoking have benefits?	22.514	10.196	.285	2.208	.032	.939	1.065

a. Dependent Variable: cigs+cigars+tobac with <20&>200 removed

Collinearity Diagnostics^a

Model	Dimension	Eigenvalue	Condition Index	Variance Proportions		
				(Constant)	Smoking have benefits?	Occupation: Cambridge scale
1	1	2.157	1.000	.07	.07	.09
	2	.596	1.902	.11	.07	.91
	3	.247	2.956	.82	.86	.01

a. Dependent Variable: cigs+cigars+tobac with <20&>200 removed

Figure 10.10 Checks for collinearity

residuals from a set of variables taken together). We explain them more fully in appendix F on factor analysis on the website. When inspecting the eigenvalues you need to ask:

♦ Do any of the eigenvalues appear *very* much smaller than the others? If so, there may be a collinearity problem, for extremely small values on a dimension indicate that virtually all the variance has already been taken up by other dimensions in the model (which can only mean that two or more variables must be sharing a lot of variance in common). In our case, eigenvalues of 2.2, 0.60 and 0.25 are fine.

♦ How high are the scores on the *condition index* derived from the eigenvalues? High index scores indicate collinearity.

♦ Is there any evidence of shared variance in the *variance proportions* for the independent variables? In figure 10.10 we see that 86 per cent of the variance in *Smoking has benefits* is mopped up by one dimension (number 3) while 91 per cent of the variance in *Cambridge scale* is mopped up by another (dimension 2). This is heartening, for it shows that the two variables are hardly related to each other (the dimension which fits one of them very well hardly fits the other at all) – in which case, there is no collinearity problem.

CONCLUSION

Least squares regression is the workhorse of social science modelling. We use it both to test hypotheses and to explore data, for it helps us distinguish the relative effects on a dependent variable of several possible independent variables that may be associated with it.

Although it is widely used, least squares regression does have a number of disadvantages. One is that it is only appropriate for interval- or ratio-level data, but many of the variables used in sociology and related disciplines are measured at a lower level than this. To some extent this problem can be overcome by converting categorical variables into a series of dummies, but this is a clumsy procedure and some statisticians warn against relying too heavily on it.

As computers have become more powerful, so more elegant methods for analysing multiple associations among categorical variables have become available. One of the key ones is loglinear modelling, which is explained in appendix I on our website. Also on this site you will find extended explanations of logistic regression (a multivariate technique for modelling data when the dependent variable is dichotomous), path models, structural equation modelling and factor analysis. Once you feel comfortable with the techniques covered in the last four chapters, we invite you to download these appendices and work through them (again, they are based on examples from the Smoking Survey), for they open up even more powerful possibilities for exploring and analysing associations between variables.

There is a lot more to data analysis than we have been able to cover in this book. Nevertheless, if you have come this far, and have understood the logic of what we have been doing, then you are well on the way to becoming a competent social researcher.

Many of the most common tasks in data analysis can be discharged perfectly adequately using the basic statistical tools and procedures outlined in this book, and when we use more complex statistics, we often end up with much the same results as would have been achieved by using simpler ones. If a finding can be adequately demonstrated using a simple technique, there is no reason to use a more complicated one.

In chapter 1, we noted the resistance and antipathy which exists in much of British sociology towards survey research and quantitative data analysis. Hopefully, having read this book and gained some hands-on experience of generating and analysing some survey data, you now share with us the view that much of this criticism is misguided. There are, of course, many pitfalls to guard against when doing quantitative research, but the potential pay-off if you get it right is considerable. Even our small-scale, rough-and-ready project on smoking behaviour, carried out by a group of students who had no previous experience of this sort of work, generated some fascinating results (we summarize the major findings in Section 1 of our website where we indicate which of our initial hypotheses were disproved and which survived).

Now that you have a basic familiarity with the techniques involved, we hope you get the opportunity in the future to generate and analyse some data of your own. But even if you don't, you can feel reasonably confident that you will be able to understand and evaluate most of the quantitative survey research findings that get published by others – and that is itself an invaluable skill. Congratulations – and welcome to the world of quantitative data!

"Okay. I feel sick. Let's go and sue the tobacco companies."
Mac [Stan McMurtry], 18 Apr 1997

Glossary of Technical Terms

analysis of variance (ANOVA)   A collective term covering a variety of different kinds of tests, all of which assess whether a difference in mean scores *between* different groups is great enough to be considered statistically significant given the variance in scores *within* each of the groups. In one-way ANOVA designs, there is one (categorical) independent variable, which may have several values. In more complex designs, there can be more than one independent variable and we can test for interaction effects.

analytical research   Research which aims to identify the causes of phenomena. This will usually involve testing of hypotheses derived from a causal theory.

bar chart   A chart displaying a frequency distribution in the form of separate vertical bars, each of which corresponds to one value of a categorical variable. Category values are plotted on the horizontal axis while the vertical axis measures the frequency or proportion of cases found in each category.

binomial distribution   The distribution we would get if we took an infinite number of samples, calculated for each the proportion of cases falling into any one category of a variable, and plotted these proportions on a graph. The result would be a histogram which has the shape of a normal distribution.

bivariate analysis   Statistical analysis of the association between two variables. With nominal level data, this normally involves cross-tabulation (*qv*). At interval level, it may involve procedures such as correlation or simple least squares regression.

box plot   A visual tool in data exploration which allows you to check for skew and for outliers.

categorical variables   Literally, variables whose values consist of a (limited) number of discrete categories (as against *continuous* variables). Usually, such variables will be measured at nominal or ordinal level, although some interval-level variables may also be considered 'categorical' (e.g. a variable divided into age groups of equal intervals).

causation   A relationship between two or more variables where change in one is found to be associated with change in another, and where prior theory suggests that this is due to a connection between them. The variable which is said to bring about the change is 'independent'; the variable which is said to be acted upon is 'dependent'.

Chi Square   A statistic summarizing the amount by which the expected frequencies in the cells of a contingency table differ from those observed. Chi Square is used in various measures of the strength of association between categorical variables (e.g. phi), and it is the basis of the Pearson Chi Square test of the significance of association between two variables.

cluster sampling   Drawing a sample of groups (clusters) rather than individuals (e.g. a sample of parliamentary constituencies). Often used as the first stage in a sampling strategy which then goes on to sample individuals within the selected clusters.

coding   Classification of responses to questions into a limited set of numbered categories. All codes are identified in a 'code book'.

collinearity   The extent to which two independent variables used to predict a dependent variable vary with each other. Multiple regression requires an absence of collinearity.

concepts   General mental categories into which we fit various specific experiences of things. Concepts are the way we think about things; they are the abstract categories of thought around which our theories are constructed.

confidence intervals   The range of estimated values of a population parameter, at any given level of probability. Calculated on the basis of the sample mean and the standard error of the mean (e.g. at a 95 per cent probability level, the estimate will be the sample mean, plus or minus 2 standard errors).

contingency table   see *cross-tabulation*

continuous variables   Variables measured on a numerical scale (interval or ratio) with no breaks or gaps in its sequence of numbers (e.g. a natural age distribution or an income scale). Distinguished from *categorical* variables, which, even at interval level, involve a clustered rather than a smooth distribution.

control   A test for spurious associations between two variables by seeing whether the association still holds when a third or further *control variables* are taken into account.

correlation   A statistical procedure for calculating the strength and direction (positive or negative) of an association between two variables.

correlation coefficient   A number between 0 (which indicates that there is no association between two variables) and 1 (which indicates complete association). The higher the number, the stronger the relationship between the two variables in question. The most commonly used correlation coefficient is Pearson's *r*.

covariance   The average amount by which the values of one variable vary in proportion to a change in the values of another.

cross-tabulation   The process of producing a contingency table which cross-classifies the different values of the categories of an independent variable with those of a dependent variable. When it is used as a noun it is synonymous with 'contingency table'.

data cleaning   The process of identifying and rectifying errors in a data set.

data crunching   A colloquial term, sometimes used perjoratively by critics of survey research, that refers to the necessity of reducing a wide range of different responses to a small number of coding categories.

data file   A computer file containing all the data on all the cases in a sample. In SPSS, the data file takes the form of a spreadsheet with individual cases listed in separate rows while individual variables are listed in separate columns.

data transformation   The process of changing the values of an existing variable, or creating a new 'derived' variable. Can involve mathematical functions like square roots, logs and cubes of numbers, which are used to compress or elongate a scale. Achieved in SPSS by means of the 'Recode' and 'Compute' commands.

deduction   A form of reasoning which begins with a theoretical generalization and then tests this against specific observations. Rather than searching for evidence to confirm our theories (as inductive logic requires us to do), Karl Popper said that science should follow a deductive logic involving repeated attempts to prove theories wrong.

degrees of freedom   The number of observations that need to be determined before the value of all the remaining observations in a table are necessarily fixed as a result of the marginal totals.

derived variable   A variable which has not been directly measured in a questionnaire but which is constructed from other variables which were directly measured.

descriptive research   Research that seeks to measure the incidence and describe the character of phenomena without trying to explain their causes.

descriptive statistics   Statistics (like one-way and two-way frequency distributions, or exploratory factor analysis) which summarize variables and the relationships between them. They are contrasted with inferential statistics, which calculate the likelihood that any given finding would be reproduced in the whole population from which a sample was drawn.

dummy variable   A dichotomous variable entered in a model as an interval variable. The two values (0 and 1) are treated as equal intervals on a scale, but the scale has only one interval.

eigenvalue   A measure of the amount of shared variance accounted for by a single component or factor comprising several different observed variables.

elaboration   The process of investigating partial associations by adding new control variables to the analysis.

empiricism   The philosophical tradition which believes that (a) we live in a real world of objects; (b) these objects have their own characteristics and properties which exist irrespective of what we think they are like; and (c) our knowledge of these objects is developed through direct experience with them.

epistemology   A branch of philosophy which concerns itself with claims to knowledge. Epistemology asks: 'How can we claim to know that something is true or false?' We look to epistemology to help us decide what is to count as an accepted fact.

error   (1) Inaccuracy in the estimate of a population parameter based on a sample statistic (may arise from factors such as interviewer bias, miscoding of responses or mistakes leading to selection of an unrepresentative sample). (2) Any variance in a variable which is not explained by other variables in the model (may arise from imprecise measurement of the variables and/or from failure to include relevant independent variables).

ethnomethodology   A sociological approach concerned to understand the methods used by people themselves for making sense of the world in which they live. In the view of ethnomethodologists, ordinary people have already made the world meaningful and all that remains for social scientists to do is to understand *how* people invest social reality with meaning.

exploratory research   Research which is not driven by hypotheses, but which seeks information on a phenomenon about which relatively little is known. Data may also be explored in the early stages of hypothesis testing, where the aim is to check for normality and to inspect outliers before proceeding to bivariate or multivariate analysis.

factor analysis   A family of techniques, some exploratory, some confirmatory, which identify underlying patterns (or *latent structures*) in data by looking at the covariances between variables. New 'latent' variables, called *factors*, are created out of larger numbers of observed variables.

falsification   Associated with Karl Popper's idea of scientific method, this is the attempt to test theories against evidence in an attempt to prove them false. Popper claimed that we can never be certain that an empirical claim is true (for it may be undermined by some future observation), but we can be certain that an empirical claim is untrue. Science must therefore seek to falsify theories rather than confirming them.

Grand Mean   The mean of the sampling distribution of the mean. In other words, the average value of the means from an infinite number of probability samples taken from any given population. One important property of the Grand Mean is that it is equal to the mean age of the population from which all the samples were drawn.

histogram   Graphical representation of a frequency distribution used to represent interval-level data. The vertical axis represents the frequency of each value, while the horizontal axis represents the scale on which the variable is measured.

homoscedasticity   The requirement in regression modelling that the dependent variable should be normally distributed at each value of the independent variable(s).

hypothesis   A statement about an assumed causal link between two or more things. Hypotheses are constructed so as to enable the causal links posited by a given theory to be tested against observable evidence.

index   (1) A summary number derived by combining the values of two or more variables and used to express the overall magnitude of a phenomenon. An index becomes a 'scale' when its constituent measures can be shown to be 'structured' or patterned in relation to each other (e.g. scores correlate and are consistent). (2) In mathematics, the number of times a number is to be multiplied by itself.

induction   Generalization based on the accumulation of factual evidence from repeated observations.

inferential statistics   Statistics used to determine whether and how patterns in a data set generated by means of a probability sample can be generalized (inferred) to the whole population. Contrasted with descriptive statistics which summarize patterns in a set of data.

interview   The process of gathering information by asking people questions, either face-to-face or through a medium such as a telephone or email link. Interviews may vary in the degree to which they are 'structured'. Unstructured interviews do not make use of a formal list of questions; structured interviews generally use questionnaires.

interviewer bias   The influence of interviewers on the answers that respondents give in a survey.

latent variables   see *factor analysis*

leading question   A question which, by virtue of its wording or its placement in a questionnaire, is likely to encourage respondents to give a particular answer.

least squares regression The method of expressing the relationship between two or more interval/ratio-level variables by means of a straight line graph. The line is drawn through the scatter of plots so as to minimize the total vertical distances between it and all the plots. The equation of this line allows us to predict the value of the dependent variable (Y) from the value of one or more independent variables (X_1, X_2, etc.).

levels of measurement Data may be measured at one of four different levels. Nominal measures are at the lowest level – they use numbers simply as labels for different values, and no mathematical significance attaches to the numbers themselves. Ordinal measures also use numbers as labels, but the numbers form a rank order of ascending or descending size. Interval measures also use numbers to represent a rank order, but ensure that the intervals between each value on the scale are the same. Ratio measures are the highest level of measurement. Here numbers form part of a scale with equal intervals and a base of zero such that they can be expressed in proportion to one another.

Likert scale A method of measuring people's attitudes by combining their scores on a variety of items into a single index. Scaling is achieved by ensuring that high-scoring and low-scoring individuals differ in their responses on each of the items selected for inclusion in the index.

linear equations Any straight line plotted on a graph can be expressed algebraically. The equation for a straight line on a two-dimensional graph is $Y = a + bX$ where a is a constant (the point where the line intersects with the Y axis) and b is the amount by which the value of X increases for a 1 unit increase in Y. In theory (though not in practice), graphs could be extended from two to three, four or more dimensions by adding additional X axes. While such graphs cannot be plotted, they can still be expressed by linear equations (e.g. the equation expressing a linear association between four independent variables and a dependent variable is $Y = a + b_1X_1 + b_2X_2 + b_3X_3 + b_4X_4$), and such equations enable us to assess the relative predictive power of different independent variables.

linearity Having the property of a straight line. A requirement of correlation, and of regression models, is that the relationship between dependent and independent variables should be linear.

listwise deletion A procedure for the removal of missing cases in which *all* cases for which information is missing on *any* of the variables to be included in the analysis are deleted.

logistic regression A method for predicting the probability of being in one or other category of a dichotomous dependent variable from the values of one or more independent variables.

loglinear analysis A modelling technique used for analysing patterns of association between several categorical variables. It involves calculating coefficients for all of the effects that explain observed cell values, and then removing effects in order to find the simplest possible model that adequately fits the observed data.

Mann-Whitney U test A non-parametric significance test which allows us to compare the rank order on an ordinal measure achieved by the members of two groups, and to decide if the difference between the groups is likely to exist in the population from which the sample has been drawn.

marginal frequencies   The row and column totals in a cross-tabulation.

mean   One of the statistics used to summarize the 'central tendency' of a distribution. The arithmetic average of a set of numbers, it is calculated by summing the values of all the cases and dividing the result by the total number of cases.

measures of central tendency   Statistics (typically, the mean, median and mode) which summarize the values in a distribution by measuring a 'central' or typical value.

median   The middle value in a range in which all cases have been sorted into ascending or descending order.

methodology   The logic or philosophy underlying particular research methods.

methods   The technology of research, the tools by which data are gathered and analysed.

missing data   There are several reasons why an answer to a question might be missing. It could be that the question was not relevant to this respondent and therefore was not asked; or the question should have been asked and answered, but for some reason was not; or the question was asked, but the respondent refused to answer it; or (in a newly created variable) the information is not available to identify a value for this respondent (in which case it is said to be 'system missing').

mode   The value which occurs more than others in a frequency distribution.

model   A deliberately simplified representation of the pattern of association between two or more variables. The aim is to produce a simple model which can nevertheless successfully predict (within a given margin of error) the value of a dependent variable (or the cell frequencies in a contingency table) from a small amount of additional information.

multiple regression   Least squares regression with more than one independent variable.

multivariate analysis   Statistical procedures which attempt to distinguish and measure the relative strength or significance of the association between several independent variables and a dependent variable.

non-parametric statistics   Statistics that make no assumptions about the population from which a sample has been drawn, and which can therefore be used to analyse any relevant variable or set of variables, irrespective of their distributional properties.

normal distribution   A perfectly symmetrical frequency distribution which forms a 'bell-shape' curve when plotted on a graph. When data are normally distributed, most cases cluster around the middle of the distribution, there is an even and declining spread of cases towards the extremes, and the mean, median and mode are all identical.

normal plot   A tool for exploring data. Plots the values of the residuals on the horizontal axis and standard deviations (above and below the mean) on the vertical axis. If a variable is normally distributed, the plots should form a straight line.

null hypothesis   The hypothesis that there is *no* association between two or more parameters in a population (and hence that any statistical association found in a sample drawn from that population could have arisen due to random error). The null hypothesis is tested in a significance test; if it is falsified, then we can have some degree of confidence that there is an association in the population as well as in our sample.

odds ratio   The ratio of two sets of odds. Used to calculate the strength of association between two categorical variables in a contingency table (including tables in loglinear models).

one-tailed/two-tailed tests   Tests of significance based on probability distributions. A hypothesis which specifies that two variables are related in a particular way (either positively or negatively) will be tested using a one-tailed significance test (for you are testing the null hypothesis that your sample lies at one end of the sampling distribution). If a hypothesis does not specify whether the association is positive or negative, then use a two-tailed test.

open-ended questions   Questions where respondents have been free to say what they like, and interviewers have written down their answers verbatim.

operationalization   The process whereby an abstract concept is translated into a variable that can be measured in empirical research.

pairwise deletion   A procedure for the removal of missing cases in which cases are retained for the analysis of association of pairs of variables on which they provide complete data, but are removed from the analysis of association of pairs of variables on which information is missing.

paradigm   A distinctive approach in science which has its own theories and methods (which may be incompatible with those of other approaches), and its own criteria of scientific adequacy and rigour.

parameter   A characteristic of a given population. The *size* of a population, for example, is one of its parameters; the *distribution* of incomes across the different members of the population may be another. A parameter is distinct from a statistic. A 'statistic' refers to the value of a variable in a given sample, whereas a parameter refers to the value of a characteristic or attribute in the population from which that sample was drawn. Generally speaking, we calculate statistics on samples in order to make estimates about the parameters of populations.

parametric statistics   Statistics that are based on certain assumptions about the population from which the sample has been drawn (and hence about the sample too, assuming that it has been selected randomly). Commonly, such statistics assume that a phenomenon is normally distributed.

partialling variance   The process in data analysis whereby we separate out the proportion of variance in a dependent variable that is explained by one variable from that explained by another.

path analysis   The mapping of patterns of association between a series of variables arranged in a causal sequence – a 'path'. The exact pattern of this sequence depends on the theory that is being tested.

Pearson's *r*   see *correlation coefficients*

phi coefficient   A standardized measure, based on Chi Square, used for assessing the strength of association between two dichotomous variables.

pie chart   Graphical representation of a frequency distribution in the form of a 'pie' which is divided into 'slices'. Each segment of the pie represents the proportion of the total cases which falls into each category.

pilot study   A small-scale test-run for a planned piece of empirical research. A pilot survey will normally involve drawing a sample, carrying out interviews using the full questionnaire, coding the results and even carrying out some data analysis so as to check on the viability of the planned research strategy.

population All the individuals, households, groups, organizations, institutions, nation-states, or other objects which fall into the scope of a study and about which the study claims to generalize.

positivism A view of science which emphasizes that scientific knowledge comes from observing things as they are ('phenomenalism'), and that theory is important only in classifying facts and making them more intelligible ('nominalism'). Positivist social science concerns itself only with facts, not opinions or beliefs or wishful thinking (it is 'value free'), and it claims to model its procedures on the example of the natural sciences.

pre-coded questions Questions where respondents are obliged to answer in terms of one or more of a set of given responses.

probability sampling Also known as random sampling, this is the selection of a sample that should be representative of the population from which it is drawn because every individual in the population has an equal and known chance of being selected for inclusion. Provided the sample is big enough, it is likely that its make-up will reflect the make-up of the population from which it is drawn.

probes Instructions to an interviewer to delve deeper into an informant's initial answer to get richer information.

prompts Follow-up questions which can be used by an interviewer to clarify an informant's response to a questionnaire item, or to gather more detailed information.

questionnaire A prepared set of written questions, directed to the participants in a social survey, for purposes of statistical compilation or comparison of the information gathered. Questionnaires may be administered by interviewers, or they can be completed by participants themselves.

quota sampling The attempt to draw a sample that will be representative of the population from which it is drawn by ensuring that it resembles the wider population on a number of stipulated dimensions.

random sampling see *probability sampling*

regression see *least squares regression* and *logistic regression*

reliability The likelihood that a research instrument will produce similar results each time it is used.

representativeness The degree to which all the characteristics of a sample accurately reflect the characteristics of the population from which it has been drawn.

research design A strategy for collecting and analysing data. It must be appropriate for answering the questions which the project is seeking to address, and it must take into account the practical constraints which the project is likely to encounter.

response rate The proportion of people in a sample who successfully complete a questionnaire. Non-responses can be due to non-contacts, refusals or non-completions.

sampling distribution of the mean The distribution which is achieved when the means from an infinite number of probability samples are plotted on a graph. The result is always a normal distribution (*qv*).

sampling fraction The size of a sample divided by the size of the population from which it is drawn.

sampling frame   A complete list of all the individuals in a population who are eligible to be included in a sample.

scatterplot   A graph in which the value of every individual case is plotted on two axes corresponding to two interval- or ratio-level variables. Scatterplots are produced to check visually on the pattern of association between two variables (in particular, to see if the relationship is linear, and to see how strong it is).

scope   Definition of the range of individuals eligible for inclusion in a survey.

significance test   A statistical test to determine whether a relationship between variables found in a sample is likely to apply to the population from which the sample was drawn.

skew   The extent to which cases cluster towards one end or the other of a frequency distribution. Measured by the *skewness* statistic which compares the value of the mean with that of the median.

social class   The British government has classified occupations in terms of 'social classes' since 1911, but its schema has recently been revised and now comprises eight discrete class categories which are distinguished on the basis of their labour market situation. A different approach, giving rise to the Cambridge scale, is to arrange occupations on a continuous scale on the basis of typical patterns of sociability between them.

socio-economic group (SEG)   The British government's classification of occupations into 17 SEGs dates from 1951 and aims to categorize people in terms of their 'social and economic status'. To allocate an occupation to an SEG, you need to know somebody's occupational title, which gives you a 'standard occupational classification', or SOC, code and their 'employment status' (i.e. whether they are an employer, self-employed, or an employee).

sophisticated falsification   The idea, associated with Imre Lakatos, that theories are never rejected on the basis of disconfirming evidence until some better theory emerges to take its place.

Spearman rank correlation coefficient (rho)   A non-parametric statistic measuring the strength of association between two ordinal-level variables.

SPSS   Software package for analysing survey data. Stands for Statistical Package for the Social Sciences.

spurious correlation   A correlation between two variables which are not really linked to each other, but which covary due to their association with a common third variable. The 'spuriousness' only arises if the analyst imputes a causal association between them from the fact that they vary together.

standard deviation   The average amount by which each case in a distribution differs from the mean of the total sample. A way of measuring the degree of scatter or dispersal in a distribution.

Standard Error of the Mean   The standard deviation of a sampling distribution of the mean. The average amount by which the mean of any one sample varies from the Grand Mean (*qv*) of all the sample means. Can be used to calculate confidence intervals when making population estimates based on a statistic generated by a probability sample.

standardization   The process whereby values of variables measured on different scales are made comparable by expressing them on a common scale as *z scores* (*qv*).

stem and leaf plot   A tool for exploring data, particularly well suited for checking for normality. Also identifies outliers.

stratified probability sampling   A method of sampling which ensures that certain key categories of people will be included in the sample in a known and predetermined proportion. The population is first divided into different groups (strata) on the basis of known parameters such as their sex or age, and probability samples are then drawn from within each group.

structural equations models   Models produced in software programs like LISREL, AMOS and EQS which identify hidden structures in data by identifying common factors from the covariation of error terms.

structured interviews   In structured interviews, the interviewer works through a predetermined list of questions in a set order and enjoys only a very limited freedom to depart from the questionnaire.

survey, social   A method of gathering information about a specified group of people (a 'population') by asking them questions.

symmetrical statistics   Measures of association between two variables which make no assumption about the direction of causation between them. The opposite, asymmetric statistics, measure the extent to which change in an independent variable is associated with change in the values of a dependent variable.

syntax   The SPSS command language. SPSS commands can be activated via the menus and dialog boxes, or by typing in commands directly using the Syntax Editor window.

systematic probability sampling   Rather than selecting individuals completely randomly from a population, the sample is selected by taking every nth case from a complete list (where n is the sampling fraction).

t test   A test of the statistical significance of a difference in mean scores between two groups. Assumes that the dependent variable is normally distributed.

Type I error/Type II error   A Type I error occurs when we erroneously conclude that a pattern of association between variables in a sample indicates that such an association exists in the whole population. A Type II error occurs when we erroneously conclude that absence of association between variables in a sample means that there is no such association in the whole population. Type I errors are most likely to occur if we set probability levels too high; Type II errors occur when we set probability levels too low.

unit of analysis   The 'object' about which information is gathered in research. In a survey, the unit of analysis is usually the individual person.

unstructured interviews   Interviews in which the interviewer engages respondents in a conversational style, dispensing with a formal questionnaire, and referring instead to a set of prompts (an aide-mémoire) or even allowing the conversation to follow its natural course without any fixed agenda.

validity   The degree to which a question or construct succeeds in measuring what it claims to be measuring. There are four criteria: face validity (the subjective assessment of whether a measure adequately expresses the characteristics of a phenomenon); content validity (whether it successfully operationalizes the key dimensions of a concept); construct validity (whether the elements that make up the overall measure appear consistent with each other); and external validity (whether it is consistent with other evidence).

values (1) The range of different attributes or characteristics of a variable (e.g. the variable 'gender' has two values, 'male' and 'female'). (2) The personal commitments of a researcher.

variable Some feature or characteristic which varies between individuals and which can be measured. Variables are said to be 'independent' if a theory predicts that they will cause change in other variables, and 'dependent' if a theory predicts that their value will change due to the influence of other variables.

variance A measure of dispersal in a distribution, equal to the square of the standard deviation. Calculated by finding the sum of the squared deviations from the mean.

weighting The process whereby the influence of one (or more) variable or group is deliberately exaggerated. Weights can be used in stratified probability sampling (*qv*), to increase the representation in the final sample of one or more subgroup in the population. Weights may also be used to correct for unintentional biases arising in the process of sampling itself.

z scores Standardized values, expressed in standard deviations, or parts thereof. Z scores are calculated by expressing the difference between a given value and the mean of the whole sample as a proportion of the standard deviation.

THE SURVEY METHODS WORKBOOK WEBSITE

A website accompanies this book. To find it, go to: www.surveymethods.co.uk and follow the onscreen instructions.

Password protection

Some parts of the site are password protected and in order to access these pages you will need to type the following when prompted:

access

The site is divided into eight sections. Seven contain files which you can download free of charge, including research materials for the Smoking Survey, additional appendices on different aspects of data analysis and research design, and a summary of key findings from the survey. The eighth contains links, updates and material submitted by other readers (including results replicating the Smoking Survey on fresh data sets).

SECTION 1: SUMMARY OF FINDINGS FROM THE SMOKING SURVEY

This book has covered the design of a survey, its execution, and the analysis of results, but the final stage is missing – the write-up. In the file Summary.pdf you will find our brief summary of the key findings from the Smoking Survey. Each hypothesis is examined using procedures discussed in the chapters in part III, or using some of the more advanced statistics and techniques introduced in the additional appendices included in section 5 of the website.

SECTION 2: SMOKING SURVEY FILES AND DOCUMENTATION

This section contains all the material you will need if you want to replicate the Smoking Survey by doing your own survey, or if you want to work on the data our students collected. The material is contained in the following files:

Dirtydat.sav: The original version of the Smoking Survey SPSS data file, as it was entered from the questionnaires by our students.

Cleandat.sav: The final version of the SPSS data file, following cleaning. This also includes all the derived variables referred to in this book.

Question.doc: The final version of the questionnaire as it appears in the appendix to chapter 3. Downloading this will enable you to make any amendments that you want and to print out multiple copies if you intend to use it in interviewing. It is not copyrighted, so feel free to use it any way you want.

Codebook.doc: The code book for the Smoking Survey which gives information on all of the directly observed and derived variables included in the cleandat.sav data file. Includes variable names, value labels, missing value codes and level of measurement, plus information on how derived variables were created.

SECTION 3: ISSUES IN RESEARCH DESIGN

This section contains two appendices: appendix A follows up on chapter 2's analysis of research design by considering longitudinal survey designs. Appendix B is designed to complement the discussion of coding in chapter 5. Social class is one of the most common variables in social research yet coding it can be rather more difficult than it may appear. This appendix describes a number of class schemas and considers how they are coded.

SECTION 4: FURTHER STATISTICS AND CHOOSING STATISTICAL TESTS

This section deals in more detail with some statistical issues discussed in part III of the book. Appendix C describes why and how to standardize variables as z scores – an issue which was touched on briefly in chapter 8. In chapter 9 we used the binomial distribution to calculate statistical significance in a Chi Square test. Appendix D describes what the binomial distribution is and how it is calculated. Finally, given the confusing array of statistical tests that exist, appendix E gives advice and guidance on how to choose appropriate statistical tests. It covers the factors you need to consider when choosing the appropriate test and indicates the appropriate tests for univariate, bivariate and multivariate analysis.

SECTION 5: FURTHER TECHNIQUES IN DATA ANALYSIS

The website includes a number of additional appendices dealing with more advanced techniques of data analysis than those covered in this book. Like the chapters in part III, these explain the logic of each procedure by testing hypotheses from the Smoking Survey, and results are presented using our survey data:

Appendix F: Principal Components (Factor) analysis

Factor analysis is used mainly as an exploratory technique (simpler techniques of exploratory data analysis are covered in chapter 7). It analyses covariances between variables in order to identify any hidden 'factors' (latent variables) that they express in common.

Appendix G: Path models

Path models trace associations between variables arranged in a causal sequence. Regression-based path modelling uses partial coefficients from a series of multiple regression models (see chapter 10), but this is being displaced by structural equations models which can estimate covariances in errors. Both are covered in this appendix.

Appendix H: Logistic regression

Logistic regression is a modelling technique used when the dependent variable is dichotomous (when least squares regression is inappropriate). It works by calculating the odds that any given case will take one or other of the values of the dependent variable, and it measures how these odds change as different independent variables are brought into the model.

Appendix I: Loglinear modelling

This is a multivariate modelling technique for use with categorical variables (it is therefore an alternative to cross-tabulation, covered in chapter 8, which can be used when several variables need to be analysed). It aims to find the simplest model that satisfactorily fits the data (i.e. where predicted cell frequencies are not significantly different from those that are observed).

SECTION 6: GUIDE TO FURTHER READING

Appendix J is a guide to further reading for those who wish to read about topics covered in this book in greater depth including research design, data collection and data analysis.

Section 7: SPSS updates, links and reader inputs

The website includes links to other useful and related sites (both survey organizations, such as the Office for National Statistics and the ESRC Data Archive, and organizations which can offer background material on smoking, such as ASH and FOREST).

It is our intention to keep this book up to date through the website. In particular, as new editions of SPSS are published, we shall provide a commentary on the changes that have been made as compared with earlier versions. In addition, you will find a basic guide to using Syntax in SPSS. This is a 'language' that SPSS uses which enables you to run complex commands and batches of commands in a way that is not possible using the usual drop-down menus.

If you have replicated the Smoking Survey (either exactly, or with a different questionnaire or sampling strategy), we invite you to submit your own data set and supporting research materials (code book, questionnaire, etc.). We shall then post this on this section of the website so that other users can access it for teaching or research purposes. In this way, it might be possible to build up a series of comparable samples which will allow for repeat testing of findings, comparison of differences in findings resulting from different research strategies, and (possibly) integration of data sets to produce larger, single samples for users to analyse. We shall, of course, give full and clear credit for the authorship of any materials submitted in this way.

To find out how to send us materials (or to communicate in any other way with the authors), email us at the following address: admin@surveymethods.co.uk

Section 8: Guide for teachers

Guidance and suggestions for teachers wishing to use this book as the basis for their own survey methods classes.

INDEX

Where subjects are dealt with on the website their placing is shown in italic, with the section number followed (if applicable) by the appendix letter: for instance, *3B* stands for the website, section 3, appendix B.